D1264491

THE THRESHING FLOOR

THE THRESHING FLOOR
An Interpretation of the Old Testament

JOHN F. X. SHEEHAN, S. J.

Foreword by
J. COERT RYLAARSDAM

PAULIST PRESS
New York   Paramus, N.J.   Toronto

Library of Congress
Catalog Card Number: 72-81574
ISBN 0-8091-0167-X (cloth)
ISBN 0-8091-1731-2 (paper)
Cover design by Morris Berman

Published by Paulist Press
Editorial Office: 1865 Broadway, N.Y., N.Y. 10023
Business Office: 400 Sette Drive, Paramus, N.J. 07652

Printed and bound in the
United States of America

CONTENTS

to
John J. Collins, S.J.
and
Francis X. Lawlor, S.J.

"Blest is the man . . . who studies Torah night and day"
Psalms 1, 1-2

FOREWORD

It is a source of personal pleasure to have a share in sending *The Threshing Floor* on its way. The author, Reverend John F.X. Sheehan, S.J., is a valued colleague and friend in the Department of Theology of Marquette University. That puts an accent on my satisfaction. But the substance of it inheres in the special character of the work itself, and in its potential role in the current ecumenical and cultural situation.

Protestant Christians have discovered that Roman Catholic scripture scholars publish a good many books about the bible that are not confessionally distinctive. They closely resemble publications with which they have been familiar in their own circles: Critical and historical studies of an "objective" sort that are not designed to show how scripture functions in the life and thought of the authors or their communities.

The Threshing Floor turns out to be a happy and stimulating exception . to this general state of affairs. It is in no sense a confessional apology; nor does it intend to be that. But it does show how the Old Testament functions for a modern man of faith, how he uses it to illustrate his own understanding of the meaning of life. Thus, indirectly, and in a very unobtrusive manner, because it contains a personal statement, the work enables the non-Roman reader to sense and ponder the ethos of the Roman tradition of faith and thought, with special reference to scripture. The "spirit of Catholicism" pervades this book; it is there as a distinctive cultural "style" that will strike the sensitive non-Roman as both winsome and intelligible.

Father Sheehan interprets representative themes and portions of the Jewish scriptures. Virtually every page of his work carries implicit reminders that he is both a modern biblical scholar, masterful in his philological erudition, and a Christian theologian in the Jesuit tradition. Nevertheless, his book is not a volume of theological essays, either biblical or dogmatic; nor does it consist of a series of philological or historical treatises. It is the sort of book that appears rather rarely in university circles today. That may serve as a cue to the nature of our cultural crisis.

Perhaps the best way to describe *The Threshing Floor* is to say that it is the work of a humanist in the classical sense of the word. It is a wise book, rather than simply an erudite one. It is the product of a lively, creative imagination and of serious reflection. It correlates learning and human self-

ix

understanding. Father Sheehan has drawn on the results of a lifetime of study in many disciplines to say something about what the bible of ancient Israel does for him: How it suggests and illustrates his own convictions about the human situation, with its ambiguities and possibilities; and how it leads into apprehensions of the Mystery along thematic paths which the Christian, too, has found trustworthy and perennially in season.

Father Sheehan has written for Everyman; his book is both personal and universal. All sorts of people, in all sorts of confessional and intellectual categories, will find it stimulating; they will find themselves in it, and it will speak to their condition. Few readers will catch all the learned allusions in the work; but even those who miss most of them will find it meaningful, for it will make them look at themselves.

The modern university finds it difficult to correlate learning and humanism. Established styles in research, teaching and curricular organization are unfriendly to it; and often those seem inseparable. All sorts of rather desperate attempts are made to reintegrate learning with reflection; or, at least, to provide surcease from an erudition that seems unbearably sterile. Recently, for example, we have witnessed the rise of an ". . . in residence" category: the poet, the theologian, the composer, the novelist, and so on. Essentially extra-curricular and temporary figures, they are brought in to relieve the drought of the human spirit apparently occasioned by the specialized demands of the curriculum proper. Hopefully, this book can help in the humanization of the curriculum in a more integral fashion.

The Threshing Floor is not a textbook. But it belongs in many courses where the scriptures play a role. It would be unfortunate if, because of its scope and many-sided relevance, it should be relegated to a list of "suggested supplementary readings"! In a long list of courses dealing with all sorts of specialized issues relating to scripture and its history, it might well be put near the center of each of them as a means of promoting the correlation of learning and reflection.

J. COERT RYLAARSDAM

PREFACE

If the dictum of show business is correct, that success requires not so much talent as courage, then the completion of a book is an achievement not of talent, but morale. Thus, it is a pleasant duty to acknowledge some debts to persons who contributed much encouragement to the author and help to the book's composition. Professor J. Coert Rylaarsdam of Marquette University read the "experimental edition" of the book and made suggestions. So also did Professor Joseph Grassi of Santa Clara University and Fathers Thomas Caldwell and Patrick Walsh of the Marquette Jesuit community. These persons are innocent of any blame for the book's deficiencies, since their very competent suggestions were always weighed, but not always heeded. Miss Lorna Rixmann typed the entire manuscript with enthusiasm and accuracy, contributed much encouragement, and avoided the typist's temptation to play editor. To all these persons, many thanks. Finally, it is in the preface that the author attempts to disarm his readers and critics. These efforts are rarely successful, but making them affords the author some modicum of comfort as the book goes to press. There is little in this book that is original. The well-read Old Testament professional will recognize many of the ideas and their sources. Encouraged by the success of such books as McKenzie's *The Two-Edged Sword* and *The Power and the Wisdom*, I decided against much documentation.

Occasionally some stray parts of the book may strike the Old Testament professional as being original and he may ask himself with some annoyance, "Where did he reach *that* conclusion and can he prove it?" Perhaps some of the original ideas in the book may eventually find their way into print in more scholarly dress. (The chapter on Ruth has already been rewritten for a *Festschrift*.) It may be objected that the more normal procedure moves in the other direction. The writer first writes the scholarly work and then does it in more popular fashion. In defense it can only be said that when I began teaching at Marquette University in the fall of 1970, I discovered the pressing need of a book for my students. That the book was completed with some dispatch was made possible only by the extraordinary cooperation of the Marquette Theology Department and its Chairman, Quentin Quesnell, S.J.

J. SHEEHAN

OVERVIEW 1

There are perhaps as many ways of writing a book of this nature as there are men to attempt it. Essentially these books would differ only in modes of emphasis. Hence, at the beginning, it will be helpful to show exactly where this author's emphasis lies. Any book for new readers of the Old Testament will be conditioned by the three major aspects of it as a book, or more properly, a rather large collection of books. These books contain material that is *historical, theological* and *literary*. This clumsy description—that they "contain material"—has been chosen by design. In our modern literatures, we tend to use specific types of writing for historical material and other specific types for matter which is theological. Perhaps we could say that the purely literary types, fictional and poetic, are a third distinct form of modern writing. Some might object though that even in modern writing, the novel or poetic form might treat material which is theological. However, what we can call "creative theology" is generally presented in a form of writing all its own. Ordinarily the reader would not confuse it with the fictional or inspirational.

In the Old Testament we find that this is not the case. Historical and theological materials are presented often in the same type of writing, if not in the same sentence or paragraphs. Also, although in the judgment of some there are passages in the Old Testament which are literarily most creative, perhaps even fictional, the Old Testament never presents these as something quite apart from theology. Many excellent books on the Old Testament begin with the avowed purpose of attempting almost equal treatment for its historical, theological and literary aspects. This the present book will not attempt. The stress in this book is on the theological and literary, historical considerations will be a distant third. To some this is not an ideal state of affairs. To lessen the demands which a firm grasp of the history entails is to risk teaching the Old Testament superficially. In acknowledging that risk at the beginning, the writer hopes to compensate for it.

Teachers and books ought to begin "where the student is." The writer admits at the beginning that he has a certain audience in mind and his views of that audience are largely conditioned by his experience with undergraduate teaching at Marquette University. There he found that his students, most of them Roman Catholics, brought a number of assets to the

1

study of the Old Testament. Among these were their sensitivity to the use of symbolic language. (This is evidenced, among other ways, by the lyrics of the songs most popular among them. They are rich in multi-layered levels of meanings, in contrast to the rather straightforward language of the ballads of a generation ago.) Moreover, they seemed unusually open to the author's treatment of cult in the Old Testament. Nor is this surprising. One with a sensitivity to mythic and symbolic language cannot but be predisposed favorably to cult. Cult is, after all, on one level, nothing more than the use of the body to act out the thought content of material often conveyed in symbolic and mythic language.

Yet with the above very real advantages, the students also brought certain handicaps to their study. Most of them had read very little of it. Many of them (some of them were freshmen) had not the vaguest historical sense of times much earlier than the Second World War. Some of them, as one gifted present-day writer of Old Testament history has put it, "believed that the Patriarchs' age lay very near the dawn of time."

They were very open to the study of theology. True, their study was not always that of the serene academician. Driven by their own problems, they tended to examine any theological work presented to them in terms of solutions which it offered to their own personal affairs. But they were quite open to reading the Old Testament on its own terms when the way was made a bit easier for them. Viewing all those factors then, the writer made a decision. It was simply unrealistic to expect that the Old Testament be covered satisfactorily on three levels in class lectures. He was fortunate that the students also met in small group sessions with a teaching assistant. In these sessions, the students read and discussed Albright's small but terse volume *From Abraham to Ezra*. The book is a difficult one, but highly recommended to the readers of this volume. For the reader who would read it without benefit of a teacher, perhaps it would be wiser to read this volume first, with its skeletal treatment of history, and then to attempt Albright.

It is worth pointing out in the very beginning that the Old Testament, even in translation, has enjoyed centuries of popularity in the modern world. Frankly, one of the reasons for pointing this out is to dispel the fear that comes on most of us in new ventures—the fear that we are wasting our time. This fear seems less realistic in the matter of the Old Testament when we reflect the unbroken history of popularity it has had in the West. It is possible, of course, that men have been wasting their time for centuries, but most unlikely. How is this popularity to be explained? What has kept men reading this collection of books despite all the difficulties which lay between them and reading the books with some degree of understanding? (Nor ought these difficulties to be minimized. A "culture gap" of seven thousand miles and some three thousand years of history stands between the American reader and the Old Testament).

For the believer, of course, the answer is very simple. He judges that God has somehow spoken through these books, that they are "his word." Many believers who are Christians believe that God has revealed aspects of his personality in the Old Testament which he has not revealed, or not revealed so clearly, in any other source. (We shall look at some aspects of this attitude in our twelfth chapter, "Old Testament and New"). But the Old Testament has enjoyed unbroken popularity in the West also among those who do not believe. How is this to be explained? A number of factors are certainly involved. Perhaps the most facile explanation is that the Old Testament became a "beautiful book" with the publication of the King James version (1611) and that is enough to explain its popularity in English-speaking lands. There is some truth in that explanation. The King James version is remarkably successful in catching much of the flavor of the original Hebrew. Still, the Old Testament has been enjoyed by millions who have read translations good, bad and indifferent in literally dozens of languages and hundreds of dialects.

Perhaps the starting point of the explanation of its popularity among nonbelievers, is that the Old Testament is an eloquent description of a deeply human problem: man's search for God. Some Old Testament readers would object here immediately that the Old Testament rather presents the matter as God's search for man. No matter. The Old Testament presents the confrontation of man with God (as the Old Testament describes him) with such clarity and force that the nonbeliever reads with interest and sympathy although he does not believe it. Again, one word is to be stressed: *confrontation.* It is the meeting of Up and Down, of Night and Day. God is the Totally Other. This is a basic theme of the Old Testament and one of its most refreshing ideas to many believers and nonbelievers alike. God is Totally Other and when he meets man, man comes for the first time to understand himself, seeing the contrast. Many modern religious writers, some of them Christian, seem at times to describe the meeting of God and man as the meeting of a weak nephew with a kindly uncle. Such writers are far removed from the religious world of the Old Testament. It is quite significant that the first instruction which the God of the Old Testament offers Moses who is about to begin a conversation with him begins, "Take off your shoes! The place on which you stand is holy ground." (*Ex* 3,5). This is perhaps the attitude which makes the Old Testament so agreeable to many nonbelievers. Although they cannot believe that the confrontation ever took place, the confrontation with such a God could only enhance the dignity of man.

Comparisons with other religious literatures of East and West are not necessary. Many great bodies of religious literature exist in the world and some in the Roman church are looking at them anew as possible sources of "revelation." Still, one comparison comes to mind. If the Koran, read in Arabic, is compared with the Old Testament, read in Hebrew, the Koran has many advantages. Not the least is the amazing fluidity of the Arabic language, certainly one of the greatest of all languages. In comparison with it, parts of the Hebrew bible seem written in a crude and unexpressive tongue. But the Koran has been virtually without influence outside the circles of pious Islam. (Although in recent years, efforts have been made in Arab countries to use the Koran as a cultural instrument of pan-Arabism). It seems, when the Koran is taken out of Arabic, the inspiration is left behind. Its asset, in any comparison with the Hebrew bible, the genius of the uniquely expressive Arabic language, seems almost coextensive with what it has to offer. When that goes all inspiration seems to go with it. This is not to disparage the Koran, whose place in world literature is secure. It is only an example of another great religious literature in the same genre as the Old Testament but quite different.

This phenomenon points up another unique aspect of the Old Testament. To look for reasons to explain its popularity in a given age is to become involved with a multiplicity of entwined causes. Perhaps it has this in common with some other great literatures, but its greatness seems somehow more than the sum of its parts.

Our own age has witnessed a special renaissance of interest in the Old Testament. Probably more good English translations have been published in the past ten years than in all previous history of bible translation. Is this simply part of a steadily growing popularity of the Old Testament through the centuries, or is this literature uniquely suited to our age? It is suited to our times. Both its literary style and its great themes fit our mood. College teachers of literature sometimes complain today that their students, bereft of any real feel for tradition are interested "only in writers who have appeared in the past fifteen minutes." This is quite false. Certainly today's college students are very interested in contemporary American and English writers. (Would we wish a college generation that was bored by the literature of its own lifetime?) To some extent too, they are not interested in certain writers who captured the interest of some other generations. Tennyson and Browning, Dickens and Thackeray are at the moment in a bit of an eclipse. On the other hand, Blake, Melville, Donne and the previously unpopular Gerard Manley Hopkins have quite seized the contemporary youthful fancy. This change in literary taste flows perhaps from the same reasons which are bringing a flowering of even deeper interest in Old Testament studies. Blake, Melville *et al.* are finding new popularity by reason of their style and themes. Their rich, symbolic language cries out to the modern mind and heart. Even where their symbolism fails to some extent with a given reader, yet there it succeeds. Its very obscurity and murkiness teaches that the writer recognizes how complex is the reality in which we are. The facileness of some earlier writers leaves the modern reader, certainly the youthful modern reader, with the impression that the writer has simply not understood how complicated the real world is.

Themes too are a factor in winning new popularity for some of these older authors. Blake and Melville were deeply sensitive to the power and might of chaos hiding beneath the surface of even an apparently tranquil world. (Perhaps this handicapped them considerably in seeking acceptance in their own lifetime. Many of the intelligentsia of their times saw the world complacently as coming more and more under intelligent human control.) Perhaps no age since primitive man has had a deeper sensitivity to the power of chaos than our own troubled times. We shall return to this topic regularly.

Both of these factors are involved in winning new acceptance for the Old Testament in the world of the seventies. The language of the Old Testament frequently involves complications. Some of these complications will be treated later under another rubric. Here let it be noted that some of them are due to its rich use of an ancient symbolism. Too, the Old Testament is deeply sensitive to the power, might, and perhaps we may even say the personality of chaos. At times this sensitivity is quite clear. At other times, due to reediting, it is nearly hidden—but it is always there. It is strange but nonetheless true that the world of the Old Testament, pretechnological though it was, seems to the alert reader uncannily like our own. This likeness is to be found in the role of chaos in the pretechnological and post-atomic ages. The young modern reader sometimes reads the Old Testament with a sense of *déjà vu*. He feels strangely that he is reading of a place where, somehow or another, he has already been.

From the above it is clear that the Old Testament may be judged "relevant" to the present age. Still, there is a caution to be observed here. An unrestrained quest for relevance can be a serious handicap in the study of the Old Testament. If we read the Old Testament, or any other body of ancient literature simply in terms of "relevance," we are exercising a kind of censorship, not unlike the biblical scholarship of another generation which sought out "proof texts" in scripture—isolated verses which were used to buttress dogmatic postures.

An example may help to point up the dangers of overstress on relevance. Let us postulate that America were to produce in the sixties and seventies a body of great religious literature which was to last a thousand years. Cannot we easily imagine the student of the year 3000 making the complaint of a course in such literature: "Every lecture touches on one of two things: Problems in America between blacks and whites and wars in some other part of the world with a people of the so-called yellow race. We have not had a race problem on this globe for five hundred years. What I want out of Literature X are answers to the Mars problem!" Of course, those of us living in the seventies realize that it would be impossible for America in our lifetime to produce a religious literature which would not somehow be conditioned by those factors. If the literature produced were great enough, presumably it would speak to another generation a thousand years removed from us and our problems. On the other hand, if that generation wanted to understand our literature *on its own terms,* it would have to develop some knowledge of the cruel divisions of black and white which our lifetimes brought to the surface and the bitter corrosion deep within the nation brought on by the Indochina war.

The strength of the above analogy will become steadily clearer in subsequent chapters. The Old Testament frequently speaks in human universals, touching the heart of any generation in almost any cultural situation. At other times, the Old Testament is the child of its own time, circumscribed by its own problems, (harassed, for example, by a nation or two which terrified the Hebrews and remembered now only because they touched on Hebrew history). By reason of cultural influences, much of the Old Testament is preoccupied with matters which our own times find insignificant: genealogies, detailed descriptions of laws and rituals, even geographical descriptions which are in fact mythical. The modern reader who steadily avoids these passages in his search of the "great themes" of the Old Testament will certainly learn a great deal. (Such is the teaching power of this book even when improperly approached.) But the reader who so approaches the Old Testament must remain aware that he is bringing it down to his own size; he is forcing it to fit within the limits of his own cultural pattern. Consequently, he will be missing out on much—perhaps most—that the Old Testament has to offer to a more open-minded reader.

The alert reader who is studying the Old Testament in translation will soon come on a number of problems and apparent contradictions. This ought not to be a surprise, in light of the manner in which most of the Old Testament was composed. A good deal of the thrust of this book will be efforts to pierce through some of these problems caused by the "social composition" of the Old Testament, to use a term which we shall later develop.

First of all, the reader should be aware that the Hebrew bible contains specimens of literature composed over a period as long as that reaching from Chaucer to *Love Story*. The Hebrew language evolved during that period, as English did in the corresponding one. Partially as a result of that evolution, we are left with a number of linguistic puzzles on almost every page of the Old Testament. The Massoretes (ca. 5-7th cent. A.D.), who were among the last editors of the Old Testament, were equipped with stern intellectual honesty and a deep love of the "traditions" which they inherited. If, in reading a text, they did not understand a particular Hebrew construction, they were most reluctant to change it to one which they did understand. Rather, they handed the text faithfully on to the next generation, hopeful that later minds might understand the difficulty which they could not, but refusing to simplify it. If all their predecessors had been so faithful and so humble, we might have been spared many problems. However, they were not. There is some evidence for scholars, as they read the Hebrew text, that the pre-Massoretic editors did indeed change some constructions which they did not understand. Oddly enough, scholars today in possession of linguistic tools which these early editors lacked are frequently able to get closer to the primitive meaning than these men were, although thousands of years more distant from it.

One observation on "social composition" of the Old Testament may be made right here. Many scholars judge that the Old Testament text as we have it, is the running together of a vast number of earlier "sources." Some of these sources may move back even before the period of widespread literacy to an age of oral composition. Some of this oral composition touches on the ancient myths of pagan nations and theologies long since forgotten, but for their having moved into the stream of Hebrew theology. For the beginner, one point must be stressed. The above theory of Old Testament literary origins holds not only that the Old Testament books differ considerably one from another, which they would have in common with most libraries of literature, but that the individual books themselves passed through long and complicated periods of composition and editing. In fact, according to this view, even a given page of an Old Testament book may show evidences of several different sources and reworkings. These complicated origins, added to the language problems already noted, bring about an enormous number of obscurities visible to the alert reader. The student who has acquired some simple knowledge of Hebrew is often surprised in comparing a page of Hebrew with the best of translations available. He may find a dozen words and constructions that he would have phrased differently. Obviously, this is no criticism of the translator. The student reading in Hebrew can juggle simultaneously three different explanations of a given word. The translator, if he is to produce a legible page of vernacular, must make a choice of one and move on. Moreover, once the choice is made, it will condition his translation of later words. If he adheres to a particular translation by reason of stylistic demands, even though the word is slightly inaccurate, he may find that this earlier translation leads him farther and farther from the Hebrew in subsequent verses. In Old Testament translations, as in the launching of moon rockets, small mistakes at the beginning tend to be massive ones at the end, by reason of the distances involved.

A further complication thrusts itself on the reader. Not only is a given page of the Old Testament derived from a number of sources, not only have these sources been constantly rewritten, but this rewriting was done from a number of different viewpoints. We have already mentioned that linguistic viewpoints differed. A subsequent editor tended to appraise a word or a construction in terms of its contemporary Hebrew usage. But this is only one factor. Subsequent writers also edited in terms of totally different historical and theological perspectives. Yet at times this rewriting was restrained by their desire to retain much of the earlier text while highlighting an entirely different viewpoint. With the greatest literary skill in the world, this could not but involve problems and obscurities. (Can one imagine for example, the memoirs of the Kennedy era being rewritten by members of the Johnson administration? If the Johnson people felt constrained to retain most of the original, while stressing their own interpretation of those years, one would have an excellent example of some of the reediting done in the composition of the Old Testament.)

Nor were historical viewpoints the only thing that changed. In the Old Testament, as elsewhere, theology goes through regular crises of growth. Some of the earlier sources were touched with paganism. Some later editors were inclined to accept the pagan images, while rinsing out the pagan theology (as that stern Christian, Milton, had no objection to classical pagan images in *Paradise Lost*). Others were quite ruthless in stamping out any signs that paganism had had considerable internal influence on various periods of Hebrew history. Some of these editors went so far as to change pagan names of Hebrew royal families. The names they chose as substitutes were indications of the pagan origins of the original and perpetuated their memory, much as pagan shrines, built perhaps to stamp out certain Christian places of worship, marked the spot of those Christian shrines with real certainty.

Literary viewpoints differed too, although this is proved with much more difficulty. There are evidences in the Old Testament that ancient pagan legends worked their way into the Hebrew tradition, were transformed and handed on. Fictional materials and perhaps some poetry written purely for entertainment made their way into the tradition. Some types of "secular wisdom" and rather cynical works of advice entered the tradition too. All of these literary types were considerably reworked and elevated to another theological viewpoint. But in the process, the secular or fictional origins of this material was often forgotten. In the earliest forms of these works there may well have been indications—technical terms, the studied use of certain cliches—to tell the alert reader whether he had in his hands fact or fiction, secular or religious literature. Somewhere in the transmission this was lost. Eventually, the latest editors came to treat the material as belonging to the form used by its most recent editors. We who read all these centuries later are frequently hard-pressed to determine the original form of the material.

The problems we have with the manner of composition are interesting in themselves. However, they lead to other and more serious problems in our grasp of Old Testament theology. A very basic question in the study of any theology is the manner in which it grew. There are two basic schools of thought on the growth of Old Testament theology. One holds that the process is relatively simple to diagram. The earliest Old Testament beliefs were quite primitive. They were refined gradually under the influence of "great men" and reach theological heights with a religion of deep thought, purest monotheism and very stern ethics only with the advent of the "classical prophets." Another school views the process differently. This school certainly does not deny the religious and theological heights of classical prophecy, but holds that such heights were in some ways a return to an earlier piety and theology. This school teaches that Old Testament theology was quite profound, almost from the beginning. This profundity is explained not through the role of "great men," although their role is not dismissed, but rather stresses the force of "community consciousness" within and without Israel. It sees the earliest redaction of Hebrew writings as reflective of a very early theology, largely molded by the great pagan theologies to which the early Hebrews were exposed. Neither school denies the significant contributions which the Hebrews, either as "great individuals" or as a thinking community, made to theology with their own particular cast of thought with which they reshaped all they received. But each school views the various steps of the process as taking place in decidedly different ways. That such a dichotomy can exist among biblical scholars is proof, if any be needed, that there are large areas of unanswered questions to be approached when one begins seriously to read scripture.

At this juncture, the reader may forgive the author for stating simply his own personal religious viewpoint. In fact, the reader may even be a bit curious about it. Some of the writer's students have asked him after a number of lectures, "You do believe, do you not?" Many of these students brought to college a somewhat "unreflective" attitude toward scripture. *Fundamentalism,* to use the word for the first and last time in this book, has never had any official approval in the Roman church. One uses the word with extreme reluctance, because it is offensive to many excellent Christians who find in the word overtones which are pejorative to some of their beliefs. As the writer understands it, this view of scripture is somewhat simplistic. In its most extreme form, it tends to accept the literal meaning of each word in the text, generally read in translation, and works on the presumption that the text as we have it can be read much as a modern work would be read and interpreted. If any reader should find the above description itself to be simplistic and faithless to any ultra-conservative positions which he holds, then he need take no further offense. The ultra-conservatism which the author would discourage in his readers is that defined above.

While this ultra-conservatism has never had any official approval in the Roman church, it has for decades flourished on an unofficial level. With good reason, the Roman church has insisted that its priests be well trained in church history, in the evolutionary process of dogmatic theology, in the deep intricacies of moral questions which parishioners would present to them. But scripture has been at times almost a minor subject. Moreover, most of the preaching in the Roman church until very recent times was considered but one—and perhaps even a lesser one—of a man's many pastoral duties. In the maelstrom of administrative duties, it was a rare Roman Catholic parish priest who did much reading in problems of scripture after he had left the seminary. (If indeed he had read much in scriptural studies while in the seminary.) Even seminary professors themselves who were teaching scripture were sometimes overburdened with other courses and with pastoral duties which hindered the kind of reading in depth that good college teaching demands. This has led to an interesting arithmetical situation. A priest ordained twenty years who was taught scripture by an overworked professor in his twentieth year of seminary teaching—not an uncommon situation—is at least forty years removed from the academic progress in the study of scripture. Depending on the nature of the professor's original education, perhaps another ten to twenty years could be added to that gap. (The latest *books*, for example, in any academic discipline run five to ten years behind the periodical literature.)

How has this affected "scriptural preaching" in the Roman church? The answer is almost obvious. With each passing year, such preachers find that their sermons grow more simplistic in their explanation of texts or—more likely—the text becomes simply a springboard to a sermon on dogmatic theology, or perhaps some social question, which the pastor really knows something about.

The writer would avoid an error analogous to that of the above-mentioned preacher, being some forty years behind the times. All of us realize happily that "summer institutes" of various kinds, and "in-service work-shops" are beginning to update the level of scriptural preaching in the Roman church. Some Catholic high schools offer courses in scripture which are near-professional. But the work is by no means complete. In the indefi-nite future, the writer expects a large number of students each year whose attitude toward scripture has been so conditioned by simplist preaching that they will continue to ask any teacher who focuses on the complexities of the word of God, "You do believe, do you not?"

Indeed he does. The writer believes (although this stance need not be adopted in order to read the book with profit) that God is somehow the au-thor of scripture; he believes that scripture is his word and that he reveals himself throughout all of it. He judges it no contradiction also to hold that there are large elements of the "mythic" in scripture. That some portions of scripture are totally "mythic" and that others have been "mythically heightened." These terms will explained later. Now let it only be noted that the writer judges God to make use of these forms to reveal his truth. For someone to judge that God can reveal only in direct address, only in the simplest of literary forms, is to attempt to place limits on the divine power. In the long sad history of biblical interpretation, many men have devoted entire lifetimes to false problems. They presented questions to scripture which it was never intended to answer and then wrestled mightily to extort the answers they sought from the answers which scripture did offer.

The writer judges himself fortunate to have been educated in a Christian tradition, that of the Jesuit Order, which finds no contradiction between se-renity of faith and relentless intellectual pursuit in all matters, including the theological and related disciplines. To avoid certain types of scriptural investigation out of fear that they will weaken cherished beliefs is to in-dulge in a timidity unworthy of the real Christian. The Jesuit tradition holds that God reaches out to the whole man, including the intellectual striver. To attempt to imprison one's intellectuality in dealing with scrip-ture, is to stifle a large area of human life which the divine truly wishes to penetrate. (This is not to say that a given student or reader, momentarily harried by certain personal theological problems of belief or morals, may not occasionally desire some respite from the crises which serious intellec-tual study of scripture may place on him.) But in the overall, this tradition judges that the truly pious Christian ought to bring to the study of scripture all that he humanly is. This most assuredly includes the role of human as restless, probing, intellectual.

Humans have made use of mythic language and cultic ritual in a number of situations. At this juncture, let us adopt the definitions of myth as "recital of the saving event" and cult as "re-enactment" of that event. The precise nature of the saving event is something we shall not presently treat. In our next chapter, when we begin to develop the notion of myth as it is applied to the exodus, the nature of "recital" will become clearer. However, even now it should be noted that recital is *not* merely the rehearsal of chronicle, the recitation of a series of facts. Myth attempts to rearrange those facts, partially to impose a certain artistic unity on them, partially because it is the role of myth to evoke the *emotional experience of a past reality*. Those who were delivered, in whose memories still lived the actual experience of the saving event, had little need of myth. The circumstances under which the need arose will be treated in the next chapter. Myth belongs to the same general area of human need as that which is satisfied by symbol. In both cases, in the use of myth and symbol (and cult is the acting out of myth, frequently with the use of symbol), a story or a thing is invested with a richer, deeper meaning than it possesses on the most obvious level. Frequently that story or thing is then related to a profound reality which humans find too difficult to express, so they use mythic language or an actual symbol.

A couple of contemporary examples may be helpful. In a film called *Lovers and Other Strangers*, a young wife is asked to explain why her marriage is breaking up. She is not well educated and not particularly articulate. After some false starts, she finally stammers: "When we first got married, his hair used to smell like raisins!" The sensitive listener knows immediately what she meant. (Unfortunately, her insensitive mother-in-law did not.) The early years had been ecstatic, certainly on a physical level, but not simply that. The two of them were on the same wavelength; they did not have to talk to communicate. To be in his presence was to be happy. Then, with the passage of time, something happened. Some harsh realities intruded and it was all over. His hair didn't smell like raisins any more. In the same film, the aging Italian father tries to explain to his young son that love goes through stages, that the ecstasy need not last forever. Explaining how conscious he is that his wife still loves him, he indulges in a long, tragicomic description of the various rich but pedestrian meals she serves him. No gourmet he. The father too fails to communicate because the son does not grasp the mythic content of the message. "Beef stew and baby potatoes" to him meant a meal for a hungry man. The father, more sensitive here than the son, saw in the food the symbolic love of an affectionate, but deeply inhibited woman.

But the use of mythic language or actual symbol is so universally human that it is not restricted to the tender emotions, as in the above examples, or in the use of the wedding ring in our society. It can have sterner purposes too. Family life in rural France is that of a stern, authoritarian society. Much used in the correction of smaller children is *le martinet,* a strap used for no other purpose. Should a tourist ask to what age a child might expect to feel the *martinet* for his misdemeanors, he is told *"En principe* (theoretically, with little real likelihood) until the late teen years." In fact, physical punishment of teenagers is as uncommon in rural France as it is in American middle-class society. Yet in homes where all the siblings are teenagers, the *martinet* generally remains hanging in the kitchen where it hung in their small childhood. Obviously, it has now taken on a symbolic value, pointing up the relationship between parent and child which continues to exist in this authoritarian society. Symbols then can be used to communicate very complicated realities in a sophisticated society, or even relatively simple ones in a less articulate society. We shall find examples of both in the Old Testament.

In our work, we shall treat of *myths* which were developed to the point of being complete and coherent stories. In other discussions of various points in the Old Testament, our treatment of the "mythic" will include small phrases and perhaps even individual words. This is because we share the judgment of those who hold that mythic and symbolic language, in almost every usage, touches on a near-universal human experience—the tendency to use symbolic expression, whether in phrases or complete stories, to relate those realities which are too complicated or too painful to admit of literal expression. The great psychiatrist Jung developed this notion to a further degree. He judged the tendency to use symbol to be so universal that certain universal human symbols arise (quite independent of cultures). In one striking example, he dissects the symbolism of the dreams of a sensitive young child and finds it parallel to the symbols of the Book of Revelation. Jung concludes that both this small girl and the author of the Book of Revelation were unconsciously aware of the rapidly approaching end of days. (The child died some days after her final dream.) In the history of biblical interpretation, ages which had grown insensitive to the use of symbol badly misread much of scripture.

To misread symbols in the Old Testament is to risk missing even the most basic message. New Testament teachers are fond of pointing out that one's view of New Testament teaching on poverty is affected considerably if the "eye of the needle" means just that, or if, as was frequently written in some of the older commentaries, it means the smallest of the gates in a large city wall. A stout camel could pass through that, with much huffing and puffing on his part and much pushing and shoving on the part of the driver. If this latter interpretation is correct, it is a rather graphic and amusing picture of how the early Christians saw the rich man making his entry into the Kingdom of Heaven.

Similarly, much of the present confusion in Christian circles on the notions of Christian poverty goes back to the Old Testament notion of the *anawim*. They were certainly poor, but frequently what the Old Testament stresses is that they were the "little people" of a society which was just starting to become economically complicated. As the "little people" they had no recourse but to cast their hope on the Lord. Moreover, the truly pious who wished to judge themselves needed only to ask: How have I treated the *anawim*? Without the help of the pious working as God's servants, the *anawim* would not survive in cruel ancient Near Eastern society. All of which is not to say that the *anawim* were not truly poor. Indeed they were. But to read that word constantly as "poor" and to lose sight of its attendant cluster of connotations is to understand the word as a computerized item and not to grasp it as a human idea with symbolic potential.

Hopefully, this first chapter has not been too abstract. The book will deal with other literary forms in the Old Testament, interpretative history, poetry, novels and legends. Problems connected with each, and some of the solutions, will be relatively easy to see when one form or another is being treated. But the basic thrust of this book is that for many readers myth, symbol and analogous literary aspects have been largely ignored areas. Consequently, the writer wanted, at the very beginning, to spell out some of their significance for him as he approaches the Old Testament.

THE EXODUS MOTIF 2

The exodus account given in the Old Testament is considered to be substantially historical by a large school of respected Old Testament scholars. Their arguments run as follows: The Hebrews seem to have a unique respect for tradition. The stories of their ancestors, while they may contain certain elements of "heightening," are rich in details of periods much earlier than any of the great writing periods of the Old Testament. This must mean that those details go back to the period under discussion. Just how rich this detail is may be best understood by comparing the early traditions of any comparable Near Eastern people. We find nothing like these detailed accounts of ancestral origins in Egyptian writings or in the Assyrian records. For some reason, the Hebrews began early to develop a profound respect for their beginnings. For this reason, the Hebrews did not have to retroject details into myths created out of nothing. In fact, one of the arguments for the substantial historicity of these early accounts is that some of the details would not have been available to a writer, creating in a later period, unless the details had come down with the stories themselves. Egyptian names, for example, would surely not have continued to be recognized in later Israel as Egyptian unless they had been traditionally handed on as part of the exodus account.

C. H. Gordon in his eminently readable book, *The World of the Old Testament*, offers as argument for the authenticity of the narrative:

> The Exodus and the incidents leading up to it have authentic Egyptian elements. The Hebrew taskmasters, for example, go to Pharaoh and say: "Behold thy slaves (i.e. we) are beaten." (Ex 5:16.) The expression is not idiomatic in Hebrew, but rings true for Egypt, where beating was not so much a matter of brutality as it was a normal expression of relationship between men of unequal status in their daily work. Collecting taxes, educating scribes, or getting any work done without beating was rare in Egypt. (p. 144)

Again, because the above mode was quite foreign to the Hebrew mentality, the idiomatic expression and the reality it involved would not have been preserved in Hebrew traditions unless attached to some authentic tradition

15

of Egyptian origins.

There is another argument for the substantial historicity of the exodus narrative in the Old Testament—the unlikelihood that men would create such an ignominious tale as the core of their nation's history. First, recognize the role which the exodus account plays in the history of Israel. It is seen as the basic event in all of Israel's history. All pivots around it and its role in Israel's creative history is unique. To see how unusual is the exodus account in world history we need only note that the great themes of exodus history state: "We were slaves! We were in bondage, weak and imprisoned. Through no power of our own and through no merit of our own, we were set free. These were the origins from which we became a mighty nation." With good reason, scholars ask if this does not conflict with all that we know about men and their memories of national origins. Would men create a past for their nation involving personal slavery, weakness, disgrace and eventual freedom which involved no heroism on the part of the ancestors? Would men hand on such a tradition of disgraceful national origins *unless it was founded in fact?*

Since we have used the term "substantial historicity," the reader may profitably be reminded of what history is. It is assuredly not chronicle, no mere recitation of names and dates however accurate. The historian attempts to find a basic unity in the movements of a given period for a number of reasons. The first is that without such a unity, the complexities of even the shortest span of history become unmanageable and pedogogically impossible. One extreme example of the interpretative role of the historian is Churchill's *Marlborough.* With his extraordinary skill in marshalling the English language to his purpose, Churchill presents a terribly complex period of history with extreme simplicity. He has managed to attain this simplicity because of his fidelity to a basic theme: The struggle for the maintenance of the Protestant succession. Churchill's heroes are willing to make great sacrifices for that succession. His villains either oppose it or support it for the wrong reasons. In this latter category he so categorizes some of the most venal figures in the Parliament of the age. The parliamentary struggles, European royal contests, extremely complex questions of rival personalities, ambitions, the emergence of political parties which were to dominate for centuries—all these factors Churchill subordinates to one basic pattern.

The reader may or may not be sympathetic to the above. However, there is in American history an example which many of us find quite sympathetic. Our own Civil War was a complication of tragedies. How many and how complex is evidenced by the wounds of that war which are still with us. Certainly some very basic economic factors were involved. In Lincoln's

Second Inaugural, however, he viewed all these complexities with the serenity of simplicity:

> These slaves constituted a peculiar and powerful interest. All knew that this interest was somehow the cause of the war. . . . If American slavery is one of those offenses which in the providence of God must needs come but which, having continued through his appointed time, he now wills to remove and he gives to both North and South this terrible war as the woe due to those by whom the offence came . . . as was said three thousand years ago, so still it must be said "the judgments of the Lord are true and righteous altogether."

Lincoln's Second Inaugural is a better example of what is involved in the composition of the exodus narrative than is the example of Churchill. Lincoln was actually engaged in healing the consequences of the history of which he spoke. This is the role of the great leader. He stands in the eye of the hurricane, interprets what is going on, finds a basic unity hidden to other men and explains it to them. Rightly or wrongly in our own lifetime, friends of Adlai Stevenson II and of Eugene McCarthy among other leaders, have so hailed these men. Their supporters saw them as leaders who understood the present maelstrom. They judged that if these men gained the presidency, by reason of their vision they would be able successfully to shape events. They did not gain the presidency and the accuracy of their unifying vision of events was never put to the test.

It is also in light of the above that many scholars tend to accept Moses as historical and to affirm that he had a real hand in the composition of the Pentateuch. The events of early Israelite history were extremely complicated. Somehow or another a small and weak band did escape from the control of a world power. Some great figure did see in those complications a certain unity, the saving hand of Jahweh. Moreover, he then persuaded his fellows that his vision of the unity was the correct one. From this vision, came the unity of a nation which was to last—under various forms of self-government—for over a thousand years. From it came a religious family which exists to the present day.

Finally there is an argument from the nature of the Hebrew language used in the Old Testament's exodus account. The language is archaic, poetic and bears an admixture of Egyptian linguistic features. These arguments from language then bear out the general supposition that the basic thrust of the account must be derived from a tradition moving back in time very close to the events described.

It may be said of a nation, with apologies to Descartes, "We remember;

therefore we are!" Our own lifetimes have revealed most clearly the fragili-
ty of the national fabric. The unity of a nation rests on its consciousness of
the past and its ability to integrate the present into that past. When persons
or peoples join themselves to a nation, they become part of the *united* nation only if they can graft themselves into that nation's past and share
somehow its collective memory. So later peoples did who joined themselves
to the "tribes of Israel." So immigrants did who came to the United States
after the Revolution and even after the Civil War. For some immigrants it
was easier than others. The Irish immigrant peasant identified easily with
the Revolutionary War fought against the British and with the Northern
side of the Civil War—a war fought to free slaves (so Lincoln contended).
America's blacks, ironically, have found this grafting into the national consciousness much more difficult. The Revolution was fought and won with
no gain to the blacks here present; the sad decades which followed the Civil
War make it difficult for them to accept the Lincoln interpretation as being
of much consequence. These examples highlight how important were the
ancient Hebrew traditions. They served to unify a nation which continued
to attract conglomerates of peoples to itself long after the invasion of Canaan. These people and their children continued to share in the vivid national memory which was the bond of unity. In Israel, as in any nation, anything which happened later either to dim that national memory or to make
difficult the sharing of it by latecomers, would threaten the nation's ability
to remain one.

The exodus account involved a dual dynamic in the development of the
Old Testament. First, the Mosaic tradition found as unifying element in the
complexities of the exodus event, the powerful hand of the Lord. Then,
once the exodus narrative reached a certain stage of firmness in the Hebrew
traditions, it came to have a kind of coloring effect on almost all other
events. Such liturgies as the "first fruits" festival, which the Hebrews probably took over from the Canaanites, became bathed in the light of the
exodus. Exodus affected laws governing dealing with strangers, "You were
strangers in Egypt!" Even an author as far-removed as the so-called "Second Isaiah" speaks of the new and coming redemption in terms of a "new
exodus" (*Is* 43,16-20). The psychological phenomenon at work here is commonly evidenced in the lives of nations—and of individuals. Most adult
men and women tend to view some particular life event as the beginning
and certainly the center of their adulthood. All that preceded the event is
seen as prelude to it; all that followed, as logical sequence. And this event is
generally not a chronological milestone, e.g., one's twenty-first birthday,
but a dynamic life-event. Many happily married couples so regard their
wedding day. Happily ordained priests so regard ordination. A physician,

to whom the medical profession is both life and vocation, may so regard the day he obtained his M.D. Such persons, with no effort to distort the truth certainly, tend to regard all the rest of their lives, prior to the event and consequent, through the prism of that event itself. Consequently, happenings of one's earlier years which are not easily related to the great event tend to pass from one's memory. On the other hand, incidents which might have been considered minor when they occurred, sometimes acquire at a later date a much greater significance, when the subject begins to view that minor happening as prelude to the wedding, ordination or medical graduation. This phenomenon may help to explain the "heightening" of certain details in the exodus account, as a later generation came to see some objectively minor events through the prism of the great reality: "We were delivered from Egypt!"

Today, many look back on the American doctrine of Manifest Destiny with a kind of helpless sadness. Living in an age which is very sensitive to the injustices done to the American Indians in the name of American growth from sea to sea, we cannot take the pleasure in Manifest Destiny which was taken by an earlier and simpler age. Yet that age, with an attitude closer to primitive Israel's attitude than is our own, saw the hand of God as facilitating the growth of the great American republic.

It might be well to note two things here. First, regardless of what stance one may take on the overall theological growth of the Old Testament (profundity from the patriarchal age or only beginning with the classical prophets), almost all are willing to grant that there is a gradual evolution of ethic. In the most primitive portions of the Old Testament, there are evidences that the Hebrews followed their own weak inclinations and later hailed this as divine command. (There is some evidence of this certainly in the notions of holy war and in the conquest of Canaan in general.)

But something else of importance is to be noted too. A colloquium was held some years ago at the Swedish Theological Institute in Jerusalem. The main speaker was Prof. N.W. Porteous of Edinburgh and he delivered some papers which have not yet appeared in print. In the course of one of these papers, he noted that certain attitudes in the Old Testament ought to be understood clearly as presented to us from the primitive Hebrew viewpoint and not from the divine viewpoint. (So far this is fairly obvious; it ought to be clear that at no point does the Old Testament text present us with the Divinity, but with the Divinity as the Hebrews of a given age understood him.) Then Porteous made a particular application. The Old Testament presents a series of names, ancient nations whose role as the Old Testament presents it was but to serve a function in Hebrew history—to chastise the Hebrews, to assist them, to fall before them or whatever—and then to disappear. Porteous stressed that nowhere does the Old Testament proclaim that it is presenting *all* of salvation history and the precise role which these obliterated nations played in the divine economy can be known only in the fullness of time. When a questioner from the audience suggested one amplification to him, it was accepted eagerly. "Yes. In Old Testament studies perhaps even more than is usual in the rest of theology, there ought to be *a respected place for ignorance.* There are some answers we just do not know."

The sensitive reader is strongly advised to keep the above points in mind as he reads: The limited viewpoint of some of the earlier Hebrew authors and the large gaps in what the Old Testament teaches about the role in salvation of these other nations. Some may think this caution naive, but one may find intelligent, adult readers who cannot surmount this emotional obstacle to fruitful reading of the Old Testament.

Also, if the point be not too controversial, in light of the above, it is difficult to share the acritical enthusiasm of some good Christians who see in every modern Israeli victory another fulfillment of Old Testament prophecy. The age of primitive ethics is over; no nations can now be considered as nothing but foils in the fulfillment of God's plan for a favored group. Moreover, such acritical enthusiasm for alleged prophetic fulfillment in modern Israel runs counter to the loftiest ethical and religious teaching of the Old Testament itself. There are legitimate hopes and aspirations in both parties now disputing in the Near East.

With all the above as preface, then, what is the literary nature of the exodus account as we have it? Our age has such an uncritical respect for technology (muted recently by a growing awareness that technology frequently creates problems which other disciplines must solve) that the following statement may be somewhat difficult to grasp. *Under certain circumstances, sober scientific statements may be less accurate than poetry.* An example may help: If two lovers share the experience of a long evening walk, they will be left with many residual memories, among them the coolness or mistiness of the night and the visibility or dimness of the stars. With the passage of time, the memories of that evening may grow weak and need some assistance to become once again alive and vital. Perhaps two means are available: A meteorological report of the evening in question or a poem written by an artistically gifted member of the couple. The point to be stressed here is not that the poem is more beautiful, but that it is in fact more *accurate* because it *evokes a past experience,* actually felt, and evokes it to a degree that the most skillfully written meteorological report could never do. If the report falls far short of the experience, it is simply inaccurate. There is no other word to describe it.

There may be a certain "exaggeration" in the writing of such a poem. There may have been mildly distressing elements present to the walk (he was vaguely aware that his hay fever was bothering him, or shyness made him nervous). When memory of the reality is fresh, his joy in it is so great that he need not suppress the vague recollection of the stressful elements. Nor need he exaggerate the beauty of the beloved. When the memory was fresh, her reality was enough. There was no need to make her prettier than life. But if the lovers part (or get married, as in *Lovers and Other Strangers*) time does something to the memory of the ecstasy. The simple memory of the actuality is no longer enough to evoke the experience of the past. If the lover is truly gifted, he writes a poem. At any rate, his memory becomes selective and exaggerating. Small blemishes disappear from the beloved; her virtues are heightened. And all this with a strange result. In his memory now, she is somewhat different from what she actually was. But this different something is now necessary to evoke the same emotional experience which flowed from the actuality. Nor is this phenomenon limited to lovers. Readers with deceased and beloved parents may realize in critical and reflective moments that their memory of the late parent differs from the reality. But this difference in memory is keyed to evoking the same emotions that the presence of the real parent did evoke.

This is the phenomenon which the writer considers "mythic heightening." Unlike the use of total myth, which we shall see subsequently also to have a major role in Old Testament literature, "mythic heightening" begins from a concrete reality and by a judicious selection of some details and a mild "heightening" of them, along with the elimination of other details which detract from the total pattern, an account calculated accurately to evoke a deep past emotional experience is created. This is honest, human and acceptable. How acceptable is perhaps best evidenced by fairly contemporary events when the entire nation watched a legend in the process of being made. In the days following the assassination of Martin Luther King, much was made of the last sermon which Dr. King gave, only hours before his death. In it he had spoken of being "on the mountain" and having seen the promised land which it might not be his to enter. He spoke also of his willingness to accept a short life, of his readiness for death, while admitting that "longevity has its grace." In the earliest newspaper accounts of this sermon, it was admitted that the sermon was one he had given frequently before—had given with such frequency in fact, that it was not an extraordinary coincidence that he should have given it once again. Shortly though, this fact began to disappear from the newspaper accounts. The "mythic heightening" had begun.

Rev. Ralph Abernathy, preaching the eulogy at the King funeral was quite restrained in his "mythic heightening." He had eaten with Dr. King in a restaurant shortly before the assassination, a meal which proved to be Dr. King's last. The item which both of them wished to order was in short supply; there was in fact only one portion of it left in the kitchen. For this reason, the two of them shared the same portion, eating, as Mr. Abernathy related, from the same dish. Some few cynics criticized this story as untrue and as a patent effort to place Dr. King in the "Last Supper" tradition. In fact, it seems that the story was quite true. Because of Abernathy's restraint, he went on to say that Dr. King and he had shared many prior meals in this fashion. Of course, the "Last Supper" did not create the tradition of sharing food as a gesture of intimate union and sacramentality. This notion is not only pre-Christian but is pre-Hebraic. In the ancient Near East it goes back to the earliest times of which we have records—and presumably far earlier than that.

Preaching the eulogy, Abernathy noted that he had eaten nothing since that meal, that his physical force the day of the funeral might be supplied by the very food which he had so intimately shared with Dr. King in the course of his last meal. Obviously this too was an effort at a kind of "mythic heightening." In the question of "succession" to Dr. King's leadership, this act was an almost perfect symbol that Dr. King's strength was being transmitted to his assistant. However, the symbolism seems not to have been very effective. Abernathy has never attained the kind of control in the movement which King had. Partially for this reason, the second of these two details, the "shared meal" as opposed to the "last sermon" has never really worked into the mainstream of the Martin Luther King legend. It may be of course that the "shared meal" was never seen as terribly important by the followers of Dr. King, since Abernathy had not effectively projected himself as a symbol of *all* the followers of the late leader. Only under that formality could he hold a place in the legend during his own lifetime. But there is another reason, too. Since he has not come to exercise anything approximating the leadership role which King exercised, the *reality* of the situation was too far removed from the symbolism which he was using.

This long excursus may be of some real assistance in coming to understand the formation of the Old Testament. Living in the communications age, no one in America really objected to the kind of heightening which took place before their eyes, *provided that it matched their emotional experience of the reality*. It seemed fitting that King's last sermon should touch on death. It seemed fitting to his stature as "prophet" that he should have some inkling of his approaching death. This was all so fitting that his earlier deliveries of that same sermon disappeared from the national memory. On the other hand, although Abernathy's relating of the events of the last meal was totally "honest" and restrained, it never entered into the legend in a heightened fashion. The fact that the two had shared many meals in this fashion continued to be related. This episode never grew into myth, as we have said, because it did not correspond to the nation's emotional experience of the reality. As pure reality, as the experience of King's relationship with one dear friend (who has not succeeded in becoming a symbol of anything else), the incident simply was not important enough to support much further heightening.

Something very akin to this dynamic was operating in the social composition of the Old Testament. For this reason, no believer ought to fear the word "mythic" or "heightening" as applied to Old Testament composition. It is not as though the growth processes of the Old Testament were unchecked by any forces. Forces very much like those just described were at work. Myths could not be created out of nothing; there was a preexistent reality. Moreover, growth of the myth was steadily checked against the nation's emotional experience of that reality. Something which did not help to evoke that reality, as the nation had emotionally experienced it, did not long remain in the tradition. This emotional experience had to have a broad base within the nation; it was not enough that a single man should so have experienced the reality, that his consciousness of it became part of the national heritage.

Another factor, however, is involved in the Old Testament dynamic which has not yet been involved in the contemporary matters just described. The Old Testament stories (as we shall examine in the next chapter) began fairly early to grow in a cultic situation. This added a number of other elements to their composition and modification. Perhaps the most important was the function which the cult served in transmitting the religious heritage to the young. We have noted before that, at least in the earlier years, for those who had actually experienced the reality, that reality was enough. They had seen the might and terror of the Egyptian empire from close at hand. They knew that in one point of time they were enslaved to that empire—as were dozens of other peoples—and that at another they were free, delivered. For persons who had actually experienced this, simple memory of the reality was enough, perhaps for a long time, to bring back the emotional experience. Even if that memory remained fresh through a long lifetime—which is not altogether consonant with human experience—there arose eventually the problem of transmitting that emotional experience to the young. If the young could not share that memory with almost the same intensity as their elders, ultimately there could be no national or religious unity. The logical focus for this transmission was the cult. Almost by its nature, cult stands in the present and stretches in two directions: Toward the past where the commemorated reality occurred and toward the future generation who must accept that past experience as their very own experience if the religious heritage is to live. The cult must make it possible for the young to graft themselves onto an ancient reality.

This book may differ from others in placing the dynamic of the heightening almost at the beginning of the transmission of tradition. Whether this be true or not, there is a certain dynamic at work which makes the heightening an ongoing process—up to a point. The process continues as each generation finds it necessary to heighten somewhat in order to transmit its own emotional experience of the (now long past) reality. The process ceases at a certain juncture for a number of reasons. The artistic process is now complete. Like the finished poem, the heightened narrative is now sufficient for future generations to evoke that past experience which even their grandparents did not personally witness. To touch the story any further would be to risk ruining it. Moreover, by this time one or two generations have shared the same emotional experience through the medium of the inherited narrative. (In earlier times, perhaps, the generations would have shared the experience in different ways. The older generation might share it partially through personal experience or partially through the personal narrative of elders now deceased; the younger generation shared it almost totally through the cultic narrative.) At this point, the narrative becomes canonized and acquires a certain sacredness of its own. Since this particular narrative has served as the medium by which a couple of generations shared in that past experience which was holy, because it involved the Divine Presence, the narrative itself eventually becomes holy too.

It is to be hoped that more conservative readers may not find all this excessively speculative. It is not out of the question of course that the events of the exodus narrative be accepted directly as we find them in the Old Testament. Only nonscholarly *a priori* judgments would deem it impossible that rivers should turn to blood or that frogs and locusts, from no visible natural cause, should appear to bring disaster on a mighty land. The writer shares no such *a priori* judgments.

On the other hand, the Old Testament text itself seems to have a certain ambivalence toward some of the wonders wrought. There are evidences in *Exodus* 7-12 that a number of differing accounts have been brought together. These evidences are one of the starting points for the theory of "sources" which sees great ancient streams flowing into the Old Testament text as we presently have it. Certain of the wonders wrought the Pharaoh's magicians seem capable of producing. Some conclude from this that the wonders of the Lord ("Our God is a better magician than your god!") have been considerably colored by the magical atmosphere of the Egyptian world. Still some commentators have been rather cavalier in their treatment of this material. One sometimes reads that all these motifs can be found in contemporary Near Eastern literature. Documentation for this statement is not easily found. There is for example, good documentation for the "Moses in the Bulrushes" story in Akkadian literature. But the Akkadian account is several hundred years removed from the Moses story. It is true that some aspects of the plagues can be attendant on the annual flooding of the Nile. Certain types of silt produce a reddish color in the river; inundation provides ideal opportunities for the breeding of insects. The plague of darkness may be explained to some extent by the Near Eastern phenomenon of the *Hamsin*. This is a kind of sirocco, a wind blowing in from the desert and creating a sandstorm at a great distance above the earth. This of course causes the phenomenon of noonday darkness, mildly distressing to the modern mind and perhaps terrifying to the pretechnologiral. But there is more to the phenomenon than that. It is accompanied by a change in air pressure which is reminiscent of the *Föhn* in parts of Austria. This change has such palpable psychological and physiological effects that (in *Föhn*- afflicted countries) certain notable provisions are made for it in law. Examinations may not be held during a *Föhn;* judicial trials are interrupted; medical operations are performed only in case of dire necessity. Since the modern Near East is less organized than modern Western Europe, such legal provisions have not been made to protect against the rigors of the *Hamsin*. But the effects are very similar and joined to a frightening darkness.

A moment's reflection, however, will show that the above can hardly be an "explanation" of the exodus event. If some of the phenomena were attendant on any given inundation of the Nile, it is most unlikely that all of them would be attendant on any given inundation. (It seems most unlikely that the nation could survive if these were annual traumata!) But if they were an annual event, one would be hard-pressed to find a connection between these events and the deliverance of the Hebrews, which is of course precisely the point which the biblical authors are making. One would have to define "miracle" pretty strictly to remove the extraordinary timing and confluence of such a series of natural events from the "miracle" category. In interpreting these events, one ought to be careful in avoiding all dogmatism, whether it flows from uncritical religious belief or uncritical atheism.

The Hebrew bible provides us with some evidence that the miraculous crossing of the sea was originally a more modest tradition. The Hebrew text (*Ex* 13,18) speaks of a "Sea of Reeds." The same phrase is related in the

Septuagint as "Red Sea." Here, as always in treating with the Septuagint, we cannot be certain that the translators were dealing with the same Hebrew text that we have inherited through the Massoretic tradition. Even if they were, they may have interpreted it in light of other and more exciting traditions. Until very recent times, the Septuagint has won the day and its phrase has influenced almost all subsequent translations.

The difference of course is enormous in its consequences. For the Hebrews to cross the Red Sea without benefit of ships would require a feat something like a Cecil B. DeMille production. But if a Sea of Reeds is under question, the situation is quite different. The Hebrews traveling on foot and lightly equipped could make their way through a swamp safely to the other side. A highly mechanized army, using chariots, the most complex weapon of the age, would be at a great disadvantage. If the Egyptians tried to cross the swamp with their chariots, driven by a blind conviction that such superior weaponry must always be advantageous (a kind of inflexibility which the military has not ceased to display in the twentieth century), the results could easily be disastrous for the Egyptians. How extraordinary is it that the pious Hebrews saw in all this the "hand of the Lord" and saw in the military lack of imagination not a weakness common to generals but a "hardness of heart" brought about by the Lord?

To a certain extent, miracles are in the eyes of the beholder. The most religious of us lives in a totally nonreligious age. It is difficult for us to perceive the mentality of an age which judged that it saw the Lord frequently at work. The expression *mal'ak Jahweh* "angel of the Lord," which we read in the Old Testament can frequently mean the "natural" appearance of a person who served as the Lord's mediator in getting something done. A later age, partially to heighten and partially perhaps through simple misunderstanding, has converted these figures into awesome appearances, the direct intervention of the Lord.

To live among pious modern Christian Arabs in the East is to be exposed again to this more ancient mentality. One may witness the process by which a skilled lawyer in a difficult case, or a physician in a serious illness, came to be hailed—even by educated Arabs—as an "angel of the Lord," sent by the Lord to see that justice was done or that his children were healed. In some of the incidents, the matters accomplished may be so remarkable that the observer would be hard-pressed to prove that the term "angel of the Lord" was not a rather accurate description. Then, one could easily see that if the actions of this lawyer or doctor were to work their way into a tradition, that their basic "natural" origins could easily be lost sight of, since they were so insignificant in the events that transpired.

Some of the heightening in the course of transmission was pretty casual. Some of it took place, perhaps, in the small family circle. Much of it however, took place under the auspices of public cult. To examine some of the notions of the extremely complex question of cult among the ancient Hebrews will be the purpose of our next chapter.

THE PASSOVER LITURGY AND
ITS PRE-HEBRAIC BACKGROUND 3

We have already mentioned that the Passover cultic meal is at least partially perhaps, derived from a Canaanite festival. It is probably also derived partially from some kind of nomadic festival. This festival the Hebrews would have experienced long before entering Canaan. The nomadic aspect of the feast is indicated by the details of preparation and serving of the sacrificial animal and the vegetables (bitter herbs) which would be characteristic of a nonsedentary society.

This partial derivation from preexisting cultic patterns involves us in a notion which is quite foreign to the twentieth century. "Originality" was something generally rather suspect in the ancient Near East. Living in an age which has somewhat lost its sensitivity for traditions, the modern reader must make a genuine effort to grasp the strength of this notion in biblical times. It was the effort to be nonoriginal in literature which contributed largely to the "social composition" of the bible. This same desire to fit into the preexisting pattern accounts for the phenomenon—visible today in the Near East—of building "holy shrine on holy shrine." The Mohammedans built the Mosque of Omar on the ancient site of the Temple not, (as we might have thought in the preecumenical West) to show disrespect for Judaism, but because they reverenced the soil on which the Jews had worshiped. It is a common phenomenon today in the Near East to find many smaller mosques dotting the countryside, built on the sites of ancient synagogues. As we shall discuss later, the building of the Temple of Solomon on the "threshing floor" which David had purchased may well be an indication of this same mentality, since it seems likely that the ancient threshing floor was a major cultic center. (In fact, the widespread Christian judgment that the building of pagan shrines on Christian centers was principally intended to blot out the memory of the Christian site is open to some question—at least in the East.)

In David's time, there was further good reason for the Hebrews to embrace the external format of the Jebusite Cult which served Jerusalem before his conquest. However, even in the earliest years, this tendency to embrace the preexisting format was strictly part of a pattern. An interesting judgment in specific proof of a strong tendency toward *liturgical traditionalism* is evidenced by certain textual studies. Within a given religious framework, the religious texts of the ancient Near East are generally written in language which is archaic or archaized. This is an indication of the truism that liturgy is traditional by nature and strongly resists change. Even in the twentieth century, which generally tends to equate change and progress, liturgical reforms among Catholics have met strong opposition by reason of this dynamic, even though those reforms were sponsored by an authoritarian church structure. This resistance to change may even be greater if the religious personnel move across boundaries from one religion to another and bring their own fixed patterns with them. There is some evidence that this happened in the Old Testament and that it is part of an ancient religious phenomenon. There may also be some indication of this phenomenon in an observation which Homer makes. (In the judgment of some, the works of Homer offer interesting insights into cultural patterns of the "heroic age," since Homer is writing of legends which long predate him in the West. Some of these legends, at least, show signs of Eastern origin.) Homer notes that four ancient guilds are "welcomed wherever they go . . . architects, storytellers, physicians and religious personnel" (*Odyssey* 17:382ff). This last indicates that the religious personnel were among those guilds which were somehow "boundary free." What they had to offer was sufficiently in demand that they could move with a kind of freedom not given in the ancient world (or the modern one) to all citizens.

The Old Testament itself gives an indication of an analogous cultural pattern. Chapters 17-18 in Judges tell of a wandering Levite who is hired by a private citizen to tend his self-made shrine. (The private citizen had previously installed his non-Levitical son.) Later in the episode, the Levite is taken away by the Danite tribe, through threat of force. Some may view this episode as a bit removed from the internationally mobile personnel of Homer (although not really; the extent to which the Danites can be considered a "tribe of Israel" at this point is open to serious question.) At any rate, the story certainly indicates the hold which the priestly guild maintained, and the use of guild members across theological boundaries which we might consider fixed and inviolable.

Obviously, this is not to say that the Hebrews simply took over one pagan rite (or a combination of them) and adopted it as the cultic Passover meal, any more than one could say the Christians simply adopted the Passover meal as their eucharist. No nomadic ritual or first fruits festival would have come down to our own day if the Hebrews had not made their own specific adaptations of it. For one thing, the significance of the symbolism changed, as the Christians were later to change it further. The smearing of blood, the "bitter herbs," the "unleavened bread," all of which came into the Passover meal from a host of diverse origins, received a unity within the Hebrew liturgical framework. All of them were related to the great historical events which stand at the center of the Old Testament religion.

This symbolism then was early accompanied by a "cultic recitation" of these great events of the past. Doubtless, cultic recitation of the ancient confessional formulas had some existence among the Hebrews prior to their liturgical adaptation to these pagan cults. The use of these cultic formulas was of immense significance even prior to their being joined to more elaborate rituals. Some Old Testament scholars go so far as to say that some small cultic phrases in the Old Testament constitute the kernel of the Pentateuch as we have it, "and the rest is commentary." This is perhaps an exaggeration but, like many exaggerations, probably founded in truth. In an oral tradition, it is the memorable lines, the striking phrases (or even the humorous ones), which tend to have the longest life span. It may be that the most discerning literary critic can find in the Old Testament as we have it, a certain "core" of ancient traditions which has been considerably amplified. On the other hand, such discernment is sometimes hindered by subjectivity and perhaps not worth the effort.

The most important part of these cultic recitations antedates their inclusion in the meal and continues to live among pious Jews to the present day —the role of "memory." Such terms as "memory," "memorial meal," and "remember" must be understood in the Hebrew context. These words do not simply mean "recollection." It is not that the cult is intended to bring to mind past events or freshen an old memory. Rather, memory in these texts means that the past is to be *re-presented, actualized,* somehow made real and present. This notion, which has come to have immense significance in many Christian liturgical traditions, is fairly clearly indicated throughout the Old Testament itself. In Deuteronomy 5 for example, the Hebrews are reminded that the Covenant, to which we shall devote a later chapter, was made with them, not with their fathers. In an analogous tradition, Deuteronomy 29 notes that the Covenant is made not only with those present, but with future generations who stand now "in the presence of the Lord," to use the Jerusalem Bible's effective translation.

This notion of "re-presentation" is something which has grown clearer and clearer in Jewish traditions. It is illustrated very clearly in some passages to be found in the various editions of the Passover *Haggadah,* the Jewish liturgical textbook for Passover. As in any liturgical religion, there are variations in editions of the *Haggadah.* The following points are not always found in all editions.

This *Haggadah* picks up the theme of the Old Testament that the great events of the exodus involved the present participants in the Passover meal. These participants are to note that God brought *us* out of Egypt. The phrase "our fathers" is occasionally used, but the refrain in the most vital passages of the *Haggadah* is that God brought *us;* we were there; we were delivered. The smallest (male) child present at the Passover meal plays a vital liturgical role. He is to ask a series of stylized questions in the course of the meal, that the great events of the past may all be brought to mind. His role, of course, is to fulfill one of the two ambivalent directions of the liturgy. It reaches toward past and future generations, striving to make all things present to the liturgical participants as they are to the Divinity. Just how young, this "youngest child" may be is indicated by some editions of the *Haggadah* which give the instructions on how he is to be coached, if need be, during the meal itself. The *feminine* imperative is used. This is significant, because the feminine role in the liturgy is quite secondary. Still, the stern rabbinical editors knew from experience that if the child was really very small, success in getting him to ask the right question at the right time was enhanced if the coaching was left to his mother.

We have stressed how young this child might be, in order to make the following point. Some texts of the *Haggadah* permit the child to use the phrase "our fathers" as a kind of deliberate mistake, until he is firmly corrected by the president of the liturgy. He is instructed that *he* was there! That he must say *us,* no matter how young he is. While the correction is kindly, it is very firm. This mistake cannot be tolerated without detriment to the most basic idea of the Passover meal—re-presentation.

The more philosophically minded may be bothered by the above. Professional philosophers, in both Christian and Jewish circles, have not been too helpful. How real is the reality of this "sacramental re-presentation"? The philosophers who treat the subject insist that it is not a fiction, that this is a real re-presentation. If pressed to answer the question "what kind of reality"?, some of them have recourse to the expression "sacramental reality," which the reader may or may not find helpful. At times, the author wonders if that answer does not bring us "back to square one," as the British say. Perhaps it is not wise to be asking such a metaphysical question here: What is the nature of the reality under discussion? That the re-presentation of past events *is* real in cults like the Passover meal is a firm human conviction, which is over three thousand years old (and perhaps much older, since we know so little about pre-Hebraic cult). Perhaps the metaphysician ought not to be asked the question, "How real?"

The idea that the past is being made present is illustrated by certain specifics in the course of the meal. At one point, the president of the meal picks up the unleavened bread and says, "This is the bread of affliction which our fathers ate in the wilderness." (In fact, the verb *to be* is not expressed in this type of construction in most Semitic languages; since the tense of the

Semitic verb *to be* is quite ambiguous; it is replaced in this kind of construction with an unambiguous particle, accurately translated *is* in English.) This particular phrase, of course, is of deep interest to many Christians, who see it as a kind of backdrop to "This is my body" of the Christian liturgical formula. In this phrase, the use of "my" is but another indication of the ancient notion of re-presentation. The president of the Christian liturgy is seen as simply making present again a past action of Christ accomplished once-and-for-all.

It may also be (although this is less clear) that the concluding words of the Christian liturgical pericope, "Do this in memory of me," are also an indication of the re-presentation notion. If this idea were being presented in a polemical context—which is hardly the purpose here—the following objections would have to be noted. Even if we are dealing here with the very words of Christ (which is by no means clear), the words could be an echo of one of two basic Semitic notions. If the words are an echo of *zikkaron*, the "memorial feast," we have fairly clear ideas that the notion of reactualization of the past is indicated. On the other hand, there is a Jewish synagogue service today, the *'azkara*, simple recollection of the dead, or "memorial service" as modern English understands the term. Old Testament occurrences of the word seem to carry no deeper meaning. The *'azkara* is found in Aramaic texts at least as far back as the fourth century. Does the word (and the reality) of *'azkara* as a simple recollection service antedate the fourth century? By how much? If the word was in use in early Christian times, did the Church understand the liturgical formula in terms of *'azkara* or the much older *zikkaron*? To attempt to answer these questions is to pile speculation on speculation.

In light of the above, then, there is some evidence that the modern Christian liturgy stands in a chain of tradition reaching back to the Hebrews and well before, to the Canaanite liturgical tradition. How ancient this tradition is, we do not know. The number of clearly liturgical texts at our disposal from this tradition is small. To what extent the Canaanite liturgy is indigenous and perhaps original is consequently largely unknown. We do know that in these three liturgies, Christian, Hebrew and Canaanite, we are dealing with large areas of similarities. Is this offensive to the pious reader? It really ought not to be. Both Christian and Jewish theology tend to insist that the scriptures are simultaneously truly divine and truly human. But if they are truly human, they ought to reflect common human values—values of a sort which we would find reflected in any human liturgy. This is precisely the case here. While we are dealing with diverse realities, the ritual used to express them remains very largely the same in three religious frameworks. The late Monsignor Ronald Knox, teasing his staid British congregation, remarked that "what our forefathers liked about the Holy Saturday ritual was its delightful pagan flavor." Less ironically and more accurately expressed, we might say that what the Hebrews liked about the Canaanite ritual and what the Christians liked about the Passover was their delightful *human* flavor.

Old Testament scholars regularly point out something else involved here, which makes the ultimate theological victory of the Hebrews over the Canaanites rather extraordinary. There was an enormous cultural gap between the two. The culture of the Canaanites by almost any criterion was decidedly superior. Their crafts were so superior that it is a cliche among archaeologists to note, "the Hebrews won another victory here!" when examining a site and finding an inferior culture thrust on a superior one. One detects traces yet in the Old Testament of the faint admiration of the Hebrew "country bumpkins" on first exposure to the superior cultural level of the Canaanites. This admiration can be detected only in traces; it is something which earlier editors at first did not wish to record and which later editors simply did not believe. The total misunderstanding of the basic thrust of paganism, which we find in the later books of the Old Testament, is doubtless the sincerity of ignorance. It is difficult to believe that the earlier religious leaders of the Hebrews could so badly have underestimated their theological opposition. In any event, the simple Hebrew folk certainly had a clear awareness of the cultural superiority of the Canaanites. This awareness made the maintenance of Israel's "theological purity" a constantly difficult task. We have evidences that the simple Hebrews asked themselves frequently the not altogether unreasonable question: "How can they be superior to us in all else and yet be less wise than we in dealing with the gods?"

All this left the religious leaders of the Hebrews with a difficult balance to maintain. They certainly made use of Canaanite ritual in later times, while eschewing most that was basic to Canaanite theology. On the other hand, there are those who note that some of the more universal bits of earlier Hebrew legislation—dealing with ecological balance, for example, the care of trees—always begin with the phrase "when you come into the land." This phrase may indicate that the legislation existed in Canaan prior to the Hebrew arrival. If this judgment is correct, we find the Hebrews then indebted to the Canaanites for more than externals.

The Old Testament scholar occasionally feels himself to be a frustrated detective. He finds traces of something or other in the Old Testament, phrases which might indicate something, then no further proof to buttress or destroy his hypothesis. One such frustrating bit is a possible interpretation of the word *pesah*, "passover," in Hebrew. What is the origin of the word and does its origin shed any light on the festival? There is a possibility, not to be dismissed summarily, that the root meaning, "limp," "hop," or some such, may be related to a kind of dance. Since the Hebrew word *haggag*, "to celebrate a religious festival," rather clearly means at least a ceremonial procession, if not a dance, this possibility intrigues. Coupled with the much later (2 *Sam* 6,14) passage where David's wife upbraids him for dancing before the ark, one may speculate a little here. Did Michal object to David's dancing, wild and enthusiastic, as a throwback to the (now inferior) early Canaanite practices? Was she embarrassed by something that had appealed to her fathers perhaps, but distressed her now after a generation of living in another culture (as American-Polish teenagers are embarrassed by their grandparents at a wedding)? We shall never know, barring the discovery of further texts. There are a couple of methodological points worth noting here. The first is the difficulty in making much solid argument from such aspects of Hebrew language studies as etymologies or tenses. If Hebrew *is* a language endowed with the extraordinary precision of, let us say, classical Greek, that precision is presently beyond our control. Still, to reject any suggestion for further understanding of the text on the grounds that the suggestion cannot be proved beyond cavil, is to reduce ourselves to a kind of scholarly nihilism.

More easily proved than the Canaanite influence on Hebrew religious practice is the presence of an influence which we might call "the agricultural mystique." A similar mystique exists among Austrian and German peasants. The most striking feature of their personalities, at least to the urban outsider, is their near-mystical relationship to land and soil. These peasants are not skilled in speech and have great difficulty in verbalizing the way they feel about the earth and its productivity, but their feelings soon became clear to the observer. It is not clear to what extent this feeling is universal and common, say, to American farmers in today's highly mechanized farm world. But the feelings of the Austrian peasants are very akin to a common Old Testament theme.

In the Old Testament, attitudes toward the productivity of the earth flow from two different sources. The first is the "quasi-mystical" mentioned above to which we shall shortly return, but there is another powerful force which impelled the ancients to reverence the earth and its productivity: The earth is not always productive! Palestine is a land of a dry season and a rainy season. If it does not rain in the rainy season, the inhabitants face a cruel year. Few readers have ever experienced the real possibility of starvation or even been hungry for a prolonged period of time (unless on a diet, for cosmetic or health purposes). This makes it almost impossible for us to grasp the attitude toward food in the ancient Near East. If it did not rain in the rainy season, the prospects were bleak indeed. Depending on the state of international trade in a given period, prolonged drought could lead to consequences that were merely severe or truly devastating. In some periods, drought could mean the loss by starvation not only of one's own life, but one's family, clan or even nation. In this light, the drama of the spring in parts of Palestine can hardly be overestimated. Once the rains cease and sunshine floods the land, a barren landscape seems to come to life overnight. The hardiest of seeds, which have lain there for a long time, leap into life at the touch of warmth. It would be hard for the pretechnological mind not to see in this the finger of the Divinity.

We are badly handicapped too, in appraising this phenomenon, since we know so little about the ecology of the land in biblical times. There has been little or no study done in this area until very recently. A modern traveler to Israel is appalled by so much barrenness and sterility in a land productive of so much religious life. And this barrenness is still quite evident, despite the remarkable Israeli achievements in agriculture. However, much evidence in the Old Testament indicates that the situation in ancient times was quite different. Though all growth did depend on seasonal rains, apparently the land was stubbed with trees, which would serve to hold much water in the earth. (One evidence for the profusion of trees is mention in the Old Testament of types of animal life which could not survive without them.) Enormous amounts of study remain to be done in the ecology of the Old Testament. Still, even in Old Testament times, the earth's productivity in Palestine was always attended by a certain caprice. That is painfully clear.

It may also be that the Semitic appreciation of "hospitality" originated in the above. What developed into a characteristic Semitic virtue, began as total necessity—if any kind of society was to survive. There cannot be much social progress without travel. In the ancient East, travel without hospitality was virtually out of the question, certainly in earlier times. (We are prescinding here from the disputed and intriguing question on *when* the camel was domesticated.) Without the opportunity fairly frequently to refurbish one's supply of food and water, there could have been virtually no travel. This involved hospitality because of the limited productivity of the land and the capriciousness of water supplies.

One of the great Old Testament theologians, Von Rad, finds traces of the agricultural mystique as late as Isaiah 28, 26 and 29. He finds the notion of man's awe at taming the earth also in Sophocles: "Man dares even to wear the earth, the eldest of the gods, the immortal, the unwearied, turning her soil with ploughs and horses year after year." This is certainly part of the agricultural mystique. The ancient/peasant/magical mentalality sees all agriculture as somehow a violation of the earth's integrity for the sake of man. The ancient notion of sowing in sadness and reaping in joy may be allied to this idea. The sadness of the sowing is of ritual origin, sympathy with the virginal earth in its being violated; the joy, sharing with the joys of "mother earth" in her fructification.

That the "agricultural mystique" influenced the earlier and more primitive worship of the Hebrews is fairly easy to accept. But it was also not without influence in what developed into the ultimately sophisticated religious worship of the Temple. We have already noted that the Temple of Solomon was built on the threshing floor which David purchased from the Jebusite Araunah. We have also cited the possibility that the purchase may have been motivated by the role of the threshing floor as cultic center. If the threshing floor in the ancient East was generally a cultic center, this may have been for reasons both pragmatic and mystical. We know from the evidence of Ugaritic literature that the threshing floor was a common meeting place. In the ancient world, especially in simpler times, the number of places available for large meetings would be quite limited. In any but a democratic and highly organized society, there would be little point in building an edifice specifically for this purpose. The threshing floor, then, conveniently served as a general meeting place. On a more poetic level, the notion of the eschatological-type judgment evident in the threshing floor imagery (an idea picked up in the New Testament), the division of wheat and chaff, the storage of one and the destruction of the other, lent itself easily to notions of primitive worship. But before this level, obviously, the threshing floor was closely tied to the agricultural mystique. The activity of the threshing floor marked the climax of a successful farming season and led immediately to the preparation of bread, the basic food and stuff of life in ancient Palestinian society, as almost everywhere else. (This notion probably explains why one of the ancient Ugaritic military epics devotes some verses to the bread being baked for the entire army. One commentator notes quite correctly that this is not the stuff of epic in the West. Perhaps not, but for someone living in the world of the agricultural mystique, the baking of enormous amounts of bread for a traveling army would certainly be a notion inspiring the "wonder" which Aristotle saw as the goal of epic poetry.)

It may be that both of these elements are alluded to in the story of the purchase. The seller wishes to include in the transaction both "threshing sled" and "oxen for the holocaust." The former is precisely the instrument used by Arab farmers today in Palestine to do their threshing. But the seller wished too to offer the materials of cultic worship. The episode begins with a pestilence of the Lord visiting the people in punishment for David's offense. The Lord has sent his "angel" to inflict the punishment. David sees the angel of the Lord standing beside the threshing floor of Araunah the Jebusite. The Greek text, which occasionally offers "glosses" or lines of commentary which are valid and helpful, notes "it was the time of the wheat harvest."

This episode was to be of enormous significance as long as the Jewish nation lasted. Solomon's Temple and all that followed it was always to stand on this site. Moreover, it is today the site of the Mosque of Omar. It may be that today this mosque contains evidence of the ancient liturgy which certainly long predated Hebrew use of the site and possibly long predated the Jebusite threshing floor cult. The West calls this building today the "Mosque of Omar" but the Muslims call it "the Dome of the Rock." Within today's mosque, there is a massive natural rock formation which makes a kind of enormous natural altar. Pictures of the rock do not do real justice to its awesomeness. Since the Rock is a holy object to the Muslims, much of it has been surrounded by iron fencing and glass enclosure to prevent its gradual destraction by relic-hunting pious faithful. Because of the glass and fencing, the size of the rock and its altar-like formation cannot be reproduced in photographs. A circular staircase leads the pilgrim some distance to the bottom of the rock where he may study its base and the natural concave pedestal which leads to the altar-like top. Even granting the rockiness of the Jerusalem area, this formation is still extraordinary. Its size, shape and location may well have given birth to the legend that Isaac lay bound on its surface awaiting sacramental execution. (Granting for the moment the historicity of the biblical account, geographically this would be most unlikely.) When one visits the Dome of the Rock, it is precisely the massive altar-like natural rock structure which seizes one's attention. Coupled with the work which has been done in the cultic notion of the ancient threshing floor, the Eastern notion of "holy place on holy place," and the general religious conservatism of the area, this striking natural rock altar leads to interesting questions. It is most likely that worship took place on this altar almost as long as there were inhabitants in the area. Was the threshing floor then built here, since the site was already a "holy place"? What function did this natural rock altar serve in Solomon's Temple? (That it served *some* function is perfectly clear. It could hardly have been ignored in the Temple. The efforts which would have been required to disguise it in the Temple would have been so great as to suggest another site for the building—unless the builders wished to utilize the rock.) In any event, the building of the threshing floor in close proximity to this ancient natural rock altar increases the probability that the "agricultural mystique" in the East is very ancient.

To note one last indication of this mystique. Exodus 24, 12 observes of Moses and Aaron, who have been on the mountain with the Lord: "They had experience of the Lord; they ate and they drank." The word we have translated "to have experience" is the Hebrew *hazah*. No felicitous English translation comes to mind. This is the word used of prophetic "vision" and seems to imply some extrasensory experience. Neither prophets, nor Moses, nor Aaron could be described as "seeing God" unless some kind of qualification is added. True, the line is brief, almost fragmentary, but it is a sound principle that little nonessential survives in the transmission of the Old Testament. In the account of the covenantal ratification as we presently have it, the ceremony is completed in two ways. The priestly account, drawing on much later sources, has the ratification completed with a complex ritual of sacrifice and sprinkling with blood. The Jahwist account, here as frequently drawing on more primitive sources, describes a sacramental meal: "They had experience of the Lord; they ate and drank in his presence." At least one of the overtones of this fragment seems to indicate: Food is holy.

We have touched on much material in this chapter beyond simple description of the Passover liturgy in a given period. This was by design. Much modern writing on the Old Testament seems to opt for one of two choices, as though they were mutually exclusive: substantial historicity in the Old Testament or preoccupation with ancient myth and cult and their vestiges in the Old Testament as we have it. It is the basic thrust of this book that such a dichotomy is a false one. There is much evidence that both of these elements are living and present in the Old Testament. The Hebrews certainly were endowed with a strong sense of history, but it was a *religious* history. (The Hebrew division names Isaiah, Jeremiah *et al.* as "latter prophets." Books which the Western mind names "historical," the Hebrew tradition gathers under the title "former prophets.") Endowed with their strong sense of history, which they viewed as religious, and sharing the appreciation of all in the ancient East for tradition and the nonoriginal, the leaders of the Hebrews made a felicitous choice. They took the best cultural values of the world they found, its deep religious awe and sense of wonder. They took its insight into the sacredness of the human, as in the holiness of food for men. Into this cultural framework they inserted their own great religious insights and transmitted the combination to the subsequent generations, in their tradition and outside of it, who have not always appreciated the splendor of what it was the Hebrews had done.

PRESENT AT CREATION

CHAOS: 4

There is one significant explanation of the continued popularity of the Old Testament which ought at least to be mentioned in passing, though we plan to return to it in the twelfth chapter, "Old Testament and New." One of the classical Protestant explanations of the living role of the Old Testament is the clarity of its portrayal of God. The focus of the New Testament is rather on Jesus. All treatment of the Divinity is refracted somehow through the prism of Jesus. For that reason, the Old Testament continues to have a vital role in Christianity. There is much to be said for this. Ignatius of Loyola (no Protestant) is preoccupied in *The Spiritual Exercises* with themes which seem colored by some kind of Old Testament exposure: The greatness of God, the distance between God and man, the monstrousness of human sin and rebellion. If we have little direct evidence that Ignatius read deeply in the Old Testament (and we have little such evidence; he does not often quote the Old Testament) still, his spirituality seems redolent of Old Testament attitudes and his hermeneutic of the New Testament much colored by the Old Testament. This may be an example of the rich dimensions which the Old Testament offers to Christian spirituality.

Still, as remarked earlier, there seems a better explanation for the vitality of Old Testament studies in our time: The Old Testament's open admission of the role played in human affairs by unreasonable and very powerful forces of evil. To our earlier names of presently popular pre-twentieth-century authors who touched on these themes, we might add the somewhat dour Hawthorne. To be sure, Hawthorne's evil frequently focused itself in the hearts of men. But in some of his works, "The Dark Veil," for example, there are hints of a brooding force of evil which comes to live in men predisposed to receive it.

It is not so unreasonable as might seem at first blush that the twentieth century is more in sympathy with this notion, present in the most ancient Old Testament myths, than were many other centuries which stand between us and the Old Testament. The common human psyche feels itself troubled and insecure almost in direct proportion to the gap between its technological and humanistic achievements. A relatively simple age, but with some humanistic sensitivity, had some degree of security. A pre-technological age, but primitive also in humanistic growth, would have

39

deep experience of man's dark possibilities for evil. A sophisticated post-technological age, whose humane growth had not equaled its technical attainments, would feel equally troubled. It is perhaps in the relative balance of these factors that our age and the age of the Old Testament have so much in common. Even as a physically strong man is more frightened by his rage than is a weakling, the twentieth century is more frightened by its capacity for evil than any preceding century in history.

Moreover, rightly or wrongly, modern man is afflicted with a vague, troubling thought: The ever-present danger of cataclysm and apocalypse is not totally of man's making. It seems to him that forces are at work conspiring toward evil, forces that he cannot understand and whose effects consequently he cannot predict. Fear of The Bomb and the resulting twilight of civilization brings man psychologically back through the centuries, back through the age of evolutionary optimism, back through the centuries of serene (albeit not always profound) faith, past the birth pangs of Christianity with its joyous hope of an immediate eschaton, past the splendid legalism of the late Old Testament toward the awe, wonder and fear of the early Old Testament period.

Nor is it simply The Bomb which makes us fearful. The horrors of the Second World War, the slaughters of the innocent, the fear growing out of Indochina that even America is capable of national moral evil—all these have contributed. All these fears have been made infinitely less tolerable in our lifetime by reason of our superb communications network. One evil act, distant from us by thousands of miles, can instantaneously through TV become present to our consciousness, perhaps to dwell in our unconscious forever.

One of the classic Near Eastern experiences with chaos (occurring even today, if one does not listen carefully to the weather reports) is the flash flood in a *wadi*. The *wadi* is a river bed, flowing with water in the rainy season, but quite dry for large parts of the year. Over the centuries, the bed, filled with water flowing from distant mountain streams, has worn a deep path through the wilderness. For this reason, the *wadi* is still used as a road by travelers, whether riding on camels or trucks, since it is much more passable than the surrounding landscape. This can be quite dangerous. Even in the normal dry season, the distant mountains occasionally receive quick and heavy showers. This leads to a rather remarkable phenomenon. The water builds rapidly to a short-lived torrent. Racing down the mountain it comes to the sunbaked surface of the *wadi* and moves with incredible speed. This large mass of water may roar by a given point in the *wadi* within two or three minutes and the *wadi* is then again dry. For a traveler caught unaware, the result is a sudden and terrifying death. For an ancient traveler, with no knowledge of how this is possible, with no awareness of the distant mountain source, simply to hear of the *wadi* flash flood would be to experience terror unrelieved. One moment the *wadi* was dry; the next a death-laden torrent; and then total calm. And all this without a cloud in the sky. The emotional effect of this on one man's small world would be not unlike the effect of The Bomb in our lifetime. In recent years, a busload of pilgrims was wiped out not far from Jerusalem in a *wadi* flash flood. Someone had failed to check the weather report. One may meet today educated moderns who seem emotionally scarred by being in the vicinity of the disaster, despite their knowledge of how the disaster occurred and how its recurrence could be forestalled. This offers some insight into the way that such disasters would have affected the man of the Old Testament.

The alert and thoughtful reader may present one serious objection to the comparison being made: in fact, ancient man feared a powerful nature which he could not control. Modern man fears the activities of other men. Is it from these two disparate experiences that ancient and modern developed or deepened their conviction that a powerful, unreasonable chaos broods over the affairs of mankind? But is this difference really significant? What the individual man fears is the power over which he has no control. Is it a meaningful difference that the Old Testament man felt himself weak in the presence of flood or famine and the twentieth-century man feels so standing in the presence of The Bomb or impending social explosion? In both cases, the individual feels terrified and helpless partially because he cannot control an impending disaster, but even more because *he does not understand it*. This is the key to the analogy. Nature's ancient capacity for irrational, massive disaster is not today possessed by an individual man, or by mankind, but by a group of nameless persons living somewhere, motivated by God-knows-what. This is precisely the psychological substratum for the original fears of chaos.

"In the beginning, God created Heaven and Earth," so do many translations of Genesis 1,1 begin. This translation may well be correct and there would be many competent scholars found to defend it. One is reluctant, too, to offer another less familiar translation, because these words in English have had such an enormous emotional effect over the centuries. Many of the classical Protestant "conversion accounts" have the protagonist saying something like the following: "When I first came to college (or to adolescence, or to serious study of the bible) all of my problems centered on the opening words of Genesis. Once I had accepted those, I had little problem with anything else." Despite all the above though, there is an alternative and at least equally probable translation of Genesis 1,1. Although this translation has achieved publicity recently, it is an old explanation of the opening verse and common among the Jewish medieval commentators: "In the beginning of God's creating, the earth was void and empty." We can call this a translation which teaches a *relative* beginning. Before examining the significance of this translation, we should note how it is possible. Translators of the Old Testament are faced with a strange situation. It is fairly commonly agreed that the *consonants* of the Old Testament text, as we have them, are extremely reliable and quite ancient. There is less agreement on the fidelity of the *vowels* to the ancient traditions. How this discord is possible in Hebrew shall not be presently treated. This can be accepted as fact however: Most Old Testament scholars have less confidence in the vowel pattern of the text than in the consonantal pattern. The two translations mentioned above result from a relatively slight change in vocalization. (Analogous differences are possible from vowel changes in English, too. English composition teachers over the years have compiled long lists of words, radically changed by a single vowel, to refute the complaint of the poor speller: I only missed one letter! But the power of the vowel in Hebrew is much, much greater.)

If the second translation is accepted, then the following results: "in the beginning of God's creating, the earth was *tohu wa bohu* and *hoshek*."

What is the difference in translating as in the above paragraph or saying: In the beginning God created Heaven and Earth. And the Earth was *tohu wa bohu* and *hoshek*. Obviously in the second translation, God is credited clearly with being the creator of *tohu wa bohu*. It is a stage in the creative process. The first translation somewhat prescinds from the question of who is responsible for the existence of *tohu wa bohu*. There is a possibility in this interpretation that *tohu wa bohu* preexisted or that it coexisted with the creating God. What then is the significance of the mysterious phrase?

It does not admit of easy translation. Many English translations say "void and empty" which is rather inaccurate. Each of the words alone can mean something like, "desert, wilderness," as the first word means in Ugaritic. Taken in tandem, they seem to mean something like, "disorganized, chaotic." In light of this, it might not be a bad paraphrase to state: "When God began to create, the earth was disorganized and chaotic matter." Further on, some translations make use of the word "deep" to translate *tehom*. In a way, this word is a further explanation of the meaning of *tohu wa bohu*. The *tehom* is a "watery abyss," it is the primeval deep. This primeval deep is clearly preexistent in other ancient Near Eastern literatures. In one of them there is the goddess *Tiamat* (which philologically corresponds to *tehom* of the Hebrew text). She is the adversary of the creating divinity in the ancient cuneiform account. In the pre-Hebraic accounts, the disorganization and chaos at the beginning of creation is not merely neutral. It flows from active combat between (equal) forces of good and evil. Here we have a good example of the fruitfulness of studying the pre-Hebraic accounts. While it is easily demonstrable that the Hebrew account owes much to all the ancient narratives which preceded it, the special genius of the Hebrews is most clearly seen in light of the process of selection and rejection which they employed in editing these old accounts. To some extent, we can argue from what the Hebrews clearly omitted toward an idea of what they were trying to emphasize. Here, for example, they took over clear accounts of a powerful struggle between equals. Hints of the struggle occasionally remain, but any notion of equality between the two combatants is totally washed away. We can argue then from what the Hebrews refused to copy and refused to integrate into their theology to the uniqueness of their accomplishments.

It is somewhat difficult now to grasp what all the excitement and fear was about in the nineteenth century when the discoveries were made that the ancient world had texts predating the Hebrews and bearing analogies to Hebrew religious texts. If one reads the pre-Hebraic texts today and engages in any kind of comparison, the pre-Hebraic texts do nothing but enhance the dignity of the Old Testament. The quasi-hysteria of the nineteenth-century scholars, religious and atheistic, may be another indication of the need which men have to admit a gap between the philosophy or religion which governs their daily lives and the current intellectual speculation. Of the latter, some will be proved correct and ought then to be integrated into one's personal religious or philosophical framework. Some of it will be proved incorrect and can then be safely ignored. In the meantime, the process of integration ought to respect the distance between the two.

If there is dispute on the real meaning of *tohu wa bohu,* there is no dispute on the meaning of *hoshek* in the same sentence. It means "darkness." The small child's fear of the dark reflects an ancient human pattern. Egyptian and cuneiform hymns to the sun worship the sun only partially in terms of its role as life-giving source. They spell out also that the sun dispels some of the possibilities open for the actions of evil men. The evil man loves the darkness as a cover for his evil. Each day the rising of the sun puts to flight the murderer, the thief. In a world where man-directed powers of illumination were quite limited, this is reasonable enough. But from this calm and rational basis, the mind of a man moved on. The setting of the sun makes possible man's evil deeds; there is a correspondence between darkness and evil: Darkness *is* evil. Judas went out from the upper room, "and it was night!" (*Jn* 13,30).

If we read the Old Testament on its own terms, then, what is it that

Genesis is specifically teaching here? (Granting the relative translation now as at least probable.) When God began the creation of the earth, there was already present disorganized, chaotic matter. This disorganized chaos, certainly was not the equal of the creating Divinity. On the other hand, it was powerful. Left to itself, it was a dynamic of disorganization. What God brought into the world was organization and unity. The notion that there is a time and place for everything is of divine origin. The destructive tendencies of the chaos are chained. The waters are to come "so far and no farther." The destructive dynamic of chaos is chained, *but it is not extinguished.* The moon and the stars are placed in the heavens to light the darkness of the night, but night is not destroyed.

As we have noted, one of the reasons why men have not learned as much as the Old Testament wished to teach, is their persistence in asking the wrong questions. In Genesis studies, the more philosophically minded West has constantly asked the question: "Does the account treat the question of creation-out-of-nothing?" Commentators sometimes state that the Old Testament mentality would not understand the question. This perhaps is not too accurately expressed. Better put, the Old Testament man would not be interested in the question. He might be puzzled by the mentality which would raise it. Whether God created out of nothing or out of something is of little pragmatic significance. The relationship between God and chaos in a world where nature is not under any kind of human control is of immense significance. (A Christian Arab friend commenting on some Western interpretations of this passage remarked with ironic Semitic insight: "The Hebrews are asking Moses, how shall we survive? and he answers, Behold! I am inventing the science of metaphysics!")

If creation of the earth from nothing is not of interest to the Hebrews, the Old Testament theologian Anderson notes that another type of creation-out-of-nothing is of deep interest: The creation of the Hebrew nation, through the exodus. Some Old Testament theologians have seemed puzzled that after this initial noting of creation in Genesis, it is treated only in conjunction with some aspect of exodus. This is not really too puzzling. Everything is treated in terms of exodus. Exodus is the central, and for the Hebrews, the historically solid event of all that preceded them. In a religion which pivoted around historical reality, accounts of creation (whose veracity the Hebrews never questioned) had to be treated in terms of events which the Hebrews considered verifiable, since creation was seen correctly as something in a distant and nonverifiable past.

"And the spirit of God brooded over the deep." Fairly recently, another translation for the phrase "spirit of God" has attracted some attention. Some would translate the "spirit of God" here as simply "a mighty wind."

A little reflection, however, will show that the two translations would not be significantly different. *Ruah elohim* as mighty wind would simply be an idiomatic way of expressing "spirit of God." Living in the West, and possessing some three thousand years of speculative research which the Hebrews did not have, we sometimes forget the difficulty which men had in attaining notions of the abstract and the spiritual. En route to purified notions of an abstract divinity, the two great ancient languages of the West, Greek and Latin, used the words for *wind* or *breath* to express the abstractness of the divine being (*pneuma* and *spiritus*). These are clearly near-universal symbols. The wind is invisible, but powerful. On one level of apprehension, breath seems coequal with life. When it is present, there is life; when it is absent, there is death. So man has tended to use the words for wind or breath as clear symbols of the Divinity. Hence, whether we translate the words here as "mighty wind" or "spirit of God," there is little real difference in the meaning. The second is a more abstract notion (perhaps). The first is more symbolic. Both describe the same reality.

The spirit of God then is said to brood (*merahepeth*) over the deep. The meaning of this word, whose Semitic root is *rhp*, is most interesting. The verb is most commonly used of birds in flight. One commentator suggests "hover." In the Ugaritic texts, the same root has the meaning, "soar." It is from this common root meaning that a pre-Christian symbolism of the dove developed, portraying the "spirit of God" as a dove. With subsequent Christian use of the same symbol, and a considerably different notion of "spirit of God," Jewish use of the symbol diminished, perfectly understandably. In like fashion, much beautiful New Testament imagery disappeared from Catholic writing because a given image had become particularly associated with a Protestant interpretation. Being "washed in the blood of the Lamb" for example, is an image that few Catholics would use until very recent times, because they had come to associate the image, not with the New Testament, but with a particular Protestant notion of redemption.

Despite the fact that Hebrews came to use the dove as symbol of the spirit of God long before Christians did, the Old Testament notion of spirit of God is not too clear. There is a temptation here for Christians to read back into the Old Testament all that the New Testament teaches about the concept. (There is a similar temptation to read into the New Testament what Chalcedon taught.) Jewish theologians tend to explain the idea of *ruah elohim* in the Old Testament as very clearly something less than God himself. This is not so clear in the Genesis passage, but there are many others where the *ruah elohim* falls upon a man. The man then seems to have a kind of personal relationship with the *ruah elohim*. To some extent, it seems to become his spirit. Jewish theologians, with their deep sensitivity toward anything which would seem even remotely to compromise the unique oneness of God, prefer to consider this *ruah elohim* as a kind of divine attribute, like his goodness or justice. For analogous reasons, some of the Christian Fathers of the Church tended to equate the *ruah elohim* of the Old Testament with *sanctifying grace* of the Roman tradition, grace in this context being defined as the divine life insofar as it is shared by men. Certainly there are some passages in the Old Testament where such an equation seems not impossible.

The Old Testament picture, then, is that of the Divinity or the power of the Divinity brooding over the dynamic power of chaos. So does the picture of the creative process begin. Many questions are left opened and unanswered. Where did this chaos come from? In the creative process, chaos is subservient to the Divinity, but is it always subservient? Was there a previous struggle? Is the creative process a picture of the aftermath of that struggle? The Old Testament seems deliberately to avoid considerations of these questions. This avoidance of large theological areas is characteristic of the temperate theology of the Old Testament. G. K. Chesterton, in an age simpler than our own, spoke of the Roman church as a great chariot careening down the highways of history, "ever-reeling, but erect." In context, he referred to the church's willingness to take a variety of theological positions on disputed questions without worrying over the ease with which a given theological position might be consonant with previous positions. The Old Testament theology, at least of creation, is quite different. The sacred authors deliberately refrained from answering large areas of questions. In concluding this chapter, we shall stress the one vital question which the Old Testament creation narrative, even in Genesis, does answer. For the moment, it is important to notice the many topics which are ignored.

The Genesis account is directed toward a prephilosophic or "primitive" mentality. It should become clear very shortly that these words imply no pejorative connotations. Living in a post-philosophic and scientific age, we must be aware constantly that the Old Testament, insofar as it offers explanations, is not aimed at our mentality.

What then is the difference between the prephilosophic and the scientific mentality? One of the essential differences would seem to be the manner in which an explanation of a phenomenon is treated, once the explanation is attained. (Both mentalities work eagerly toward explanations.) The prephilosophic is satisfied with the mythic explanation, the description in poetic language of something which might account for the phenomenon. (We shall see an example in chapter five, "Sin and the Fall.") Why does the world seem to work against man, God's creature? The first parents of us all sinned and . . . The scientific mentality will not rest with the mythic, but probes and tests until some kind of answer is found on an empirical level. If this explanation of the difference between the two is accepted, there is some question that all twentieth-century scientists are working from a genuine scientific mentality. For example, modern efforts to explain thought processes on a totally materialistic level, opted for the "electrical discharge" theory to explain thought processes. Subsequent research proved that this was helpful to explain thought in the instantaneous present, but not helpful in explaining long-range thought, memory, creativity in terms of past learning. Some researchers then simply opted for "chemical locking," noting that we need now only to find the key to such chemical activity. This conclusion of course rests on the premise that the thought processes are to be explained totally in terms of matter. (A premise not granted by many researchers who find indications of a certain nonmateriality in the psyche.) The present stage then of the "chemical locking" theory is not scientific but *mythic*. But it is being accepted by some as though it were not to be subjected to further test. This is an intellectualism vastly inferior to the prephilosophic which accepted myth as myth, not as empirical truth.

Perhaps more important is the realization that there are times and places for one sort of thought or the other. An excellent example of the prephilosophic mind at work in the wrong area is found in Kozinsky's novel *The Painted Bird*. The protagonist, a small gifted Jewish child, spends the Second World War wandering through Europe. At one point, he falls into the hands of an emotionally troubled peasant who regularly becomes angry with him. In efforts to avoid the peasant's wrath the child applies his gifted, but prephilosophic mind to the problem. He decides to avoid such things as scratching his nose, shaking his head, blinking his eyes, because each of these actions had sometimes been followed by the peasant's unbridled rage. This is perhaps a good example of the times when myth is not to be employed. Myth's proper function is to be used as an explanation of a reality where an explanation in terms of cause and effect is not at hand, or where the reality is simply too complicated or too painful for human comprehension and expression. In this example, of course, the small child was ignorant of something which a more experienced observer would have known. The causes of rage are many in the emotionally disturbed. Nothing that the child was actually doing provoked these rages; they were brought on by events completed long before the child was born.

Freud, on the other hand, makes a use of myth very much like the use made of it in the Old Testament. Faced with a mass of data which did not admit of easy control but demanded some kind of explanation. Freud began to use myth as a kind of "open-ended" explanation. On one level,

Freud's myths were descriptive of something which, had it been historically so, could have explained the phenomenon he was handling. On another, the myth was deliberately vague; the connection between the myth and the phenomenon not spelled out. Freud used myth as a pedagogical device. If Freud's myths are interpreted or studied literally, we have the same problems with them that we would have with the Old Testament myths if we took them in literal fashion.

The great student of comparative religion, Eliade, makes the remark that Judeo-Christianity differs from all other religions in one attitude toward myth. For the Judeo-Christian, the great events recaptured by mythic expression are historical, once-and-for-all. Other religions view their great events as cyclic. This is not totally acceptable; Eliade later modifies this when he treats of the notion of sacramental re-presentation. We have already seen that for many Jews and Christians, the liturgical year involves a kind of reliving of past events in sequence. For the Christian the sequence is perhaps clearer: The birth, death and resurrection of Christ. It is true that the Christian confesses that these events did happen historically in the past. Still, his participation in them is renewed each year; moreover, the language of the liturgy encourages the Christian to believe that this year's participation is a unique event for him. The Roman Easter vigil service, for example, makes use of the baptism of the catechumens to recapture the experience of past baptism for the Christians. And the baptism is then used emotionally to evoke the experience of the death and rebirth of Christ. One of the major readings of the service is then addressed to catechumens and formed Christians alike, assuring them that as they have been buried with Christ, so they ought to rise with him (*Rom* 6,3-4).

The Old Testament myths are deeply satisfying because they deal with realities which are far too complicated to be handled by any other literary form. Moreover, the value of the Old Testament myths is enhanced by the restraint with which the sacred authors use them. What they state is true. What they refrain from stating remains open-ended so that our ability to use them more than three millennia later is not handicapped. One more problem which the Old Testament does not treat ought to be mentioned here. Could God always control chaos? This is not answered. That God in fact does not always control chaos is too clear in human experience for the Old Testament to spend much time on the question. This is the common human experience. Chaos asserts itself constantly, but irregularly, in human affairs. It is this last which makes chaos particularly painful for men, long after they have come to terms with its existence. If only chaos could be kept constantly in its place. When Macbeth cries out, "She should have died hereafter!", every listener knows immediately what he meant. The mature adult comes to admit the role of chaos in the world, but most never come to live with the irregularity of its intrusions. Theologies have tried to handle this in various ways. It is pointed out that chaos is irregular only from our viewpoint; from a higher viewpoint we could see that chaos is in fact part of a larger pattern. This is scant consolation, since it is only in terms of our own viewpoint that we suffer.

For the peasant mentality, the rhythms of time and place sometimes afford consolations which do not assist a mentality not shaped by the agricultural mystique. For example, in Pearl Buck's classic, *The Good Earth*, the husband of the heroine kneels at her grave and sighs with satisfaction, "You are at last, again, part of the good earth!" For a peasant, the return in death to the soil, the source of life, was not terribly frightening if it came in the proper season. For the nonpeasant mentality, the notion of return to the earth can be frightening. But the peasant has seen too many seeds die in the earth and leap into new life to be frightened by the prospect of returning to the source of life. Still, there is a time and a place. It may be concern with this last which gave rise to the Old Testament notion of the value of being buried "in the land of my fathers" (*Gn 50*), though perhaps the point ought not to be pressed.

The Old Testament is too wise to teach that chaos will never explode out of due season. But it does teach in the Genesis creation account that chaos is somehow subservient to the divine. He imposed a kind of order on it in the creative process. At the end of the flood narrative, the Lord promises that chaos will never be allowed so to burst forth as totally to interrupt the seasons (*Gn 8,22*). With this we return once more to the agricultural mystique. The peasant mentality becomes so attuned to the rhythms of time and place that even the unexpected boon is undesirable, because unexpected. The Western mind might feel that rain in the dry season would be an unexpected blessing. Yet in 1 Samuel 12,16ff, the prophet terrifies the people by the act of bringing rain, though the season is dry. In the narrative, there is little hint of any disaster brought about by the rain, but it reduces the people to total fear. It ought not to rain in the dry season! When it does, something is amiss.

Interestingly enough, the notion that faithfulness to God is not a *guarantee* against the intrusion of chaos is spelled out in the much later work of First Isaiah (28,15). There the unbelievers are chastized precisely for having made a covenant with Mot (god of the underworld) and for thinking that they have assurance that "the destructive whip" will not catch them as it goes by. In the context, where the prophet has been disabusing the people of false notions of covenant, it is clear that what is being reprehended here is the notion of total guarantee against the powers of darkness. The mainstream of Old Testament thought is far too wise to promise that to the believer. Respecting the power of the Lord, the Old Testament is aware that he has never promised total control over chaos. For this reason, it mocks any other god who would make such a promise and despises the adherent of any religion who would be foolish enough to believe it.

What then is the chief lesson of the creation narrative? It may well be this: Chaos is present at creation, but in a totally subservient role. Yahweh uses chaos as he uses everything else—as an instrument to achieve his own purposes. Since the present world is but the continuation of the creative act, man ought not to fear chaos. The Lord controlled it at the very beginning; he controls it now.

As in all religious writings, the Old Testament notion of who is ultimately responsible for evil is not always clear. Psalm 46 (1-2) states precisely enough:

> "God is our shelter and our refuge,
> a timely help in trouble;
> so we are not afraid when the earth heaves
> and the mountains are hurled into the sea."

The above is described as "precise" theology, since the question is left open: who causes the sea to move violently? The answer does not matter, whoever does, it is the Lord who controls all.

On the other hand, a difficult passage in Amos (3,6) may read (as in the New English Bible translation): "If disaster falls on a city, has not the Lord been at work?" If the New English Bible translation is correct, this verse represents a more primitive view.

Most accurately expressed, the lesson of the creation narrative (which is not always grasped by the writers of the Old Testament) is that chaos continues dark and powerful to thrust itself into the affairs of men. It is an awesome and capricious certainty. It continues to win victories in this world. (Each nightfall is a brief victory for chaos). Still, its powerful activities are somehow or another subject to *divine control* (though the Lord may not choose always to exercise it) and that makes its power to inflict pain on men almost humanly tolerable.

SIN AND THE FALL 5

We shall now admit that we are using a less-than-ideal approach in treating some of the topics in this book. One can with some accuracy, for example, speak of an (implicit) doctrine of sin in the novels of Dostoevski. Presumably, the author's attitude toward human rebellion fluctuates throughout his works. Still, his time span of literary activity is fairly limited and he is writing with a considerable degree of originality. One could present a fairly accurate digest of his "doctrine" throughout his novels.

But when one treats of a topic like "sin" in the Old Testament, the situation is much more difficult. The time span of literary activity is enormous, the influence of the pre-Hebraic literature considerable. It would be a good deal more honest to treat sin, and many analogous notions, with serious attention to history. One ought in the ideal order to treat sin as it is discussed in various individual books of the bible. Better yet, one should treat sin as it is discussed in various definable literary units within the Old Testament. These units are quite small, although at least one of them (the succession narrative) overlaps the end of one book and the beginning of another.

However, in matters of pedagogy, the ideal order is rarely coextensive with the real. The reader using our approach can still learn a good deal about "sin in the Old Testament" particularly if he bears ever in mind that the approach is a certain compromise with reality, and of necessity involves simplifications and certain consequent inaccuracies.

Hemingway once remarked that there are no synonyms in the English language. If this somewhat depressing idea is correct, the reader can more easily understand the difficulties in trying to find an approximation of words between languages. Words differ between cultures because men differ not only in their attempts to express realities, but also in their very apprehensions of realities. A striking example of this phenomenon is the two different ways in which the color spectrum is divided in the Western languages and in Arabic. The Arab apparently perceives the spectrum somewhat differently and tends to describe as one color a phenomenon which the West sees as two. (We are not here describing one color-blind Arab, but an entire group of peoples and their language.) Within the Western family of nations, we may have an analogous phenomenon in Homer's description of the "wine-colored" sea. This description has produced a host

51

of doctoral dissertations, alleging that the favorite Homeric wine was green! This may have been the case; still there is the simpler possibility that a dark enough green and a dark enough maroon seemed to the Greeks as *oinops* which we translate, "wine-colored."

In theological matters, this phenomenon leads to extreme difficulties. For example, "sin" in English means a deliberate human violation of a divine law. "Guilt" is the quality which accrues to the person who has committed sin. No precise equivalent is found in biblical Hebrew for either of these two words. We find the same word used as "sin" in contexts where the act is quite indeliberate. The word "guilt" is sometimes used to describe the consequences of sin which fall on an innocent party. Finally this last word, sometimes meaning guilt or consequences of sin, may also mean the sin itself (the willful act). To the extent that the abstract root meanings of any Hebrew word are accurate, the chief words for sin seem to mean *failure, infidelity* or *rebellion*. The word we have described as *guilt* (or *distortion*) has a root meaning of *twistedness* or *bent out of line*.

To the extent that these basic meanings are really there, they do offer some insight into what the Old Testament thought of sin. For example, *infidelity* and *rebellion* certainly point out that sin involves movement against God. On the other hand, *failure* and *distortion* point up that sin hurts man. Morality is for the sake of man, not for the sake of God. Still, one may seriously question the validity of any discussions resting on the root meanings of these words. In New Testament studies, one has the advantage of the wide world of Greek literature. In large areas of writing outside the New Testament and uninfluenced by it, some of the key New Testament words occur. Their non-New Testament usage offers some insight into what they mean in the New Testament. This is almost totally impossible for any of the key theological words in the Old Testament. There is little helpful prior use of these key words (in cognate languages) and any subsequent use is largely colored by the significance which the Old Testament gave to them.

These basic difficulties with words for "sin" show the enormous difficulties in grasping the Old Testament meaning of the narratives of sin which begin with Adam and end with the flood. In the simplest sin accounts to be found in the Old Testament—David and Bathsheba—one has difficulty distilling a basic idea of what sin meant to the authors. In the primitive accounts of Adam and his immediate sinful descendants, the difficulties are even greater.

James Barr, a noted Presbyterian scholar (whose solid critical competency and acerb wit make him a kind of Protestant John L. McKenzie) has observed that most biblical Hebrew word studies up to the present have been somewhat inaccurate. Part of the difficulty is that many scholars, whose grasp of a wide spectrum of languages is quite limited, have been content to use dictionary occurrences of words. In dictionaries, the context given is so small as to be almost useless. More important still, even the dictionaries, according to Barr, have missed an important point. They have been content to illuminate Hebrew usage in terms of occurrences which *preceded* the bible only, ignoring those which followed. Barr's point here may be a bit difficult to grasp. The advantage in studying usages of the word which occur after the Old Testament occurrences is that they include meanings, probably current in the spoken language of Old Testament times *which did not work their way into the written Old Testament literature.* Therefore, by studying post-biblical literature, we come to understand background and "flavor" of Old Testament words.

This is a remarkable insight. It is especially valuable because of the nature of the subjects treated by the Old Testament as opposed to those treated by the post-Old Testament Hebrew literature. The Old Testament subject matter is quite limited; the post-Old Testament Hebrew (and Aramaic) is almost without limit.

The reason for the wide scope of post-biblical Hebrew is this: Unlike ecclesiastical Latin, rabbinic Hebrew had to move into the kitchen and pantry, bathroom and barn. The Hebrew religious code governed all areas of human life. Pots, pans and shovels are not worthy of religious saga so they are not prominent in the Old Testament. Such words abound in post-Old Testament literature, presumably handed on by an oral tradition.

Evidence of this is the reconstruction of the modern living language of the State of Israel. The great lexicographer, Eliezer Ben Yehuda, found words for at least ninety percent of the concepts of a modern world, resting in the Old Testament or post-biblical texts. (He first looked for the word he wished in the Old Testament, then in later Hebrew, then in Aramaic, and —all else failing—he would locate the word in Arabic.) The fidelity to Hebraic language structure of what Ben Yehuda did is indicated in a rather interesting way. Modern Israeli language studies constantly appraise the role *in the living language* of the words found by Ben Yehuda (and subsequently by the Hebrew Academy). If the word found or "created" (from an ancient usage) is not accepted and used in speech, radio, TV and in the newspapers, the word is dropped from the Israeli dictionaries. Some of Ben Yehuda's most ingenious contributions (long and involved words, say, for airplane) were rejected by the people and a transliteration of a modern word adopted (*aviron*). But meanings of an ancient word which are faithful to the basic idea of the word continue to live (even though the meaning does not exist in the Old Testament).

One example may suffice, in interesting confirmation of Barr's contention. The Akkadian (Babylonian-Assyrian) verb *rabasu* shows up in the Old
Testament with a meaning of "sprawl," the act of animals lying down. It is
not used of humans. The Akkadian also uses this verb in a causative form
with a meaning "to beat." Modern Hebrew, picking up a post-Old Testament usage of the causative, *harbis* (from the root *rbs*) uses the word with
the meaning "to spank," i.e., "to lay a child across one's knee," "to cause a
child to lie across one's knee." This word has been accepted by the Hebrew
speakers of the past few decades because it seemed to them to "fit" the language structure somehow or other. If there were an obscure occurrence of
this word with this meaning in the Old Testament (there is not) the meaning would be as clearly illustrated by post-biblical usage as by pre-biblical.
However, until the philologists come to realize this and to rework their
basic studies we shall be handicapped. In the matter of such technical theological words as "sin" there is still the question of how helpful later usage of
the words would be, since these usages would always have been colored by
the original Old Testament usages of the words.

In 1969 an English edition of the work of a German exegete appeared. It
was given the rather poor English title: *Is Original Sin in Scripture?* The
German author, Prof. H. Haag, ought not perhaps to bear full responsibility it. The German title was much better: *Biblische Schöpfungslehre und
kirchliche Erbsündenlehre* (Biblical Teaching on Creation and Ecclesiastical Teaching on Original Sin). The English title is poor because, as we
have already noted, it is extremely difficult to say that scripture, or certainly the Old Testament, has a doctrine of anything. The Old Testament
presents accounts and narratives, but rarely doctrines. It was certainly
not worth Prof. Haag's time to write a book proving that the doctrine of
original sin is not to be found in the Old Testament. Prof. Haag belongs to
that rather large school of Roman Catholic exegetes who persist in finding
new proofs for the judgment that the Roman church and her councils were
somewhat naive in the use of scripture prior to Vatican II. (One of America's most gifted New Testament exegetes, Rev. Raymond Brown, S.S., has
upset many of his fellow exegetes by pointing out in his recent little book,
Priests and Bishops, that Vatican II was equally naive.) These judgments
have some validity, but it is possible perhaps to put a benign interpretation on the conciliar use of scripture. Frequently the church councils used
a few verses of scripture as the *occasion* for authoritative teaching. The
councils believed this to be legitimate for them, even as many of the early
Church Fathers believed that they had the right to teach something in the
light of certain verses. To subject the verses so used either by the Fathers
or by the church councils to scientific scrutiny is to misunderstand the use
which Fathers and councils made of them. Father Brown observes that it

is interesting to note that scholars who are quite stern in judging the "non-scientific" use of scripture by councils prior to Vatican II are quite broad-minded in accepting the use which Vatican II made of texts. It is equally interesting to note that scholars who are exacting in criticizing the exegesis of some earlier church councils are mild and tolerant of the "unscientific exegesis" of the Fathers. We should be very clear that there are ways and ways of using scripture. Most dogmatic theologians would grant that the Fathers and councils of the church had certain *charismata* not given to the rest of us. Those of us who are neither Fathers nor councils must be careful to teach either in their light or in the light of the best that scientific scholarship has to offer.

Is there any clear reason why the modern preacher may not utilize the exegetical method of the Fathers? Some very capable scholars think there is none (Henri deLubac, for example). But there is one serious objection. Beyond the noted possibility that the Fathers may have been given certain *charismata* limited to their times, there is a certain criterion affecting their work, as we have it. We have reason to believe that these men taught a good deal tentatively. What has survived in their writings, or in the quotations which others make of them, is their teaching *as it came to be accepted by the living church*. If this is true, one could be rhetorical with any who urged their right to preach and teach today, using the scriptures as the Fathers did. Perhaps they do have the right, if they are willing to let us wait for some centuries before we listen to them with any conviction.

Haag's work is interesting as an example of the kind of mistake which some modern exegetes are making. On the one hand, Haag accuses the church of reading into scripture her own theology of a given period which he finds deficient in sophistication (e.g., that prior to "original sin" man's life was totally idyllic, as it would have remained if the "first parent" had not sinned. Death, disease, hard work, wars, famine, etc., all stem from this sin.) On the other hand, Haag persists in reading into the Old Testament the more sophisticated (not necessarily better) theology which has colored the past decade. (Man is the cause of his own evil. There was no "first parent." Death, disease and the rest are part of the human condition.) However, what principally interests the reader of the Old Testament is not what the church read into it (although the teaching of the living church has considerable validity of its own), but what the *Old Testament is teaching*.

So what does the Old Testament teach on the matter of Adam and the "first sin"? On the most basic level, what does the Old Testament teach in the form which we presently have? It ought to be clear by now that we have considerable respect for the judgment that the Old Testament, as we have it, has a long history of composition and transmission. This history is eminently worthy of study. Still, no study of this history can justify replacing an account presently given by the Old Testament with one which the reader might have written had he been engaged in the "social composition" of the Old Testament.

Now what is it that the Genesis account is teaching? 'Adam can be a proper name or can mean *mankind*. The Genesis account edits this somewhat by noting that Adam named his wife Eve, "since she is the mother of all the living" (Gn 3,20). This would seem to imply the judgment that 'Adam is the father. The editor of the story, as we have it, highlights other features. Even as the problem of chaos colors the creation accounts, the problem of evil colors the story of Adam and Eve. The writers of the Pentateuch knew God to be gracious, though awesome. They judged that man's relationship with him ought to involve a certain serenity, a real growth toward filling up the "image and likeness" of this good God which man was. But the most pious of religious authors was handicapped in holding such views. He was handicapped by the known reality. Early death and a life of hard work were so characteristic of the ancient Near East that no one could write without taking them into account. To be sure, there was a possibility that these were nothing but further manifestations of the power of chaos. Still, chaos had been chained at the creation; had something loosed the bond?

Against this framework, the story of Adam and Eve presents an eminently satisfactory answer. The sacred authors do not deny that men sin on their own account. (The sin of Adam and Eve is followed by a host of other examples.) Yet, the sacred authors do present a case of a single couple who seemed to sin almost from the beginning. This is a mythic statement of the proposition that something had gone fundamentally awry very, very early. To get involved in this question, once again, is to introduce a host of questions which the Old Testament authors would find boring at best.

Beyond the argument for solidarity just cited (Eve is the mother of all the living, hence, not likely married to "mankind" but to Adam) the Old Testament stresses constantly the notion of family, clan (and ultimately national) unity. The sacred authors would be astounded to hear someone say in defense of one of his activities, "I am hurting only myself!" How can one hurt only oneself? Each is a member of the human family. What hurts one, hurts the family. If one soldier violates ritual purity, the ban falls on all Israel (1 *Sam* 14,27ff). If it is true that the Adam and Eve account must be understood in light of the chapters which follow, giving the account of other sins, it is equally correct to say that the Adam and Eve account must be understood in light of the rest of the Old Testament. If no man can sin without endangering his family, clan and nation, obviously Adam and Eve could not sin and harm "only themselves."

Only one point is to be made here. It is not that Adam and Eve were a single set of parents from whom all mankind descended, not that "original sin" is thus to be explained; not that men were destined by a conditioned divine will to lead idyllic and carefree lives until Adam and Eve ruined it all. But it is that all of these statements seem implied in what the Old Testament is teaching. Limited by its own framework (and spared the limitations of later ages) the Old Testament begins with the vague human feeling that something had gone fundamentally awry somewhere. Operating out of two basic convictions that the creating God was all-good, that there was much suffering in the world, even among the apparently innocent, and believing the human family to be one with an awful oneness, the sacred authors speculated and reached some valid conclusions. Something had gone wrong in the beginning; an early family (if not "first parents") were at fault; the fact that anything at all had gone right since then was convincing proof of the ineluctable goodness of the God of Heaven.

Does the Old Testament really say that there was once a world without pain, severe toil or hardship? Granting the literary style of the Old Testament, this may not necessarily be what it is stating. A mankind which had not sinned might have viewed the same world quite differently. The Old Testament may be explaining that a change has taken place, but it is in *man*. This has altered his relationship to the world and so the same world seems different. This is possible because what affects man really is not the world as it is, but the world as it seems to be. And sin has altered his vision.

What was the nature of the first sin? There is certainly the possibility that the story, as it worked its way into the Old Testament corpus, involved some sexual aberration. Fr. Louis Hartman presented some argumentation for this (*CBQ*, 1958, pp. 26-40). He argues largely from the imagery of the story and the role of the serpent to conclude that a sexual violation is involved. One other possible indication for this view is the Hebrew pun which introduces the story. The serpent is described as being more shrewd (the Hebrew almost says "sneaky") than any of the other animals. The Hebrew is *'arum*. After the sin, the couple note (for the first time) that they are "naked," *'erom*. This would be a fairly typical use of a Hebrew pun.

Others see the account as simply mankind's living through the ignorant innocence of the prepubescent to the tumultuous knowledge of adolescence. Still others argue from the serpent imagery to a repudiation of Canaanite fertility cults (whose essentials were scorned by the Hebrew religious authors in much of the Old Testament period). But even this type of sin too might not be too far from sexual aberration, granting the nature of the Canaanite religious practices.

Still posing our question, "What does the Old Testament say on this matter?", we may wonder at the singling out of a sexual motif (of any kind) which served then to rupture a happy relationship between God and these creatures. The Old Testament has some few ambivalences on the subject of sexual activity. In general, it seems to praise sexual activity within the framework of marriage (the Song of Songs) and to judge it sternly when the activity takes place outside of marriage (*Prv* 7,6-27). There are euphemisms employed, however, in some passages where later editors seemed more shy about the subject than some of the earlier writers. So the Old Testament is ambivalent about sex. Is this a surprise? The Old Testament on a very real level is human, and ambivalence on this subject is a deeply human trait.

Still, there may be real wisdom in taking the first human sin to be a sexual violation. Could it be that the Old Testament here teaches something important about sexual sin? We must make a real effort at this juncture to stand outside the inhibitions of the twentieth-century world, in and outside the Roman church. Many moralists are still overreacting against the errors of earlier centuries, which seemed at times to teach that sexual sin was the only sin. That of course was quite false. But could it be that the Old Testament uses the story to teach that sexual sin is unique in that its possibility is almost always with us, unlike many other sins? Most of us receive relatively few opportunities to defraud widows and to deprive orphans, to begin unjust wars or to separate our neighbor from large sums which are his in justice. If any sexual motif is involved here, the Old Testament may be teaching an unfashionable lesson, that sexual violations can harm not only individuals, but society. It is interesting to note in passing that Will and Ariel Durant in one of their works which includes the line, "as long as there is poverty, there will be gods!", also conclude from nonreligious arguments that society reasonably requires sexual mores to be determined by the greater good and not by the powerful drives of the sexually aroused. The Adam and Eve account may be stressing the same lesson.

But perhaps again we are asking the wrong question in seeking to find the nature of the sin involved here. The ethico-religious patterns of the Old Testament are sometimes totally different from ours. (As evidenced, for example, in Leviticus 19, 18-19 where two commandments are juxtaposed, "Love your neighbor as yourself! Do not sow two different kinds of seed in a single field!" The Old Testament sees these commandments as related, perhaps, since it is viewing them from a totally different vantage point.)

So maybe the last editor of the Old Testament account of Adam and Eve was not thinking of a precise sin. All sin involves *pride*, i.e., willful estrangement from God. The mode which that estrangement took may not have interested the biblical authors. It certainly did not intrigue them as it does intrigue us or presumably they would have made their position more clear.

Many in the Roman church today are badly handicapped in trying to understand the Adam and Eve account and its consequences, so badly have we lost any feel for community. Someone has remarked that "the Roman church is discovering the individual in an age which is rediscovering community." If there is any truth in this mildly cynical dictum, members of the Roman church ought to be aware of the problem while reading the Old Testament, which assumes that all understand the meaning of the oneness of community. Here as always, the Old Testament indulges in something which readers may find comforting or infuriating. It never bothers to prove its position, but states it with serene confidence. In the Adam and Eve narrative as much as anywhere in the Old Testament, the modern reader asks, "How is this possible? What is the internal intellectual consistency between the actions of a sinful couple and harm to the entire human family?" The Old Testament does not hear the questions and never really answers.

The Adam and Eve account is not really complete in itself, but introduces a number of other tales of sin building to a crescendo and concluding with the flood narrative. Some, as previously noted, have argued that this diminishes the force for evil that the sin of Adam and Eve is supposed to be. However, the argument from the subsequent narratives of sin cuts two ways. It is at least possible that the subsequent sin narratives, ending in the flood, are indications that sin became easier after the disaster of Adam and the mother of all the living. It should be noted though, that this conclusion is certainly not clearly stated in the text.

With the flood, chaos reasserts itself. The Lord's promise, mentioned in previous chapters, always to maintain the major rhythms of the earth cycle, is a promise never to unleash chaos again to this extent. God's kindly promise is motivated, according to Genesis, by his awareness of man's weakness "whose thoughts and imaginations even from youth are so bent to evil" (*Gn* 8,21). Throughout the rest of the Old Testament there will be tension between this notion and the idea that man is created in God's image and likeness.

Certainly in comparison with pre-Hebraic texts, the "personification" of chaos in the Old Testament is a dim one. If there is any justification for the founding of this notion in the earlier Old Testament works—and many would dispute this—it can only be in hints of a kind of activity which is close to "personal." In the ancient song of Moses and the Israelites (*Ex* 15) and the Song of Deborah (*Jgs* 5) stars, rivers and ocean struggle against the enemies of the Lord. Possibly even the crossing of the Reed Sea itself is an indication of the subservience of chaos to the Lord. The chaotic sea which had hitherto been given a place of its own and kept separated from the dry land (*Gn* 1,9) now is forced temporarily to yield some of the place it has been given that the "dry land may appear" (*Ex* 14,21). Some see in this co-operation of the violent side of nature in doing the work of the Lord a hint of previous struggle in which the Lord mastered the violence of nature and forced it henceforth to do his will. If this is so, the previous struggle obviously implied some clear notion of personality on the part of chaos, since only persons or living things are capable of struggle. However, it must be admitted that there are only hints of the prior struggle and any clear indications of "personality" in chaos have been rinsed away before their insertion into the Old Testament text as we have it.

With these notions on chaos, we conclude our treatment of sin and the fall. At this point, it may be noted why *myth, mythic heightening,* and *symbol* are being treated here with some overlapping. First of all, because these notions form a spectrum, as it were, in the human judgment. It is not always clear where one ends and another begins. Even more important for the purposes of these chapters, the Old Testament is quite vague on the distinctions between one and the other. To thrust a clear distinction between them is to intrude into the Old Testament something which is not clearly there. This is to be avoided at all costs. Any resulting ambiguity, distressing though it may be, is an ambiguity which flows from the Old Testament itself and ought not to be avoided.

SOME PROBLEMS
FOR THE STUDENT OF JUDGES

Until now, we have not introduced any notions that might serve to explain some problems of composition and inspiration. Most of us tend to reject unnecessary knowledge, and until this point, there has been no real need for a fuller understanding of these difficulties. However, with Judges, the reader meets a few problems. It might be well to touch on some answers now.

Once again it may be helpful to begin by noting what the point at issue is *not*. Inspiration does not mean that all of scripture is a word-for-word communication of God's message to man. In fact, many problems which students (and scholars) have had with the notion of inspiration might have been avoided if the answer to a simpler question is sought first: How large a body of scripture is required for the inspiration to take effect—by *communicating?* If one admits that a certain size is needed, a full paragraph, often, or a *pericope* (a longish section dealing with a united theme), many unnecessary problems can be avoided. For example, in Genesis 7,17, Noah's flood lasts forty days and forty nights. However, in Genesis 7,24, the flood lasts one hundred fifty days. If one insists that no particular size is needed for effective divine communication, and that the message or truth-content effect must be found in every phrase of scripture, these two verses would present some difficulties. Much mental gymnastics on the part of scholars from every religious persuasion have been used in efforts to reconcile such flat contradictions as the truth-content contained in these two verses. If we admit, however, that the communication level of scripture in which the Divinity is involved requires some length greater than that of a single phrase, scholars are free to devote themselves to greater—and soluble—problems.

Inspiration, then, is not coextensive with the communication level of scripture. Inspiration does mean that the Divinity is involved somehow or another in the composition of scripture. Even if each Old Testament book involved the work of a single human author, which is almost never the case, we could make a clear distinction between the creative act of authorship and the communication level. In the act of social composition, where the books have been written by many men, through many generations, influenced by a host of literary sources (flowing from their own respective acts of creative authorship) there is large room for the activity of the inspir-

ing Spirit, without committing that Spirit to the message level of any given
small phrase.

Some notions like the above, making possible a distinction between inspiration and message on many levels, is necessary for the ethically serious
reader of the book of Judges. Much of the literature in the book is not
"edifying." For this reason, generations of wise Sunday School teachers
have begun the instruction of small boys in the world of the Old Testament
not with the intricacies of Leviticus or the profundity of Deuteronomy, but
with the "wild, wild west" of Judges. However, to a sense of refinement
and ethics more delicate than that usually found in small boys, much of
Judges is painful and threatening.

The term "judges" itself is perhaps worth a paragraph. The translator is
constrained here to use the English word "judge" in a rather poor effort to
reflect a type of pun in Hebrew. (Hebrew, as many other ancient languages, uses puns with a flavor which we do not quite get. It is not humor,
but does not seem to be utter seriousness.) The Hebrew word *šopet* (the š is
pronounced sh in transliteration) does have the meaning of judge in the
sense of one who is rendering a verdict between two people. But something
else is probably implied. The root *špt* in Hebrew frequently implies the rendering of a *favorable* verdict. The same flavor is sometimes found in the
noun *miSPaT* which is derived from the same root and frequently translated indifferently as "judgment" in English. So part of the overtone of
the term "judges" for these leaders is that they enabled Israel to find
favorable decisions at the hands of the Lord in disputes with their adversaries.

What is the manner in which the book of Judges was composed? Here, as
so often in Old Testament studies, opinions differ, but what follows is at
least probable. Long before the Hebrew invasion of Canaan, *pari passu*
with the years of invasion and conquest, and residual some time after the
conquest was complete, was the activity of small local shrines. These were
pagan in origin and continued to be sources of something less than the
purest of Jahwism. Only in the light of much later theological precision, can
we criticize the Jahwism of these shrines. The shrine priesthood and the
faithful who worshiped at them were doubtless motivated by real piety,
admixed with some confusion (like the rest of us). Their piety, however,
was free of much later theological clutter.

It is almost impossible to overestimate the role of these early shrines in
Israel's theological development. Their influence began early and lasted
late. Perhaps some of the very late effort to stamp out non-Jerusalem worship was focused on shrines whose existence long predated the Temple in
Jerusalem. This is an interesting example of the fact that antiquity does not

always equal orthodoxy. A great personality or a dynamic event can reverse historical tides. The Samaritans, for example, have history on their side for their superior claims to holiness for their mount of worship. Jerusalem, however, bathed in the light of the Davidic personality, won the claim to orthodoxy, despite its relatively late start in the history of Hebrew worship.

As each shrine developed a variety of religion all its own, so each developed a host of traditions. Around each shrine would gather a group of leaders, religious and political. The same dynamic which we have mentioned in "The Exodus Motif" would assert itself here. Selection, rejection and heightening of these traditions took place around the shrine. In some cases, the historical origins of these traditions may have been stronger than in others. In any event, with the invasion and conquest, many of these shrines were absorbed by the incoming Hebrews for the same cluster of reasons that motivated David later to make use of the Jebusite priesthood. The local priesthood was surely of real political influence; their shrine was established and a holy place; their cult attractive. Fear of syncretism (a smooth blending of religions and a blurring of lines of demarcation) is a much later arrival in the history of ideas. When these shrines came into the Hebrew domain, their traditions came along with them. It is possible to explain some of the theological failings of the "judges" as shaky Jahwism, but an easier explanation is available. Some of the stories were taken over whole from these shrines; the original heroes were Hebrew only by later adoption into the mainstream of Hebrew tradition.

The above cannot be demonstrated beyond dispute, but there is some real indication of it. For example, Judges contains a couple of references (3,31;5,6) to Shamgar, son of Anath. He is mentioned as one who "also delivered Israel." A mighty warrior, he once slew "six hundred Philistines with the jawbone of an ass." Although we have only a couple of references, the greatness of his stature is indicated by the offhand remark in the song of Deborah, "it was in the days of Shamgar, son of Anath." With this phrase, the man is used as a dating device. Such devices would be quite understandable in any society which was rather vague on years (which after all have to be counted in terms of something or someone). The expression may only mean the equivalent of, "it was the year of the great fire." Even if the phrase means nothing more than that, this makes Shamgar a rather colossal figure. The composer(s) of Judges felt that they could presume that all their readers or hearers knew who *he* was, and when he lived. But there is another advantage to the use of a name as a dating device. It can also point up the *emotional climate* of the period and that may well be recalled by the reader. For most readers old enough to remember, the two phrases, "During the opening months of the Kennedy Administration," and "During the closing months of the Johnson Administration" point up differences that indicate an emotional chasm far wider than the seven years which separate them. The national mood in those two periods was totally different. At the beginning of the Kennedy Administration, an entire nation saw in the handsome young president the leader of the new Camelot; an innovator, who would make all things new. This may or may not have been the *reality*, but it was the national mood. By the waning months of the Johnson Administration, circumstances probably far beyond the control of either president had brought a deep middle-aged depression on the entire nation. Nixon's Acceptance Speech reflected the mood perfectly with words he put into the mouths of the children of immigrants, "have we come so far for *this?*" It would be impossible for any writer to use the earlier Kennedy months or the late Johnson ones as dating devices without introducing a particular emotional color. This device may well be involved also in the use of royal names in the Isaiah(s). So Shamgar's name may have been used for an analogous purpose. His name served to call to mind not only a chronological period (which could not have meant too much to the early Hebrews, or they would have devised a way to keep track of the chronology), but an emotional climate. The violence of Shamgar's age was a particular kind of violence. The Philistines were a particular kind of adversary and the whole age suffused by a specific mood.

If Shamgar was of such massive stature, why have only two fragmentary lines survived? The one episode to which allusion is made (slaying of Philistines with the first available weapon) seems also to have been taken from Shamgar and given to another (Samson). The problem rests in his title, *ben Anath*, son of Anath. This was simply too much for later editors to stomach and they washed out most of the story.

Anath is a Canaanite goddess of violence, described in the Ugaritic literature as wading up to her knees in the blood of her fallen enemies. The fact that Shamgar was given the title was a judgment of his heroic stature. In the ancient world, the hero who is larger than life-size is sometimes given a divine parent even of the same sex as his recognized human parent. Achilles is such a hero that he comes to be known as the "Zeus-born son of Laertes." In the case of Shamgar, the case may be even simpler. The legend has him as the son of Anath, with no mention of his father; therefore, he may be of half-human, half-divine parentage, like Aeneas son of Venus and Priam. However, unfortunately for his longevity in Hebrew legend, that title, "son of Anath" stayed with him. Without it, he would not have been useful as a dating device; with it, he could not long survive. One Jewish scholar remarked of a much, much later phenomenon that "if Thomas Aquinas baptized Aristotle, Maimonides circumcised him!" Later editors of Judges apparently felt that Shamgar was beyond circumcising. Other pre-Hebraic figures, handicapped by no such recognizably pagan titles, survived easily, and their traditions worked their way into the mainstream of Hebraic tradition.

There is another aspect of the shrines which continued to have great influence on subsequent Hebrew history. These shrines were not only *religious* centers, but were also *political* centers. They were the meeting place on various festivals of the clans which surrounded them. For a logical reason, these clans were generally divided into groups of six or twelve. If the latter, each clan took the responsibility of maintaining the temple one month a year; if the former, each group was in charge twice. This is a notion which probably long predates Israel and is found outside the ancient Near Eastern world as well. The type of government which resulted is called *amphictyony* or amphictyonic league since the clans gathered around (*amphi* in Greek) a central shrine. This is the background to the grouping of the twelve tribes of Israel. If we judge from the Old Testament alone, we could conclude to a simplist account of twelve tribes marching out of Egypt. In fact, such a formulation of the nation was finalized long after the conquest was complete. In the Old Testament itself we are given a variety of lists for the twelve tribes, varying from period to period, and the names add up to more than twelve if all the lists are collated.

In the event of an emergency, the "clan of the month" would summon the others to united battle. A confederacy of this sort was, of course, quite limited. The only motivation which could bring a given clan to the aid of another in distress was the fear that under analogous circumstances the clan now being summoned would be left alone and without help if it did not now demonstrate its loyalty. This motivation would not always be sufficient. If the summoned clan was being called to a battle with a truly powerful foe, with whom it presently had no personal quarrel, it might well feel it wiser to sit this battle out and to worry about its own defense should later danger arise.

In the song of Deborah (*Jgs* 5), we find references to the weak nature of this kind of government. Four of the tribes are chastised for refusal to join the battle. Two of them (Asher and Dan), are described as lingering "by the sea," or "in ships." Since the battle took place far inland, these tribes may have felt that the struggle was none of their affair. If Dan was a clan of sea rovers, as some have thought, or if its men were employed principally in the service of a nation which did roam the sea, the tribe probably judged that not only was the battle not their business, but that the remaining land-loving clans would be of little use to them if Dan did become engaged in wars of his own.

On the general principle that the poetic parts of any composition which includes both poetry and prose are much older than the prose portions, this song is doubtless very ancient. (Among other reasons for this widely accepted principle is that poetry is memorized more easily than prose. Moreover, the nature of "primitive" Semitic languages lends itself more easily to poetic composition than to prose.) So in this poem, we have an insight into the rather flaccid governmental system which ruled early Israel. It is fairly obvious that, with the rise of stronger enemies, the nation of Israel could not long continue to exist if it did not adopt a stronger form of government.

The casual reader may get the impression that the book of Judges presents a study in chronological order. One "judge" is described and then another. Therefore, one judge lived, ruled and died, and another succeeded him. In fact, this seems not to be the case. This was a literary order imposed on the collection of stories by later editors. Some of these judges lived simultaneously; some of them, as noted previously may have been pagan heroes predating the Hebrews; some of them, conceivably, never lived at all. Perhaps this explanation makes more reasonable the behavior of some of the judges. If some of these tales are taken over whole, from a totally pagan background, then a certain ethical insensitivity on the part of some of the judges is not surprising. Certainly there is another possible explanation—that the Jahwism we are dealing with is extraordinarily primitive, and the aspects of the judges' behavior which bothers us is something that never worked into the mainstream of later Jahwism. However, this is not really sufficient in dealing with some of the major problems, such as the Jephtah incident (*Jgs* 11), which we shall examine subsequently. Such an incident, the sacrificing of a child to "the Lord" is so counter to everything in Hebrew religious history, that it seems more reasonable to take the whole story as something that happened completely outside of a Hebrew framework.

Some might object that there is a simpler explanation. The incident did indeed take place in Hebrew times. Jephtah, as the Old Testament text admits, was at best living on the fringes of Israel and was brought in by the Hebrew leaders in a desperate situation. In the situation, he responded according to his own confused religious norms and promised to his god a living sacrifice—to be determined by a chance meeting. When he met his daughter by chance, according to his own norms, he had no choice but to sacrifice her. In comparing this to the ancient story of the intended sacrifice of Isaac we see that the Jephtah incident in no way fits the Hebrew "mainstream." The Isaac story is a stern polemic against human sacrifice which has never had a place in the Hebrew framework. In this case then, what the later editors did was to take the Jephtah sacrifice story and to substitute the name of the Lord for the name of his own god to whom the promise was made and for whom it was fulfilled. These editors at least were less bothered by the human sacrifice than they were by the prospect of Israel's being saved through the military skill of a pagan.

The power of tradition and the loathing which human sacrifice has always inspired in Jewish circles is illustrated by an interesting phenomenon in modern Israel. Although land in the city of Jerusalem is at a premium, and has been for several decades, a large, well-situated plot was left without any building until fairly recent times when simple force of pressure finally caught up with local prejudice. The land, the place of *Gehenna*, was in the local judgment the site of ancient child-sacrifice to Moloch. (Something archaeologists can presently neither prove nor disprove). Three thousand years or more after the last alleged sacrifice took place, no Jew wanted to live there.

The Jephtah story also offers some insights into problems of transmission. It is clear that *some* change was made in the story, either in the description of what actually happened, its chronology, or in the religion of the protagonist involved. Living centuries after all scripture has become fixed or *canonized*, we must remind ourselves that sacred scripture was not always sacred in the mind of the readers or hearers. It took a long time to acquire this status. (For this reason, the Old Testament does not contain a word meaning "inspired" with regard to writing. Once one had begun to think of writings as *inspired*, the period of Old Testament composition was virtually over.) We have every reason to believe that before the status was acquired, the transmitters of the stories felt that they had the right to edit or amend *under the limitations* which we have discussed in previous chapters.

That we have inherited the rugged tales of Judges as we have, is due to one bit of genius on the part of all who transmitted these accounts. They avoided the mistake of transmitting only what was beautiful and fitting—according to the lights of a later generation. They were *conservative* in their transmission—to use Walter Lippmann's definition of the word, they strove to "preserve the best of the past." And they had the insight to realize that the very best of that past included the Lord's ability to move in history and to use men, even the theologically confused Jephtah, to attain his ends. They never tried to rewrite past history in terms of present categories. The earlier Hebrews may have passed on these tales with some ease, after some slight expurgation. A moment's reflection on the nature of real scholarship in the Solomonic period (and much later) will illumine how difficult some of these earlier stories must have been for the learned and the saintly religious personnel of the Temple. Did they not have some qualms on passing on certain aspects of the Samson cycle to their children? Doubtless they did. Still, they wisely passed the account on, "warts and all," long before any formal understanding of "canon." These men saw that the Lord had worked with and through people like Samson for the redemption of Israel and they would not be more fastidious than the Lord. The only change they may have made, was to turn some of these ancient heroes into Jahwists who were faithful in terms of a much later definition of Jahwism. Otherwise, they left the old heroes untouched. One wonders how many religious ages have been so wise.

Ever since Max Weber, the term "charismatic leader" has been used of the judges. Quite accurately, the term embraces the Old Testament idea of a sudden descent on a man by the Lord's spirit. Possessed of this spirit, he had authority. Although the term *charisma* has been overworked in America recently, its modern usage does spell out notions, implicit in what Weber wrote, that some have not really noticed. The charismatic leader has *authority by reason of personality*. No election is needed to give him the authority; he need not receive it by inheritance; it flows from no personal title. This is the authority which comes on a man who knows what to do at the scene of an accident. If he moves boldly enough, no one stops to question his credentials, to examine his educational background or to study his family tree. This powerful authority then, described in Old Testament symbolic language as the "falling of the Lord's spirit" on a man, actually flows from within the man's personality and his own deep personal conviction that he ought (or is called) to lead. For this reason, one student suggested as a proper title for this chapter, "How Did a Feller Know?" This is of course an excellent question. Attempting here as always to steer a middle course between simplist supernaturalism or simplist atheism, we suggest that the charismatic figures of the judges may be understood in terms of modern charismatic experience. One of the more scholarly works on American politics recently was done by three competent British journalists who wrote a book called *An American Melodrama: Elections, 1968*. In it, they treat this very problem. The charismatic leader does *not* know, effortlessly and constantly. He must keep proving it to himself. For this reason, they offer the intriguing theory that the Robert Kennedy *charisma* had been badly weakened immediately prior to his assassination. He had lost one primary contest in Oregon and very narrowly won the primary in California. These authors speculated that the *charisma* was virtually gone and that the convention would have been very difficult for him. This was so, they argued, not because his followers had lost faith in him, but because *he no longer had total trust in himself*. And this is the solid bedrock of *charisma*, that the leader trust himself. This psychological insight (whatever its validity in the case of Kennedy) may be useful in explaining the Samson cycle.

Samson's "spirit" departed when his hair was cut, because he had yielded to the woman. In his world, there was no fault in sexual dalliance with a woman, but the man must always be the master. By giving away his "secret" he had been defeated by a woman and with that defeat his confidence and *charisma* fled. With the slow regrowth of his hair, Samson felt the possibility that the divine power would return to him. So it did and he destroyed more of the enemies with his death than in an entire life. The reader will see the possibility here that the expression "falling of the Lord's spirit" is analogous to the "angel of the Lord" seen previously. It expresses the Hebrew tendency to see God moving mightily—and through personal intervention—in the midst of history.

With the regrowth of Samson's hair, one may note that there is involved here an interesting aspect of the human attitude toward objects with deep emotional significance. Frequently the *locus* of the emotional attitude remains the same, while the manifestation of the attitude is quite different. So with hair in human history. Samson was weakened because "a razor had touched his head." On the other hand, in Egypt, to appear in the presence of the pharoah without having shaved absolutely all the hair from one's body was offensive. David's captured warriors from whom the foe had shaved half the beard and half the hair on their heads, could not appear in public until both had grown back. To shave totally and then to appear in public would have been unthinkable. The fallen woman in Leviticus had her hair "loosed" by the priests. It may be comforting to note that modern preoccupations with length and style of hair (and consequent harsh judgments!) are vestiges of taboos which may well precede written history.

The expression *mal'ak Jahweh*, "angel of the Lord," which we discussed in a previous chapter, occurs more than twenty times in the book of Judges. Perhaps there are two attitudes which the reader ought to avoid in appraising this expression. Obviously, he must keep his mind free of the pictures of angels throughout the history of art (good and bad). On the other hand, he must make an effort to understand the mentality which saw the Lord operating through the efforts of men. Much of the refusal to see this, much of the desire to limit divine intervention to direct personal intervention without agency, rests on a sort of humanism second-class. Such a reader esteems the human condition only up to a point. He regards it as *unseemly* that the Lord should work through men. Especially if the men seem deficient in heroism and/or saintliness, which generally seems to be the case in Judges. For the most part, redactors and transmitters of Judges defeated this feeling in themselves and handed on the stories of the divine intervention as they received them.

The Ehud episode (*Jgs* 3,12ff) is worth noting. Ehud apparently makes a

successful escape attempt after his assassination of the enemy king since the
king's servants are faced with a mighty dilemma. They delayed for a long
time to approach the king (who had been murdered) since he had not summoned them, according to the normal custom, and they were afraid that he
was making use of the royal toilet facilities. (*Jgs* 3,24-5) This is not always
made clear by translators, but it is clearly there. Faced with this dilemma,
the servants waited and waited; meanwhile the hero made his escape. The
modern West (and this is doubtless progress) finds little humor possible in
face of the death of a foe, however much he may have deserved to die. The
ancient world has far fewer inhibitions. The song of Deborah not only
concludes with humor far too strong for our taste (the aged mother being
consoled by a flattering maid-servant as both wait for the triumphal return
of a king already dead at the hands of a heroine of Israel), but there are
snatches of humor prior to this. In Judges 5,25 the king who is about to be
assassinated rests quietly and asks only water of his hostess: "He asked
water; she gave him milk. She brought him curds in a royal bowl." Before
examining the humor, this should be noted. Humor that has to be explained to a reader or hearer ceases by that fact to be funny. Moreover,
the "humor barrier" is vast—even between modern nations of different
languages or sometimes the same (British and American). There is a
gradation in the first colon where he begs *water* and is given *milk*, but
there is deep irony in the second. What we have translated as "curds" is
the basic, common, simplest stable food of the poor bedouin of the period
—but it is served to him in a magnificient dish, "a bowl worthy of a king,"
as the Hebrew really says. To translate this into English, one would have
to make some substitutions, oleomargarine and butter in the first colon
perhaps, "peanut butter on a plate of gold" in the second. From these
somewhat inelegant suggestions, the reader can see why translators de-
spaired of conveying the humor and have left us with the somewhat stilted
phrases that were cited at the beginning of this paragraph.

Jotham's fable (*Jgs* 9,7ff) however, contains humor that is closer to our
own taste. Jotham does not speak with open criticism of the kind of man
who becomes king, but notes that the trees had a most difficult time in
finding a tree who would consent to rule over them. Fig, olive and grape-
vine were not interested in the position; they found their own productivity
eminently satisfying. The bramble, however, who obviously had nothing
better to do, consented to be king of the trees and accepted with a speech of
great humility. The fable may be interesting also as a place where the
seams show in the construction of Judges as we presently have it. Someone
involved in the composition obviously did not think very much of the idea
of kingship. On the other hand, the refrain occurs in other places that

"there was no king in Israel" and this generally precedes or follows some monstrous tale or, once, the sad conclusion that "every man did what was right in his own eyes" (*Jgs* 17,6). Principally we have cited the fable to show that humor does occur in the Old Testament, though frequently in strength or taste which does not suit us. Much of the Old Testament writing, at least at one stage or another of its transmission, was recited for its entertainment value. The Hebrews would have to be without human parallel if they did not appreciate some humor in their literature. Any time we judge another national family to be without humor, we are simply misunderstanding their humor. Some is almost always there.

The Jephtah episode in the form which it presently has, contains one other interesting feature. The daughter who is to be sacrificed desires some time "to bewail her virginity." Not to have children, to be without posterity, is the most awful of fates in the Old Testament. Such posterity is one's immortality. This notion with regard to men shows up in the Semitic world in a type of monument which our taste finds strange. The basic decoration of the monument is a faintly disguised male sexual organ. In some fashion, there seems to be a connection with that and the universal Old Testament desire for descendants, and consequently, an eternal memory. Strong as the idea is, the Jephtah incident shows the strength of another idea. Awful though the fate of virginity is, the virgin about to die (in some months' time) does not think of losing or violating her virginity. This is worth pointing out as it is sometimes argued that the Judeo-Christian ethic of sexuality is largely motivated by age-old economic considerations which are now defunct. (The young lady preserved her virginity because without it she was not particularly valuable on the marriage market.) If the attitude mentioned in the Jephtah story goes back to the story's origins, on the fringes of Jahwism or even outside, we have an interesting rebuttal of this criticism. Life-long virginity is a burden, but even under the strange circumstances of the Jephtah story, virginity is to be preserved where marriage is not possible. If our exegesis is correct, respect for the notion of virginity, outside of marriage, goes back to very ancient times—times so primitive that reverence for human life could yield to notions of religious worship and sacrifice. We would stress here, not that it is our judgment that virginity ought to be preserved until marriage, but that this idea seems rooted in one of the most ancient portions of the Old Testament, whence it flowed into the "mainstream" of the Judeo-Christian tradition.

This chapter is not intended as a "commentary" on the book of Judges. The few specifics cited are interpretations generally not otherwise available. Judges is a remarkable work, without many parallels in other literatures. The Nobel Prize-winning *Kristin Lavransdatter* of some decades ago shares some analogous flavor. *Kristin* deals with the coexisting Christianity and awful violence of thirteenth-century Scandinavia. Author Sigrid Undset had a feel for the kind of literature which Judges is. To read her work is perhaps not the worst of introductions to Judges. In both we read of strong men and women in primitive times who loved the Lord with the same primitive affection that they felt toward all whom they loved. Their deep love and faith were not attended by parallel growth in deep, ethical sensitivity—strange as that may seem to a later and more sophisticated age.

REALITY
AND THE BOOK OF RUTH
7

In a previous chapter we noted that Eliade's statement about the unique role of historical reality needed to be understood with some precision and we added a distinction to the statement he was making. Nonetheless, his basic insight is correct: Historicality or the judgment that something very real exists at the core of the religion is integral and essential to Judeo-Christianity. There is an interesting proof of this in the ancient Nicene Creed, recited regularly by many Christians. One article of the creed affirms "he suffered under Pointius Pilate." Implicit in this is the idea that Pontius Pilate really existed. It is not an exaggeration to state, then, that many Christians regularly confess in their faith, "I believe in Pontius Pilate." Many of them may not have adverted to this as part of their confession, but it is there nonetheless. Possibly there could be some other way of interpreting the phrase, but it would be hard to see how Nicaea could have understood it differently from this: Pontius Pilate was; he really existed; the passion of Christ really did take place under this man's governorship.

Since this notion of reality is so integral to Christianity, its influence has been felt in many ways. Much that is best in the classical Protestant Sunday School tradition flows from this feeling for historicity and the reality content of Christianity. The emphasis, even in the instruction of younger children, on biblical geography is founded in this notion. The Holy Land is really there. Rivers, mountains and deserts can be traced and studied. It is a real place and part of the real world. The Old Testament is sometimes confusing and not too helpful in this matter. The editors, obviously, tended to use the place names and the geographical knowledge of the times in which they wrote. However, they generally provide enough clues so that the skilled scholar can work out a good enough approximation of what modern *loci* correspond to the names under Old Testament discussion. With the rise of modern Israel, this science has grown considerably. At the present time, one may do a demanding Ph.D. at the Hebrew University of Jerusalem specifically in the field of biblical geography. The numbers of students in this program on the graduate level is such that we may reasonably hope for vast improvements in the science of biblical geography in our lifetime.

The field of archaeology has also made enormous strides in recent years. The relatively recent employment of modern technological breakthroughs gives us hope of a "great leap forward" in Old Testament studies. In any ancient field of study there is a limit to what we can learn from texts, since we are always limited by the texts presently at hand. One example may suffice. Many scholars have worked on the presumption that the literature of Ugarit, unlike the literature of the Old Testament, has no particular history of transmission and reediting. Recent archaeological work shows that the most important temple in the ancient city was dedicated to a god who is minor in the literary texts which we have. It is not unreasonable to argue that since the god is quite minor in the literary text we presently have, that this represents a change. If the literary substratum of the text is anywhere nearly so old as the massive temple, presumably there was a period when the god's role in the literature corresponded to his role in the city's temple complex. The illuminating role of archaeology in basic Old Testament studies is also enormous. It shows Saul's palace, for example, to be rustic in simplicity. We could never learn this from merely reading the Old Testament. In matters of history the Old Testament tends to a certain egocentricity, not unlike the making of modern maps, which generally show one's homeland in the center of the known world and distorted in size.

Since, as we have mentioned, the authors of the Old Testament saw all history as *religious* history and religious history as the history of Jahweh at work, the "historical" books would naturally be egocentric, since *Israel* was the center of the Lord's work. The casual reader of the Old Testament could get the impression that all ancient Near Eastern history pivoted around Israel. This would be as though one were to read American history in terms of the history of Rhode Island. Rhode Island is certainly involved in much of American history, going back to Colonial times. Still, it would take the hardiest of Rhode Island partisans to deny that American history studied simply in terms of Rhode Island would involve some loss of perspective. For this reason, the reader is strongly advised to read the Old Testament in an edition somewhat like the heavily annotated *Jerusalem Bible* or the *Oxford Annotated Bible*. Either edition would do nicely. Some may find the latter translation, which is superlatively accurate, slightly heavy reading. However, each of these editions will put at the reader's disposal the advantages offered by scholarly notes with insights from historical, geographical and archaeological studies. The reader, of course, must be careful in reading such an edition and be prepared to engage in some shifting of mental gears as he moves from text to commentary and back. The text is inspired, in the judgment of most Christians and Jews. The most satisfactory of commentaries is not.

All of the above having been said, does it follow that every book in the

Old Testament is historical? It need not so follow. The most strict of Christians has no difficulty in accepting at least one kind of fiction in the New Testament (the parables). If one can accept Jesus' use of fiction to teach in the New Testament, why cannot fiction be used to teach in the Old Testament? Actually, the only difference for the modern reader is that the fictional form of parable in the New Testament is perfectly clear even to us. The division between fact and fiction is not always clear in the Old Testament.

With this we come again to the problem of "literary form." A superb grasp of language, in any area of study, is not particularly helpful if one cannot identify the form. A native adult American speaker might be hard-pressed, in overhearing the conversation of two college students, to determine if the conversation is a friendly one or an argument. The amount of harshness tolerable in banter decreases with age. What would be insulting in conversation between two fifty-year-olds who are not close friends is quite acceptable between twenty-year-olds who are moderately close. But the outsider, who happens to overhear snatches of such a conversation may never know the meaning inherent in the sentences, although he understands all the words. He cannot interpret the meaning of the whole until he determines the literary form.

This may be a rather clumsy example, but it is helpful because it teaches that the usefulness of knowing literary forms is not limited to the Old Testament or even to the written word. (Most readers are aware that they read advertising circulars or watch TV commercials with a certain cynicism which they do not ordinarily exercise in listening to their pastor's Sunday morning sermon; they may never have adverted to the realization that this difference is based on an implied awareness of the difference between "literary forms." Some are meant to be taken as serious and factual and honest. Others are not really intended to be so taken.) Then there are other literary forms, novels or poems, where the question of "honesty" or "dishonesty" does not arise—at least not on the simple level of fact communication.

While all this may seem perfectly obvious, there remains one major problem, seldom admitted by the ardent proponents of form criticism. In the Old Testament, with what degree of accuracy can we distinguish between one form and another? In the point at issue, with what degree of conviction may a scholar state that Ruth is solidly historical or a totally fictitious short story? Proofs one way or the other are not terribly moving. For example, some scholars have seriously argued that Ruth must be fact because of the convincing tenderness of the story. Obviously, to argue this way is to have a very low regard for the craft of fiction. It is the part of the skilled author to reproduce exactly that tenderness which a factual situation would bring about. On the other hand, one argument for Ruth as fiction is not beyond rebuttal. This argument states that there is a certain artificial balance in the story, the character of Orphah and her initial, but faint loyalty is too nicely contrasted with the fidelity of Ruth to have been strict history. There is an analogous argument for the Samson cycle as fiction. It seems to strain our credulity beyond measure that Samson could have revealed one false secret after another, (with subsequent attempts by his enemies to bind him) and then been foolish enough to have yielded finally by telling the truth. Particularly bothersome for the idea that this is strict truth is the Semitic motif that some effort does not avail on a first or second attempt, but eventually yields. Still, this is not to say that the whole Samson story is false, simply because one of its details may have been somewhat heightened. But if there was an Orphah and if she did so speak, how else could an author have written this as history? In the case of Ruth, Judeo-Christianity can live with the story as fact or fiction. In closing this chapter, we shall offer some further suggestions on its basic form, but in the form it presently has, Ruth offers powerful religious insights, whatever its original structure.

What is the setting of the action in the story as it presently is found? There are good reasons for believing the book's opening verse. "It was in the time of the Judges' rule." Readers who have read Judges with some sensitivity are occasionally puzzled by this. Judges is a violent world, Ruth a gentle idyll. Can this really be the same time and place? Yes, for Ruth is the mirror image of Judges. The latter is precisely a description of the large portions of time during the Judges' rule when the nation was troubled and at war. But the time of charismatic leadership covers a great span. There were in this long period some moments of peace. Ruth describes this violent world in one of the brief respites. Boaz is described as a *gibbor hayil*, a "mighty warrior." In fact, this word seems to be a technical term describing a social class. Boaz, by reason of his wealth and lands kept a relatively large number of men in his employ. With the advent of war, he would be able to muster a good body of men and to put them in the field against the enemy. A little reflection will show that such a condition would have to exist in a country without a standing army. Easy assembling of an army of any size demands some supply of men to fill up smaller units from which the army can then be assembled. Some authority is required to get men assembled into these smaller units. The period of the Judges, as many analogous periods in ancient history of both East and West, called into being this kind of primitive feudalism. The authority of men like Boaz was based on a harsh but strong reality. In times of peace, he provided employment, hence food, to a large body of men. In times of war, the able-bodied among these men would have little choice but to follow him to war. The nature of work on the relatively primitive Canaanite farm would guarantee that most of the men would be able-bodied. So perhaps the leadership of an amphictyonic period is not so weak as might seem at first glance. It was necessary to persuade only a small body of men, the *gibborey hayil* of each clan, that war ought to begin. These men could then give a simple command and their units would follow them into battle.

Whether Ruth is fiction or merely fictionalized history, some of the most basic themes in the work lead us to believe that it was composed in one of two historical periods for one of two polemical purposes. Some think that it was composed in the period of Ezra/Nehemiah. We shall see in a subsequent chapter, "The Old Testament and the Law," that there were many real religious values in this period. One of the great themes of the period, however, led easily to a religious extreme: The religious leaders of the period insisted that Hebrews should marry only Hebrews. Their reasons were not "racist." From experience, they knew that marriage with non-Jews frequently led to abandonment of the Hebrew religion as a way of life. With all the strengths of the legalist position which they espoused, these leaders fell into one weakness. In efforts to defend the law, they continued to extend the areas which the law touched. Previous generations had made some provision for conversion to Jahwism as a legitimate entry into the Israelite family. In the period of Ezra/Nehemiah, "conversion" as a normal way of entry into the Hebrew family became more and more difficult. It was probably during this period that the principle began to arise, "he is Jewish who has a Jewish mother." The reason for choosing the mother in this dictum is probably clear. Law demands principles which admit of universal application. Given a single witness at the hour of birth, society can easily determine the child's mother, but "It is a wise child that knows its own father!"

Against the Ezra/Nehemiah position described above, the book of Ruth may well have been written. If this judgment is correct, the argumentation of the story is quite clear. "Is it so essential to have a Hebrew mother? David's grandmother was a Moabitess." If the argumentation for origin of the book during the period of Ezra/Nehemiah stands, then there is slightly less conviction for the historicity of the book than if it arose during a period closer to David's life. In the latter case, knowledge of who the great leader's grandmother really was would, presumably, have been common knowledge. Still, one must be on guard against reading Western intellectual weaknesses into this. We would find it impossible to state with any degree of certitude the genealogy of any leader back through several centuries. On the other hand, this might not be the case in the Near East where genealogies are considered important. It is not uncommon among un-Westernized Arabs (who ironically in many areas remain closer to the ancient Near Eastern Hebraic culture than modern Jews do) to find men who do not know their birth date (day *or* year) but who can recite their own genealogy back through several generations. Their birth date they consider of little importance; the origin of the parents and more remote ancestors they do consider important. In the case of a great leader like David, it is not extraordinary to think that his genealogy would belong to the common domain, being memorized by at least the storytellers or chroniclers of the times.

There is another theory on the time in which Ruth originated. This theory has the story receiving substantially its present form during the reign of Solomon. This theory too sees the story as flowing from polemical origins. One of the most serious difficulties which we have in understanding the political structure of the Israel of Saul, David and Solomon, is that we tend to read a modern type of royal succession into the reigns of these men. This is quite far from the truth. The transition from the purely "charismatic leadership" of the judges to successionism was by no means complete when Solomon began his rise to power. The leader himself had to win some kind of personal authority in order to rule with any degree of effectiveness. Solomon was considerably handicapped. At an age when his father was a shepherd boy defending flocks against wild animals, Solomon was living within the children's quarters attached to the harem of a court—albeit a modest court. It is no surprise that the toughness and oneness with the people of Israel, which was the stuff of David's *charisma*, was singularly lacking to the cultivated, but somewhat effete Solomon. But he had a worse handicap. It was common knowledge that a large role in Solomon's successful struggle for the throne was played by his mother Bathsheba. In no age has the image of a man hiding behind his mother's skirts been particularly dynamic. Even more appalling was this image in the rugged world of ancient Israel than it would be today. At this juncture, according to one theory, a skillful rhetorician wrote, rewrote (or assembled) the book of Ruth. The theme of the book shows that women have always had a large role in determining the leaders of Israel. Not only does the book expressly show that David's grandmother, by her strong will and the artifices of her mother-in-law, played a large role in determining her own future (and consequently the birth of David), but the book hints at something else. With Ruth's initiative in seeking relations with Boaz, there is a strong but veiled allusion to the story of Tamar. Much less strong, but perhaps also present, is an allusion to the role which Rebecca played in determining male succession in the ancient nation. So the author of Ruth is asking quietly: "A strong role for women in determining succession in Israel is a long and honorable tradition. Any who object to the machinations of Bathsheba on the grounds that it is unseemly for an Israelite hero to be so aided by his progenitress, do not know their Hebrew history!"

Whatever the ultimate explanation for the story's origin and transmission, its delicacy and charm in the form which it presently has would have guaranteed it a long transmission. Ruth's great line, "Where you will go, I will go, where you will stay I will stay. Your people will be my people and your god my god. I swear a solemn oath that nothing shall separate us— short of death" (Ru 1,16-18), is almost enough to have guaranteed immortality for the short narrative. But there is characterization given to the mother-in-law Naomi in a single verse which is almost the equal. Faced with the singularly cruel fate of the widow in the ancient world, Naomi struggles honestly to separate her daughters-in-law from herself. While they would be doubtless of some assistance to her, she had little to offer them and did not wish to burden them with her problems or with guilt for refusing to share them. In the face of a bleak future, she delivers herself of an heroic line. Stating that she has nothing to offer these younger people, she says: "Why, if I were to conceive twin sons this very night, would you wait until they were grown that you might marry them!" Obviously, there is no prospect that Naomi is to conceive that night or any other. This is one of the few lines in the Old Testament which touches a chord of universal humor. It is the courageous humor in face of sadness too deep for tears. From the viewpoint of the literary craftsman, it was only Ruth's subsequent history that takes the lead of the story away from Naomi who could well have been the central figure in another redaction of the account.

As the reader knows, Boaz treats Ruth with great kindness and Naomi is then encouraged to give her further instructions, "Go in at evening while he is asleep and take back the covering from his feet. Lie down, and he will tell you what to do next" (Ru 3,4). There is little doubt that we have here an allusion to an open sexual seduction on the part of Ruth. The telling of it has been modified considerably as later editors found parts of it shocking. If this interpretation is correct, it is less probable that the story arose in the time of Ezra/Nehemiah. The attitudes and practices here would have been less acceptable, even among those outside the Ezra circle, than in earlier times. The "feet" of course are frequently used as euphemisms for the genital organs; this much the latest editor of the story left intact.

The reader must be very careful in trying to understand this passage. Many of the taboos which have surrounded the sex act in the past several centuries arose from the very realistic notion that marriage ought to be defended by law. For this reason, much of Western society, as notions of law developed in strength, saw law as a proper and valuable safeguard for the powerful sexual drive. For this reason, the very valuable notion developed that the sexual act, performed other than with one's *legally married partner,* was wrong. This is a subtle, but real, difference from saying that the sex act between male and female is wrong, if it is not done *in view of life-long union.* This last attitude, with deep, primitive Semitic origins, has been preserved in the codification of Hebrew law found in the Talmud. The latter states that a legitimate marriage may be performed in one of three ways: The purchase of a bride with cash or material goods; the exchange of promises in the presence of some recognized authority; or the performance of the complete sexual act *with the intention of thus contracting a marriage.* At least one scholar has so explained the romantic tragedy of the fourth book of the Aeneid. Aeneas and Dido have spent an evening together in love. Afterward, Aeneas makes preparations to move on to the conquest of other worlds and Dido is heartbroken, protesting that they are married. Until recently, most scholars saw this episode as nothing more than a traditional pattern where the male saw the love affair as nothing more than that, and the female saw it as propaedeutic to marriage. One of Vergil's comments gives an indication that perhaps something more is here involved. "She calls it a marriage!" That is exactly what she calls it and perhaps exactly what she considered it. Dido, being of Phoenician origin, would have been exposed to the common background of Semitic legal principles. It may well be that what was codified in the Talmud represents something which had a widespread acceptance in the Semitic world outside of Israel. Perhaps one of the most frustrating aspects of Old Testament studies is the extreme difficulty with which we can establish as *fact* the contact between ancient Israel and other ancient nations. This has been for some decades an area of intense (and rather heated) dispute among Old Testament scholars. One result, if constant contact between Israel and the rest of the ancient world could be proved, would be this: We could considerably supplement our understanding of sketchily described attitudes and practices in the Old Testament with fuller descriptions to be found in other literatures. (In our chapter on pre-Hebraic cult, for example, we made use of one Homeric insight. Homer as a possible source for illuminating the Old Testament is still not universally accepted.) A book of this nature is not the place for conducting disputes with other scholars or—worse yet—taking unfair advantage of the opportunity to sum up their arguments, with some weakening, and then to refute them. Suffice it to say that for some periods of even early Old Testament history, there is enough evidence of contact among Eastern and Western ancient nations, that it seems unwise to reject Homer, for example, where there is a possibility that he can shed some light. On the other hand, to argue from fragmentary lines in the Old Testament as "Dan dwelt in ships" to the conclusion that ancient Israel roamed freely over the known Mediterranean world is perhaps equally unwise. If truth is not always found in the middle of a dispute (and obviously it is not always so found) the middle is far from the worst place to remain until the dispute is resolved!

By reason of the prominence which the threshing floor plays in the story of Ruth, at least one scholar suggested over thirty years ago that the story was originally derived from a "fertility cult" legend and then cleansed and absorbed into the Hebrew mainstream. Another argument for this conclusion is the locale of the story in Bethlehem. There are many Bethlehems in ancient Canaan. Most probably the name (house of *lhm*) implies a shrine where *lhm* was the central object of worship. The Semitic root *lhm* means bread. Thence some have concluded worship of a fertility god connected with grain and bread. In the Ruth story, this is enhanced by the timing of the story to coincide with the grain harvest. This possibility is enhanced by the following set of intriguing little allusions. The death of Goliath, elsewhere attributed to David, is also attributed to Elhanan of Bethlehem (2 *Sam* 24,19). Some have suggested that this proves only that David is the "throne name" of the man originally named Elhanan. But there may be a more complicated (and more interesting) explanation. Chronicles (1 *Chr* 20,5) says that Elhanan (not here defined as being of Bethlehem) killed Lahmi, the brother of Goliath. If we have Elhanan (of Bethlehem) killing Lahmi, it is hard not to see some flavor or harking to an ancient battle between heroes of opposing deities, especially since the force of *Beth lehem*, wherever it occurred, would have been much clearer to a Hebrew reader who recognized *Beth el* as the only authentic Hebrew word for temple. The mightiness of this original battle was such that two effects followed. One, it was attributed to David, and two, the stature of the other character was great enough to frighten later editors (as did Shamgar, son of Anath) and eventually even his defeat was taken away and attributed to another (Goliath). In any event, with the coincidence of these elements, Bethlehem, grain harvest and threshing floor, the suggestion that the story is of ultimate "fertility cult" origin does not seem totally shocking. Why is it that the suggestion was received with so little enthusiasm?

There are perhaps two reasons. First, most of the Old Testament as we have it rejects the essential of the fertility cult. However, to reject the essentials of an earlier religion is not always to reject its cultural form. Until very recently, the liturgy of the Roman church in praying for deceased Christians, prayed that they be delivered from "Tartarus and from the lion's mouth," two classic aspects of unhappy life in the underworld, according to Greek and Roman mythology. No one has ever suggested that the Roman church was affirming her belief in Tartarus or the lion. She was making valid use of an accepted symbol. So there is no reason why the Old

Testament could not inveigh against the reality of the fertility cult while preserving some of its external forms or popular legends.

Another reason why the suggestion of fertility cult origin for such a story is shocking to some students is that many in the West have never really come to understand the basic notion of fertility cult. While certainly such cults could—and did—lead to orgiastic excesses, their basic idea was rather profound. If the Divinity did not this year impregnate the universe, animals would not bear, fields would not yield and the universe would die. However shocking the notion of ritual prostitution may seem to us, it is not impossible that this action was accompanied by the prayerful hope that the action, through sympathetic magic, was indeed leading to continued fruitfulness of the world. (Some readers may feel that ritual prostitution was practiced with mixed motives on the part of adherents. Are not mixed motives found in most religions, most of the time?) It is only by realizing how profound were the best aspects of Canaanite fertility cults that we can properly esteem the grandeur of Jahwism which confronted them and overtook them with more than military conquest.

Four basic elements in the story point up the possibility of fertility cult origin: Bethlehem, grain harvest, threshing floor and the sexual union of Ruth and Boaz. But whatever the origin of the story, the form in which we have it has come to play an immense role in later Judeo-Christianity, pointing the way toward a real universalism for Jahweh who was to become God of Heaven (in Ezra/Nehemiah) and ultimately, Lord of the quick and the dead.

TRANSITIONS: SAMUEL, SAUL, DAVID 8

Toffler's *Future Shock* attracted a great deal of attention when it was first published. The basic theme of the book was that the widespread common neurosis of late twentieth-century America arose from the incredible acceleration of change. With considerable rhetorical skill, Toffler argued to his conclusion from a datum like the following: Transportation speed moved from 3-4 miles per hour (rate of human walking) to 10-15 miles per hour (horse and carriage) in the first 3500 years of history. In the past few decades, as airplane travel became more and more the common mode of long-distance travel, the nation accelerated from the 20-30 miles per hour of the early automobile until we stand at the threshold (perhaps!) of regular supersonic jet traffic. He argues then that absolutely nothing in history is parallel to this and the consequent "future shock" should be no surprise.

Certainly it is not to be disputed that our times are unique. On the other hand, shock effect does not arise from absolute but from relative states. One is shocked not by what happens, but by the contrast between what is happening now and what happened yesterday—or five minutes ago. If this notion is grasped, the reader can understand that there were prior ages of history which had to endure changes subjectively as shattering as our own. One of these was the beginning of the Iron Age.

With the discovery of the process of iron-making in the twelfth century B.C., the holders of the process were able, for a time, to enjoy what General Yigael Yadin says is the dream of every military leader: The ability to use superlatively good offensive weapons against the enemy, while protected by an impregnable defense. (General Yadin was chief of the Israeli general staff during the war of 1948. In the past decade he has been employed as an archaeologist at Hebrew University with a specialization in the history of war in the ancient Near East.) A nation which could produce iron could outclass any non-iron-producing nation decisively, even in matters of the simplest weaponry—spears, shields and arrowheads. When the added factor of chariots was sometimes introduced, it would be hard to exaggerate the difference that iron-forged weaponry would make. The chariot improved incredibly from age to age. It was a highly complex weapon which the Hebrews, for a variety of reasons, never quite came to understand until the reign of Solomon. However, long before the chariot became a complex weapon, simple mastery of the iron process made the Philistines hopelessly difficult enemies for the Hebrews to fight.

For this mastery was coupled with monopoly. We read in the Old Testament that the Hebrews could not make their own hoes, but had to seek hoes made by the Philistines. (1 *Sam* 13,19ff). Obviously the purpose of the hoe monopoly was to make sure that the making of superior weaponry rested always in the hands of the Philistines. Granting the nature of ancient Near Eastern total war, with death of combatants and enslavement of noncombatants as the normal thing, control of the iron process made the Philistines every bit the terrifying foe that nuclear monopoly would make a later adversary. If one's enemy has the power totally to destroy him, his clan and his nation, the means are indifferently terrifying.

In this situation, which continued for years in the ancient Near East, the only way that the less equipped adversary could win would be through ruse or some superior bit of military strategy. (Luring the enemy into poor terrain, for example.) The precise manner in which the Hebrews eventually overcame their superior foe is not related for us with any degree of precision. Doubtless here too a number of factors were involved which lay beyond the confines of Canaan's borders. The Old Testament authors, here as elsewhere, are preoccupied with a *theological* history, neither political nor military; they leave some details out, perhaps subordinate some and highlight others, creating a picture once again of a God that moves in history to the advantage of a beloved people. At our distance in time, with what legitimacy can we deny their interpretation of events?

In light of what we have said about "future shock" and the difficulty one has in adjusting to sudden change, it would be hard to underestimate the shock on a person born when the prophet Samuel was at the height of his powers, and dying, say, at the midpoint of Solomon's reign. Such a span would cover no more than seventy years and yet the emotional distance would be astronomical. As a small boy, such a person would have lived in an Israel that was only vaguely aware, at least inland, of the political movements on the world scene. At the height of Solomon's power, the King took to himself a daughter of Pharaoh as one of his many wives. Some Old Testament historians are quick to point out that this involved as much the descent of Egypt on the world scene as it did the rise of Israel. But this is churlish. No one could have foreseen in the age of Samuel that Egypt and Israel would ever be close together on the world political spectrum, no matter how much movement this would involve in two directions. This would be as if Cuba and the United States were to deal in the near future as political near-equals. What citizen would predict that today? What citizen, either Cuban or American, would not find such a reality shattering if it came to pass?

With the emergence of Samuel, the last and greatest of the Judges, Israel begins to move toward some kind of real unity and a place on the world stage. With Samuel too, there is evidence that the story of his early years has been "heightened." For example, the events that preceded his birth seem part of a common motif. The "great man" is often considered to have been so, somehow or another, even before his birth. Samuel's parents wished a child for a long time and were unable to have one. Finally, in answer to prayer, the child is born. The story is found elsewhere in the Old Testament (the Isaac episode), in the Ugaritic literature and is repeated in the New Testament (John the Baptist). There is another interesting possible evidence of heightening. Some scholars judge that certain events of the great man's later life are retrojected into his youth. David, for example, was to lead the nation to perduring victory over her foes. From this the Goliath story is taken from another and attributed to the youthful David. Analogously, Samuel was to be a stern prophet of a pure cult and defender of the rights of the cultic figure. By the same psychological process which wishes to see the victories of one's maturity foreshadowed in childhood, it may be that the shy, respectful child is described as the one who bore the message to Eli that he would be sorely punished for his negligence in correcting the cultic faults of his priestly sons. Yet, there are notes of substantial authenticity in the Samuel story, even when the theme is the events of his earliest years. We read, for example, that Samuel's mother would go up to the shrine each year to worship and to visit her small son and each year, "she would bring with her a new little garment for the boy." With this we are in the area of literary instinct, but this detail is historically so insignificant, although touching, that it seems to have a ring of truth to it. This is not the detail which one would invent. Also, Eli, on hearing the news of his forthcoming punishment, destruction of his household and consequent obliteration of his name and memory—awesome punishment in a world without notions of immortality—makes a statement of eloquent simplicity: "The Lord is God; let him do what is right in his eyes!" This statement sums up one of the great themes of the Old Testament; God is totally transcendent and owes man absolutely nothing. Yet the context of Eli's statement, its stark simplicity and freedom from rhetorical flourish, bears the mark of authenticity. Two points are worth stressing about the nature of the Samuel account. First, there is little doubt of its substantial historicity. Secondly, in treating the question of possible literary heightening, much of the evidence can be weighed, at the present state of our knowledge of literary forms, only with a certain subjectivity. The reader is well advised to read the texts for himself and to make a judgment.

It is possible to miss the significance of Samuel's cultic role. Historically, there has been an interesting connection between cultic performance and the role of leadership. This is certainly not to say that there *ought* to be such a connection, but that in fact such a connection exists and is quite human. In any cultic religion, the cultic leader stands in a singularly dramatic role. Depending on the theology of the cult in question, the leader *is* or simply seems to be in a special relationship toward the Divinity. In the cult itself, special clothing, words, gestures come to invest the human cultic figure with an awe overflowing from the Divinity addressed. (Some younger members of the Roman church might question this; the Roman liturgy is presently moving in a direction of informality, toward "communion banquet" and away from "sacrifice." In fact, the Semitic banquet on which the eucharist is based is solemn and sacred. Moreover, if "informality" continues to grow in the Roman liturgy, there will be an inevitable reaction. At least, such are the lessons from the history of liturgy.)

By what has seemed at times to be almost an inevitable dynamic, cultic leadership tends toward something else. It becomes difficult for the layman —and at least as difficult also for the cultic leader himself—to see the leader as leader *only* in cult. The drama and the authority which the leader has in the cultic situation tends to overflow in other directions. Samuel was no different from many of his historical successors in this regard. Flowing from his own cultic activity came a larger and larger share in the power structure of the amphictyony, until he had a greater share of authority than any of his predecessors. When the kingship of Saul was thrust on him, Samuel resisted with ill grace. Precisely because his own authority had arisen from the cult did he react so violently when Saul took some small cultic action into his own hands. "Obedience is better than sacrifice!" (1 *Sam* 15,22) is, so understood, less edifying than previously thought. Samuel was reacting vigorously in an effort to defend the vanishing remnants of his own authority, like many a cultic leader after him.

The scholars who hold that we can find "sources" hidden in apparently unified Old Testament compositions, point out that one judgment ought to be made on behalf of Saul. In all the accounts that we have in the Old Testament, we can detect, perhaps a "Samuel" source and a "David" source, but almost never a "Saul" source. Consequently, it is very difficult for us to make an accurate judgment on precisely the kind of king and person Saul was. With David and Samuel, we can compare the two sources and reach some fairly stable conclusions.

Whether or not there really is a Saul "source," there is one fragmentary line which seems favorable to him; we shall discuss that shortly. Otherwise, the picture given us of Saul in the Old Testament is one of extreme complexity. Psychoanalysis at a distance, even by a professional, is almost always a waste of time. In the case of Saul, most of the analyses have been made by laymen and the information at our disposal is scanty indeed. Perhaps it is not extreme to judge that Saul did suffer from some kind of depression, whether or not it met the classical clinical definitions. The Old Testament speaks of a dark spirit which settled on him periodically. The spirit seems to be more frequent in its visitations in his later life and the dark periods seemed longer. It would however be a serious mistake to judge Saul from these dark moods alone.

"From his shoulders upward, he was taller than other men!" (1 Sam 9,2) This verse and a few around it may be from a "Saul" source. The description of the youthful and handsome Saul seemed to stay in the mind of the man who wrote these verses. Presumably the verses were composed long after Saul died, although we cannot prove that, but what the author remembered was the vision of Saul in his youth. Tall, yes, but tall in a special way, with a long neck and a massive head. This is the memory that makes the stuff of heroic legend. (Even as such details are remembered by those who saw President Kennedy in person. Kennedy was not tall by twentieth-century American standards; what stayed in memory was the bronzed skin of the marvelous year-round tan or the massive chest, dramatized by the two-button suit coats.) But in the memory of Israel, those marvelous youthful memories of Saul largely died out. This happened principally for one reason. David came to occupy such a place in the Israelite memory (to the day of our writing) that there was in national legend place for only one youthful, handsome and dramatic leader. This was David. In fact, he died at an older age than Saul, but what lived in legend was the youthful slayer of Goliath, the handsome singer of songs, the vigorous warrior. David's old age and some of its attendant problems are recorded. Still, the dominant motif of the David theme in the Old Testament is the contrast between the feeble and embittered Saul and the confident, young David. David's ability to attract attention to himself, even after his death, also affected Solomon's reputation, in large parts of the Old Testament and certainly outside of it. Modern Israeli lore has taken some portions of Solomon's earned glory away from him and attributed it to David. The point to be made here is that a kind of literary dynamic is at work. Henry James remarks that the stuff of drama requires a "collection of fools" and one strong spirit in contrast. By an extension of this dynamic, Saul and Solomon, as well as the enemies of Israel, had to suffer that they might serve as literary foils for the great David.

Modern Israel has developed an oral tradition of its own in commentary on the Old Testament. To some extent, the tradition is shaped by earlier oral and written traditions. To some extent, it is new. It is not scientific and frequently not accurate. Since modern Hebrew is so close to biblical Hebrew, it is not always easy for the Israeli to realize the severe limitations on his knowledge of the biblical Hebrew text. There are in the biblical text severe problems standing between the text and even the scientifically skilled reader, equipped with some knowledge of historical grammar and a grasp of comparative Semitic languages. Some modern Israelis (obviously not the scholars who are also scientifically trained) tend to read the Hebrew Old Testament unruffled by these problems, smoothing them out and creating a polished whole where in fact there is none. Despite this, the modern Israeli oral tradition is always interesting. It is also not without insight into some of the popular feeling of ancient Israel. In the point under discussion, the modern Israeli attitude toward David is most interesting.

For the modern Israeli oral commentary, David can do no wrong. Where the bible spells out David's faults with clarity and drama, as in the Bathsheba episode, the popular reaction is: "Who is perfect? These are *human* weaknesses." Most interesting is the popular reaction in any area where the Old Testament is the least bit vague. References in the Old Testament to the *mil'o,* a building accomplishment which involved the filling of a small valley (*mil'a* means "fill" in Hebrew) admit of some obscurity. There is one text which *possibly* permits the interpretation that David had something to do with this project (2 *Sam* 5,9), but there are several clear and explicit references in the text which state flatly that Solomon managed the work (1 *Kgs* 9,15;9,24;11,27). What we are calling modern Israeli oral commentary rejects this totally. "The later texts may mean that Solomon put the finishing touches to the project, but this was David's work!" This type of popular reaction may well be in a psychological continuum (albeit with chronological interruption) with the popular reaction of ancient Israel to the handsome and charming David. He could do no wrong and much that was right was taken away from others and attributed to him.

Some readers of the Old Testament may wonder if it is possible to exaggerate the skills which David possessed and the role which he played in Israel's history. The modern world, composed of a society of professionals with real but discrete skills, marvels at a Churchill who was professionally competent in politics, perhaps also in military leadership, and in the use of the English language. Jefferson's combination of talents has never ceased to delight his biographers. But look at the range of David's talents. He was a general of the first rank in his times, a political genius, religious reformer and cultural leader, builder of cities, poet and, so far as we can determine, competent musical composer. And all this coupled with a personality of such grace and charm, "winsomeness" to use Anderson's description, that he was almost universally beloved. He had the personality, even when he erred, of the charming rogue, the culprit with whom one can grow angry, but never remain angry. It was perhaps this personality, as much as the reality of what he did, that created the David legend which lives to the present day. The "winsomeness" of Abraham Lincoln so permeates Sandburg's six volumes that the reader on finishing them feels: If it was not so, it ought to have been. I wish never to hear anything negative about Lincoln! So did the David legend grow; the reality was great enough, but added to the charm of his personality it created a saga almost without parallel in human history.

David's skill as a warrior is quite clear. Not only do we have the indication from the Goliath account (which meant that the composers of the Old Testament wished to stress David's heroism and skill in combat even from the beginning), but we have the phenomenon of David working in his early years as a hired ruffian for the Philistines. Doubtless the motives of the Philistines were mixed. They believed that they could use David as a wedge into the fissures of Israelite disunity which were always there. Still, they would not have chosen just anyone in this one. David had clearly demonstrated his ability to win and to hold personal loyalty of troops. While his own personal charm was of immense significance in all other areas of his leadership, it would be of no use to him in the personalized warfare of the ancient world if not coupled with deep personal bravery. Nor at any stage of his life did he lose the capacity for the dramatic gesture. It would be hard to exaggerate the effect on his troops when they saw, or heard about, David's pouring out on the soil, drop by precious drop, water which heroes had brought to him at risk of their lives when they heard him mention his burning thirst. That action quenched the thirst of an entire army as the Jordan River never could (2 *Sam* 23,15ff).

It is ironic to note that the Philistines thought they could use him to destroy Saul, and with Saul, any chance for a strong Israel. That David weakened Saul's national unity cannot be doubted. The irony of course is that having destroyed Saul, the Philistines found in David a leader who could unite Israel as Saul never had. Under Saul the ultimate threat of punishment for failure to cooperate in united struggle against an outside enemy was the principal source of unity, as it had been under the earlier amphictyony. This is the poorest source of unity. It meant that any concerted action had to involve a clear majority of the Israelites, or at least what constituted militarily a clear majority. Even after a successful struggle, an inevitable amount of ill will was left to fester among the minority (which might be rather large) who had been thrust into battle against their will. Here David's gifts of personality were of immense assistance. Almost as long as he lived, he could provide single-handedly a substitute for the deep internal unity which the nation never really had. He became what any charismatic leader must become if he is to rule effectively over any group—a legend in his own time. The rumored exploits of his boyhood and youth and the verified events of his romantic career as hired mercenary for the Philistines soon gave him the aura of a man who could do for his followers things which they could not do for themselves. This, of course, is the stuff of leadership.

Our age has perhaps nothing comparable to the ancient attitude toward literary (and musical?) composition. It was at one and the same time a religious and social activity. We shall touch on this again in our chapter on the Psalms. It is sufficient to note here that such activity was social and public. The very act of composing itself has a public nature in the East, even today among the Arabs. A friend foolish enough to accept a dinner invitation to the home of an Arab parent whose son was failing in the local Jesuit school listened to spontaneous Arab poetic compositions all night long. They soon began to turn on the terrible fate awaiting the boy (and his teacher?) should he fail to make the grade.) This public nature of composition and recitation gives the man skilled in composition a tremendous advantage in seeking leadership. Such composition is not only sometimes inspiring (which is obvious), but it has a high *entertainment value*. In a world which lacked the principal entertainments of the modern West, the ability to entertain would be (and was) highly prized. Since the nature of the entertainment frequently verged on the solemn and dramatic, there would be something analogous to the "overflow" effect of cultic leadership. The aura of skill and drama in one area would tend to cover the man if he moved into another. In the case of David, who had long demonstrated his ability to fight and to lead, the ability to entertain, to move, to compose in public would but enhance his enormous capacity for leadership.

If one bold judgment of C. H. Gordon is correct, the above would move from the area of sound speculation to proven insight. Gordon notes that one verse of the beautiful lament over the death of Saul and Jonathan is a puzzle for all interpreters. Most yield to temptation and, by textual emendation change the verse (2 *Sam* 1,18). As the Hebrew stands, the line reads, "he used the song to teach the people of Judah *the bow*." Most amend it to read something like "he taught them *to sing it*. Gordon notes (*The World of the Old Testament,* p. 160) that the text can be taken easily as it is. Hebrew would not distinguish between the word for *bow* and one for *archery*. David used the song and its rhythms to teach his bowmen. There is an interesting parallel to the Greek poet Tyrtaeus (chronologically far removed) whose songs inspired his countrymen to drill and to fight. The theme of the lament, the tragic beauty of death in battle, may strike us as poor preparation for fighting. In fact, large numbers of nations in all periods have used just such themes to inspire troops (as late as modern Turkey in the thirties and Japan in the Second World War). Most of us may find this strange, but then most of us do not understand the military mind. And David's mind was certainly of that ilk.

One other aspect of the poem is worth noting. In 2 Samuel 1,21, David prays that no rain, no dew may fall on the earth which dared to receive the fallen shield of the anointed leader of Israel. This is perhaps another interesting reflection of the agricultural mystique. Should neither rain nor dew fall on the hills and fields where the shields of the two lay fallen, these territories themselves would be removed from the land of the living. Without water, there is no life. It is that simple.

It is also worth pointing out that the Old Testament tells us that the entire poem is to be found written in "The Book of Jashar." Some argue from such references to a "source" theory. Here we have a clear statement that some other book existed at the time of the compilation of Samuel about which we know nothing. The most significant portions of such volumes, according to "source" critics, were copied over and used in other parts of the Old Testament. This facilitated the disappearance of some of them, since their greatest values had now been incorporated into some other work.

David's greatest skill, and the one which all the others really served only to enhance, was his ability to lead and to mold a nation. He was a master politician. There is no other word in English even though this word has some unfortunate connotations. ("Statesman" in English generally describes one's skills outside the nation.) The politician is here understood as one who has real skill in finding an attainable common denominator among the goods sought by a host of people and the ability to persuade these people to abandon their contradictory goals and unite in quest of the common ones. In any age, the politician is open to suspicion that he is insincere, since his eye is always on the *attainable*, "the art of the possible" as the cliche has it. Moreover David suffered this charge, at least from some non-Jewish readers of the Old Testament, because he was not afraid to use religion as a national unifying force. Most Jewish readers, with a deeper feel for the Hebraic unity between land and faith and nation, are gentler with David in this area.

In quest of further strength for the feeble unity of the nation, David had the wisdom to move his capitol to Jerusalem, to this day "the city of David." By the move, he hoped to centralize authority in Israel outside of any area associated with tribal control. Much in the same manner the American founding fathers chose to establish the neutral Washington,

D.C., as their new capitol. They were, with good reason, fearful that Boston or Philadelphia might be tempted to seize the national government in time of crisis. Living long after the states have been shorn of any real power, it is easy for us to forget just how strong the states originally were.

However, simply naming a new capitol and establishing the government there is not enough to create a new reality. (The unsuccessful efforts so to establish Brazilia are recent proof.) One must find a means for transferring a feeling of loyalty to the new capitol. David had considerable means at his disposal and exploited all of them. First, he could invest the city with his own personal capital, the reservoir of loyalty and goodwill he had won from the nation. For some, Jerusalem was the city of David and that was enough. He announced plans to build a central temple there, although fulfillment of these plans was delayed until Solomon. But even before erecting the new building, he managed to begin there a central cult. It seems that he used the Jebusite priesthood for this purpose. (The Jebusites were the pre-Davidic inhabitants of Jerusalem.) They were probably more skilled in cultic rite than the rustic Israelite priests, but this was only part of it. All of the priests throughout Israel enjoyed some share in governmental structure by reason of the cultic dynamic, as previously mentioned. The local smalltown priests would be shorn of their local authority by being compelled to worship in Jerusalem. The Jebusite priests, who perhaps had also shared some local Jerusalem authority, now had every reason to be deeply loyal to David. He gave them a place of pre-eminence in the Jerusalem worship. If anything happened to him, their lives would probably be forfeit—and they knew it.

When David chose to bring the ark to Jerusalem, as part of his plan for making Jerusalem a truly national capitol, something happened in the course of the ascent. The biblical text (2 *Sam* 6,6) tells us only that a man was struck dead for touching the ark (with reverent intent according to the story as we have it). The text adds that this happened "as the ark was approaching the threshing floor of Nacon." What happened here? One can only conjecture and perhaps it is best not to do so at any length. Was there something truly sacrilegious done which comes to us in this seriously bowdlerized version? (It is interesting to note how definitions of the obscene vary from age to age. One could make a good case for judging that what is *sacrilegious* is *obscene* for the ancient editors and thus deleted or changed. Even the expression to "blaspheme" is sometimes changed to "bless" in relatively harmless contexts.) If the ultrarealist wishes to say that this detail tells us nothing but that the incident did indeed take place at a precise spot, the threshing floor of Nacon, we shall not quarrel with him. Still, it is hard to dismiss the possibility that there was a conflict of some kind (a battle?) at the threshing floor of Nacon. The times in which any kind of syncretism would be officially acceptable were coming to an end. One can only wonder if an allusion to a man's death for an apparently well-intended act veils something else that happened as they approached a threshing floor which was (perhaps) presently a site of active pagan worship. Obviously this is highly speculative.

This same chapter contains the description of David's response when finally the ark entered the capitol. He began to dance with religious fervor. (Remember the *pesah* and *haggag* of earlier chapters.) Then as his fervor and excitement mounted, he cast off some or all of his clothes and danced "with all his might before the Lord." (2 *Sam* 6,14) His dignified wife, Michal, who looked on from a lattice window, "despised him in her heart." When first they were alone together, she upbraided him sharply for "exposing his person" in the presence even of the slavegirls. David strongly defends himself and the biblical redactor adds, "Michal never had a child so long as she lived!" Thus, apparently, did the Lord decide who was right in this case.

Michal was not the last to chide David for this action. Commentators in our own lifetime speak harshly of him and his dancing as calculated only to win the esteem of that common populace whom Michal derided. This is possible of course. How can we accurately judge motives from such a distance of time and space? One may wonder though, if David and his critics were both correct. Some who belong to strongly cultic religions surely are aware of analogous experiences. They have begun cultic ceremony out of obligation only to find as the services proceed that they are deeply moved and involved in a real religious experience. Perhaps David began with one motive and, like many a later cultic worshiper, found himself subject then to a higher power. According to the custom of the day, he manifested that, not as a male of the twentieth-century, with a few quiet tears in the eyes, but by shedding first decorum, then dignity, then clothing. Whether David's experience, or that of the cultic Christian, flows from a psychological dynamic, or from the "Spirit of the Lord," or both, who dares to say?

We will treat Solomon in the next chapter. Still, it should be noted here that long before Solomon's reign ended, a sharp eye could have observed that the seeds of destruction had been sown in the powerful little state. With Solomon's death, Israel's power, such as ever it had been on the world stage, was no more. Chronologies vary, but under any of them, it was only approximately a century from the high-point of Samuel's power to "Solomon in all his glory." Considering the relatively long time span of Old Testament history and the much longer span of the history of the Jewish peoples, some religious believers judge that the Old Testament is teaching something here too. The Lord of history can move within the dynamic governmental structure of a world power, even when that power belongs to his chosen people, but it is hardly necessary for him. In dealing with the Hebrew family, his first and deepest love (for is any second love ever quite the same?), he chose so to operate for but a few decades.

SOLOMON
AND THE SONG OF SONGS 9

History can be fickle in the extreme. The old Greek adage, "Count no man blessed until the day of his death," is perhaps not conservative enough. If one is considering blessedness short of immortality as the Greek adage was, one ought to wait until the man has been dead a long time, since history has a way of turning winners into losers and vice-versa. Moreover, the moods of history constantly change. It seems that men long dead are steadily reappraised in light of the knowledge and styles not of their own times, but of the historian's era, which considerably affects the appraisal. Perhaps the extreme example in American history is the modern-day appraisal of Robert E. Lee and Ulysses S. Grant. Lee is regarded as a dedicated Christian gentleman, with finely honed conscience, militarily brilliant mind and deep courage. Grant, who among other things succeeded to the presidency, is remembered as a general who sacrificed the lives of thousands of men and for little else. One has to stop from time to time in order to remind oneself who won the war. How are such appraisals and reappraisals possible?

In the case of Lee and Grant a reasonable solution is that their *image* is what has shaped history's recollection. Lee, the handsome, dignified Southerner with classic physical features, and Grant, unimpressive, grubby and somewhat soiled. So, often enough, are historical portraits made.

In Solomon, we have an example in the Old Testament itself of how history's mood changes. There is one beautiful story in the Old Testament which most of us remember from Sunday School days (1 *Kgs* 3,6ff) where the youthful king, offered all the goods of this world, prays instead for wisdom to rule his people well. In light of all that happened in his reign, one might well wonder if the prayer was ever uttered. If it was, it seems that it was not answered. The story, though, is a beautiful one and it may have perdured in history for no other reason than that. There is little enough beauty in the history of ancient Near Eastern kings; one is reluctant to be stern in appraising that story, but there does seem to be a certain ambivalence in the life story of Solomon which hampers us in accepting the story as true the way it is told.

Solomon seems to have been almost two men at once: A cultural leader and patron of the fine arts (which presupposes some wisdom) and a national leader with remarkable shortsightedness, especially in the realm of the economic. If this is the case, Solomon would not be the first of men who suffered a chasm between his speculative and practical talents. In the latter area, he simply could not grasp some basic economic facts. His plans for Israel were far too grandiose. Had he been the leader of a nation with far greater resources than Israel, his love of letters (and far more expensive cultural projects) might have been more suitable. As it was, his expenditures left the nation in a parlous state from which only a leader more prudent than Solomon (but equally inspiring) could have rescued it. The leader did not arise and Israel's days of glory were about over.

Economics in any age is a complex subject and demands professional competence. There are certainly factors of productivity involved that make Mr. Micawber's definition of happiness (a penny greater income than expenditure) not always applicable to the affairs of nations. Still, our own lifetime has taught the lesson again that not even the greatest economic power in history has the resources to do all that it wishes all of the time. Much more so Israel. What then did Solomon attempt in terms of economic balance? It is worth pointing out that few basic studies have been done in the economics of the ancient world. The study of economics is complicated enough so that serious research in Old Testament and related economic problems would require both the linguistic and historical skills of an Old Testament researcher and the talents of a research scholar in economics. At the time of our writing, no man or team of men has undertaken to solve these problems.

The balance of payments problem is nothing new. In a complex currency-based economy, its social effects may be more easily noted in terms of inflation and resultant suffering on the part of the poor. But the hardcore effect is always the same. If the importing nation over-extends itself, its basic economic unit will be more and more involved in foreign payment, with resulting scarcity and hardship at home.

Solomon involved himself in vast building projects. It is true that one of these was the Temple. However, in a budgetary ploy which is not yet out of style, Solomon's Temple was the core and most highly publicized part of an enormous building complex which included palaces for his many wives as well as military buildings. How were all these to be paid for? What did Israel have to export in order to pay for the vast amounts of raw materials and expertise needed to complete the projects?

The only thing that Israel had in the amount which these projects required was virtual slave labor. It has been estimated that Israel had enrolled at one time, either in projects at home for pittance wages or in foreign employ, an incredible amount of labor in exchange for imported goods. The number of able-bodied men so employed would be the equivalent of a peacetime draft in present-day America of 8,000,000 men! And the situation in Israel was not proposed as a short-lived emergency but as an open-ended state of affairs. While the erection of the beautiful Temple may doubtless have been some consolation to the more pious Hebrews, the palaces with foreign wives worshiping strange gods assuredly were not. The costs, economic and social, were enormous and Israel never did quite balance them.

One cannot but be sympathetic with Solomon. Few leaders, on national or much smaller scales, are surrounded with competent and restraining advice. It is the rarest of leaders who does not soon find himself hearing only a rephrased echo of his own thoughts. Moreover, at the time of Solomon's ascent to the throne, Israel was culturally retarded. This is clear even in the material in the Old Testament which praises the extent of Solomon's wisdom: "(He) was wiser than Ethan the Ezrahite and Heman, Kalcol and the sons of Mahol." (1 *Kgs* 4,31) A writer praising a wise man whose wisdom was internationally recognized would not be compelled to mention a host of lesser names telling the reader that the subject was wiser than any of them. Biographers of Copernicus and Einstein do not compare their subjects to a host of obscure names! In cold fact then, the Israelite reader had well-founded doubts that his nation belonged in the forefront of the wisdom movement. Solomon's biographers felt obliged to spell out his credentials in terms which the reader would recognize and admit. In the same passage, the extent of Solomon's knowledge is also so described. The Old Testament author does not waste his time in describing Solomon's gifts in profound speculation, which the reader might well regard as less than useful, but notes that he understood the realm of nature and was prudentially gifted as an administrator. Thus, Israel's cultural retardation is shown, too. Even if Solomon was a gifted philosopher—and this is by no means clear—the crude practicality of Israel might not hold this in particularly high esteem, so the court biographer must point out that Solomon's gifts were also eminently practical even though, as we have noted, that seems not to have been the case.

It could well be, of course, that these ambivalences in the Old Testament's description of Solomon do not flow from different "sources" but from one and the same reality—the complicated personality of Solomon himself. In this case the circumstances of Solomon's upbringing, which we mentioned in the past chapter, are worth underlining. The circumstances, royal birth and education, would explain both halves of the dichotomy: His cultural sensitivity and esteem of things artistic and intellectual as well as his total insensitivity to the needs of the nation and his people. Solomon, in a word, lacked the common touch. Because the phenomenon of the cultural gulf between father and son is so common in America, we tend to think of it as a uniquely American phenomenon not to be found elsewhere. In two or three generations, the descendant of a South Boston bartender becomes a patrician President of the United States. Perhaps even more dramatic is the rise of the Nixon family, since the time span is much shorter. As a teenager, the President was working in vain efforts to keep his father from losing the family grocery store. As ten- and twelve-year-olds, his children were daughters of America's vice-president. With the deepest respect for the powers of heredity, the environmental change is such that it is little wonder that the two daughters comport themselves in social situations with a deep calm and apparent inner poise which President Nixon seems never to have acquired. The David and Solomon succession reminds us that while the phenomenon may well be easier and more common in our nation, it is not unique to us or to our history. Could David have seen the height of Solomon's reign, he might well have regretted his son's inability to feel with the nation. On the other hand, it is most likely that he would have envied the ease with which his son corresponded with Egypt's pharaoh—in decline though the pharaoh may have been.

A firm grasp of the above is necessary to understand the phenomenon of *authorship by attribution* and specifically to understand how authorship of the Song of Songs was attributed to King Solomon. Without some notions like the above, authorship by attribution can seem a puzzling phenomenon. With these notions understood, it is not a difficult idea to grasp.

The basis of the idea is this: The reading or listening public in the ancient world wanted the author to be worthy of his work. The possibility that an author could possess only one real skill, the ability skillfully to use words, was unattractive to them. In the case of the Song of Songs, the ancient public wanted as author a man with a reputation for deep cultural sensitivity and skill in love as well as letters. Solomon was that man par excellence and authorship of the work was attributed to him.

There is perhaps something faintly artificial about this attribution. In the case in point, most of the evidence is that the work was written long after his death. In the early days of its attribution, it must have been quite clear to the audience that Solomon could not possibly have written the canticle; there was an element of pretense involved. Over a long enough period of time, at least in the popular mind, some confusion may have arisen about authorship until finally Solomon was easily accepted as the real author.

At first glance, all this may seem a bit puzzling and many commentators have noted that we have nothing like it in our society. But this is not totally the truth. At least one modern phenomenon does seem a remarkably close parallel, and its origins may lie close to the same psychological roots. This is the modern craft of ghost-writing and the attitude which the public takes toward it.

While the craft probably has a long, long history in America, it has much increased in recent decades. The demands on public figures to deliver literally dozens of speeches in the course of a year would make it impossible for them to do much else if they were to write these speeches themselves. Yet, as the name indicates, the ghost-writer for decades was just that. He had no public personality of his own and was instructed to keep out of notice. Even some of the critical editions of the collected speeches of Franklin D. Roosevelt make little mention of Louis Howe, Raymond Moley and others who wrote the most famous parts of the great addresses in FDR's earlier years as president. It is obvious, of course, that one reason for their anonymity, as with any ghost-writers, is that the man who delivers the speech wants it so. But possibly something more is involved.

Could it be that the public also wants it so? Could it be that the public really wishes to believe that Roosevelt's "fear itself" and "day of infamy" or Kennedy's "city on a hill" or Inaugural were written without much help from Howe, Moley or Sorenson? One reason which inclines us to think that the public does so wish it is the attitude toward speechwriting in most recent times. By reason of the pressure of media on the political candidate during the campaign itself, it is no longer possible for the role of the speechwriter to be kept much of a secret. Richard Goodwin's portable typewriter was far too much in evidence in the 1968 campaign to be ignored. Goodwin raised the craft to new heights with his considerable literary skill. He is quite extroverted and not particularly modest. Yet he got really very little publicity during the entire campaign, although he managed the rather incredible feat of writing speeches for opposing sides (Kennedy and McCarthy) at various points. Why did Goodwin not succeed in becoming a public figure himself during the campaign—even though all the evidence was that he would dearly love to have become one?

The answer may be found in the same psychological dynamic which explains authorship by attribution. The public wants its leaders to be complete figures. The rugged good looks and dynamic personalities, say, of McCarthy and Kennedy, when coupled to the craftmanship of the words they delivered in public, made almost the complete leader. In the case of Robert Kennedy, who had no genuine claims to being an intellectual, the public was intrigued by the idea that he spent his spare time (when not shooting rapids or climbing mountains) in reading Camus and Sophocles. And reading them with such intensity that their thoughts came easily to mind when he sat down to write a speech or arose to deliver himself of "spontaneous" remarks. The public desires to be led. If a complete leader is not at hand, the public tends to make one. Goodwin, however, was somewhat overweight, rumpled and—in the judgment of one modern historian—"consistently gravy-stained." The public did not wish to accept the beautiful words and balanced cadences which McCarthy and Kennedy delivered as being much influenced by this singularly undramatic figure of only one proven skill: The ability to write the English language superbly. The attitude of the public in this matter may not be reasonable, but it is terribly human.

So with the Song of Songs. Its author, or more probably collection of authors, was an assemblage of nobodies. If the judgment is correct that the Song went through a variety of rewritings, it is almost impossible to note at what point the literary piece moved from being a selection of rather skilled writings to being a work of art. The title itself is an indication that at some point the high literary merit of the work was recognized. Hebrew has to paraphrase in order to express the superlative. Song of Songs means the best of songs, the most beautiful of songs. (This is the same idiom involved in the expression "King of Kings".) Perhaps, in the same process that moved finally to entitle the work Song of Songs, the tendency gained force to attribute this literary masterpiece to the one man in the ancient world who seemed worth of it—the great literary patron and Wise Man—Solomon, son of David.

The Song may be an excellent example of what we have been calling *social composition*. It may have now the form of an anthology of a host of different songs, written at different periods and ultimately brought together because it seemed fitting to the national mentality that this collection should belong together. While speculation ought to be avoided where clearer solutions are ready to hand, in the matter of the Song not much clear and decisive evidence is available to us. Therefore, speculation may be permitted to us here, provided that we bear in mind that our speculative conclusions are just that—highly tentative.

In looking for informativn about a work of this nature, there are two possibilities available to us. The first is clear information from other literatures which could explain the *origin* of the piece in question. The other possibility is to study foreign materials in the hope that they will shed some light on the work in question and offer some *elucidation*, prescinding from the question of origins.

With that caution noted, we could look at the Egyptian love lyric, the Arabic wedding songs or, more controversially, early Egyptian liturgies as being of some help. The first of these certainly uses some of the phrases which seem to be of the same flavor of the language of the canticle. While it is true that there are doubtless certain human common denominators in the language of love, a few of the expressions in the Egyptian love lyrics seem closer to the canticle than merely that. The lovers are "brother and sister"; the voice of the swallow speaks and announces "the land has brightened." The situations of the lovers are analogous to the canticle; they are separated by difficulties (a stream with a crocodile in it adds a local Egyptian touch). A small selection of these lyrics is given in Pritchard's *Ancient Near Eastern Texts* (467-469), and the reader might profitably look at them after reading the canticle. Still some cautions should be noted. The nature of the Egyptian language is such that one may suspect the translator of having enhanced the cadences so that the lyrics seem more similar to the canticle than may really be the case. There is also the problem of the human "common denominator" already mentioned. This leads to the following development. The role of fantasy in normal human sexual love is enormous. This reason may be the underlying cause of a theme which seems common to the Egyptian lyric and to the canticle and is also found in the medieval love lyric. Granting that *one* of the influences on the medieval love lyric was the canticle, no one would place the Egyptian, the canticle and the medieval lyric in a straight line of historical descent. So this theme may well flow from the common—and quite necessary—role of fantasy in human love. The medieval lyric, Latin as well as Arabic, spends much time and effort in describing the longings, the strivings, the yearnings of lover for the beloved. The quiescence that follows love satisfaction is not the stuff of the great lyrics. So the theme of looking for the beloved, of losing him or her, the separation, the difficulties which seem common both to the Egyptian lyrics and the canticle may be common to something much deeper— the role of fantasy in normal human love.

One theory finds the canticle originating in an Egyptian cult of love and life (Ishtar-Tammuz) which, it is said, eventually found its way into Israelite worship and was legitimized. In fact, some scholars judge that this explains the ease with which the canticle was accepted into the Jewish canon of sacred books. This theory certainly poses extreme difficulties. While there is good argument for allowing some influence of fertility rite worship on the early periods of Israelite history, there is extreme difficulty in accepting this in any later period. The evils of syncretism had long been discovered by Israelite religious leaders, and such origins for the song would be reason to exclude it from the sacred texts rather than to accept it. On the other hand, this theory does point up something which is very interesting in light of the subsequent religious history of the canticle. The early Christian church made use of readings from it to celebrate the resurrection. Starting perhaps from one text (Sg 2,10ff) which calls on the beloved to rise, noting that the winter is past and that new life has appeared, the church went on to use other passages. One exegete has recently noted that part of one resurrection account (*Jn* 20,11-18) may well be modeled on selections from the canticle. If this is so, to what extent may it be explained?

Faced with such problems, some early Church Fathers had a solution; they said that demons put allusions to Christian writings in pagan literature in order to embarrass Christians. This theory has a certain clarity to it, certainly, but it also has drawbacks! In our earlier allusion to the work of Jung, we noted that there are certain images common to the human psyche. It may simply be that human love, spring and new life stand on a continuum. To think of one of them is to begin to think of the others. This is not to say that resurrection is merely part of the human thought process. Rather, that the early Church meditating on the resurrection found herself involved in ancient thought patterns, analogous to those found both in the canticle and in the ancient Egyptian liturgy.

In some translations of the canticle, there is a certain amount of—perhaps inevitable—literary dishonesty. It is not that the translators are mistranslating words and phrases, but there is a certain amount of re-arrangement of the whole. While a Greek text does assign the terms "bride" and "bridegroom" and "daughters of Jerusalem" to certain speaking parts, this is missing from the Hebrew which *generally* indicates the shift in sex by grammatical changes. Still, there are places where the shifts are not all that clear. Moreover, many English translations attempt to turn the work into a united whole. The Hebrew text reads much more like a collection of different songs.

Whatever the origin and nature of the songs, they were ultimately accepted by Jewish religious leaders as being books that "soiled the hands." This interesting phrase meant that the books were so holy, that the reader had to wash his hands after touching them, before using his hands for any other purpose. (Analagously, as in certain Christian cults, the minister washes his hands after touching the liturgical vessels and before touching anything else.) Sometimes Christian sources in talking about the acceptance of religious books into the canon refer to a Jewish "council" of Jamnia and attribute to it the date A.D. 100. This brings up the image of an assemblage of Jewish leaders, much like a church council, meeting in solemn conclave and making authoritative decisions. Although the result of the "council" remains the same, the reality was quite different. It seems that there was over a fairly long period of time a center of Jewish studies at Jamnia. During this period a collection of books was accepted as sacred, and that collection came ultimately to be regarded as the Jewish "canon." How then did the canticle make its way into the collection of books so regarded? There are two possibilities. Certainly at this period the allegorical interpretation was well underway. The well-intended purpose of this interpretation was to make every line and phrase of scripture applicable to the here and how. In the case of the canticle, the most dour of rabbis could not object to it if it was read as a love song between Jahweh and his beloved Israel. Certainly many of the rabbis so read it, and it may be under this rubric that the canticle was accepted.

But there is another possibility. Even as other sections of the wisdom literature were to be accepted because they extolled a divinely given human gift—the power of intellectual striving—so the canticle may well have been accepted simply as a paean to human sexual love—another gift of God. If Jamnia was a school in existence over a period of time, it seems likely that it would reflect the balance which is characteristic of the Old Testament at its best. An individual rabbi might have difficulty in accepting the canticle without resort to allegory; it seems unlikely that the mainstream of Jewish thought would have any such problem.

Still, one final caution should be noted here. There are thought patterns common in the West which seek to attain the truth through the adversary system and see truth as either/or. This is not always the case in Jewish thought which, in certain issues, sees the truth as both/and. In much, much later Jewish thought, (the Talmud) opposing positions are sometimes given one after another. Rabbi A taught X and Rabbi B taught non-X. With that the Talmud moves serenely on to another topic. The truth is often complicated and the listing of contradictory teachings one after another may not be the worst way to indicate this.

It may be that there is no conflict to resolve in the question of whether the canticle is to be accepted as allegory or simple paean to human love. There is much truth in both interpretations.

The universalism of certain fundamental ideas of the beauty and strength of human love may also explain one verse in the canticle which otherwise might be explained in terms of Ugaritic "influence." *Love is as strong as death* (Sg 8,6) appears in the Ugaritic literature at least as clearly as "Love (of the gods) is as strong as death." There is certainly a possibility of some connection between these two occurrences. The notion of "strength" in death is not immediately evident in modern English. Yet love and death have a common term with an interesting history of occurrences in even Western literature. Both are described as "all-conquering." For Homer death is *pandamator*, "all-conquering." Chaucer picks up the phrase of the Latin lyricists *Amor vincit omnia,* "Love conquers all things." This then death and love and sleep have in common with few things—

guaranteed ultimate victory. On another level, love won a victory in the canticle. Through the sheer beauty of its descriptions of what human love ought to be, the Song made its way into the canon of inspired writings and was preserved long after such works as "The Book of Jashar" and "The Book of the Wars of God" had disappeared from sight. These books were possibly more "religious" than the canticle, but less "human" and consequently not preserved.

SOCIAL JUSTICE
AND THE DIVINE TENDERNESS 10

Amos and Hosea belong to a collection of writings infelicitously called in English the "minor" prophets. This title, given to a dozen books in the Old Testament by ancient editors, means only that these writings are shorter than the writings of the "greater" prophets. It does *not* mean that Amos, Hosea *et al.* were somehow prophets of the second class. In fact, their writings are often singled out because they treat themes found nowhere else in the Old Testament or at least found nowhere else so eloquently expressed.

AMOS

In Amos' own description of his life's work, he observes that he is "neither a prophet, nor the son of a prophet." (*Am* 7,14) This can be somewhat disconcerting to the reader who finds Amos listed in his bible amidst the prophets. It raises some problems. First of all, what is the distinction between a prophet and the son of a prophet? In the latter phrase we have another example of the tendency of the Hebrew language to avoid adjectives (already noted in the phrase "song of songs"). The expression "son of . . ." frequently means in Semitic languages "a member of a particular class." The puzzling New Testament expression, "Son of Man" which Jesus often applies to himself means "a member of the class of man, a human being." (Its context in certain late Old Testament passages gives it also another meaning, but that does not concern us here.) It may also have some flavor of "a lesser member of that class." So Amos denies flatly that he is a prophet, a member of the prophet class or something a shade less than a prophet. All subsequent tradition affirms that he is a true prophet. How then is the contradiction to be resolved?

It is fairly clear from the above that the term prophet *evolved* in the course of Old Testament history. Amos understood a prophet to be one thing (one thing he clearly understood himself not to be), and later tradition has understood the prophet to be something else.

In the Old Testament itself, the term "prophet" has a host of meanings and it is not always clear that these meanings are distinct. One meaning refers to a group of people, gifted with some ability to foretell the future—sometimes for a price—but generally not too highly regarded. The reason for this lack of esteem is not patent. Perhaps this class was of non-Hebrew origins and never shook off the ill-repute of their forebears. Perhaps this group simply manifested too much of the "ecstatic" in their work and this frightened the more sober Hebrews. It was this class which gave rise to the expression "Is Saul also among the prophets?" (1 Sam 10,12). The meaning of this expression is not always clear to the reader. The idiom expresses some surprise that the dignified personage Saul was consorting with such a band. In modern Hebrew usage, the same proverb is used to express surprise when a dignified or respected person is seen associating with company that is beneath him. Here again we have an example of how modern Hebrew stands on a psychological continuum with the ancient language.

If this group of prophets is to be described as "disreputable" (at least in the eyes of many of their contemporaries), there is a second class of prophets which can be described, not altogether facetiously, as "eminently reputable." This group, by family or education or both, moved in the best of circles and was treated with consummate respect. Nathan and Elijah before Amos, and Jeremiah and Ezekiel after him belonged to this classification. If Amos looked at the first group and saw that he did not belong, since he was not given to public ecstasy and did not deal commercially in knowledge of the future, he knew that he certainly did not belong to the second group either. He was not of the higher social stratum and possessed little or no education. He was a "shepherd and dresser of sycamore trees." What he did know was that he was summoned by the Lord (Am 7,15). It did not occur to him apparently, that this was the essential note of being a prophet. In this passage, where Amos denies that he is a prophet but admits that he was summoned by the Lord, we have an interesting example of the weakness of etymological argument. The weakness is that the *force* of the etymology is not always understood or intended by a person using the word; hence, when the commentator uses an etymology in efforts to explain the fullness or richness of a given word, he may succeed in doing so. Still, he may be explaining a "richness" which the original subject of his commentary never intended. This is as though one were to explain the etymology of *understand* thus: It is to know a thing as well as if one were *standing under* it. There are dictionaries which insist that this is the etymology of the word (although it is probably only a "folk-etymology"), but it would be a rare English speaker who ever adverted to that coloration in his usage of the word.

Here, Amos denies that he is a *nabi'*, frequently translated prophet and explained either as a *spokesman*, (like the Greek *prophētes*), or *one who is called*. There are excellent etymological arguments for the latter interpretation, but it seems to have been lost on Amos and all his editors since his little speech here would then read: "I am not one who is called . . . but the

Lord took me (*lqh*) and said to me: Go! Act the part of the prophet!" There is a simpler explanation which has some adherents. According to this explanation, Amos is saying, "I *was* not a prophet . . . but the Lord told me . . ." (We have already noted that the verb *to be* is generally not expressed in Hebrew.) But this explanation is a minority opinion.

This passage from Amos touches on a theme which has intrigued religionists and atheists alike in their study of Old Testament prophecy. There is in much of the autobiographical material which the prophets offer to us a rather steady notion of *compulsion*. It is for this reason that many psychologists of other generations delighted in treating the prophets as an interesting study in the whole spectrum of human psychological pathology. Some of these writers seized on the notion of compulsion as *per se* incompatible with good mental health. Obviously, there is a compulsion which is pathological; the question at issue here is whether the hidden drives to which the prophets allude is that species of compulsion.

As so frequently, the novelist Henry James offers a valuable insight. In his work, *The Spoils of Poynton,* the "collection of fools" which we mentioned in an earlier chapter is very much in evidence. There is also the "one strong spirit." Unfortunately, all of the fools seem to be conspiring against the heroine to keep her from marrying the man she loves. To the surprise of the unalert reader, they succeed in doing just that. She finds herself in a position where she cannot marry him without compromising strong ethical principles; this she refuses to do and the man marries another for whom he is patently unsuited. Critics have pointed out two elements in James's work which are of use to us here. The heroine, in James's judgment, was the only free spirit in the entire work because she was *free to do what she ought* and the others were compelled to do what they felt like doing. Secondly, although a major theme of the work (and the title) are derived from a massive collection of beautiful artifacts, only one of them is ever mentioned in detail. It is a Maltese cross. Apparently, James intended this symbol to teach the lesson only revealed at the end of the work: There are varieties of human freedom. If one accepts that the freedom to do what one ought to do represents a very high degree of human freedom, we shall not be so distressed by the apparent "compulsion" which afflicts the prophets, nor will we make the mistakes of the earlier psychologists who wrote of them.

Even the more modern and sympathetic commentators on Amos note that Amos would probably have been happier as a shepherd or dresser of sycamore trees, but that he felt called to the prophetic vocation. The common denominator of this vocation is *the urge to interpret the will of God for the here and now.* This was to be the theme of much subsequent Old Testament religious history and to become the core of later Judaism. The true prophet was gifted in such interpretation, because he stood much closer to the Divinity than did all other men. It is precisely this that makes the psychological studies of prophets such a perilous business. Beyond the difficulties of psychoanalysis at a distance (as noted in the Saul episode), with the prophets we have a further hurdle. They have had a totally unique human experience. They have stood closer to the Divinity than any other men. By that very factor, then, how can we say what is normal or abnormal, since the experience is totally unique? Religious counsellors face an analogous problem in dealing with people who seem to be "mystics." The spurious mystic is probably mentally unbalanced (since he is pretending to be something that he is not). The genuine mystic may well seem to be unbalanced, since his response to a totally unique experience is difficult to grasp for one who has had no like experience.

Finally, there is one other point which ought to be noted, simply to be forgotten. There is no incompatibility between mental aberrations, up to and including insanity, and the gift of prophecy. If the "earth is the Lord's and the fullness thereof" (*Ps* 24,1), he ought to be able to move in the totality of all that is created, which certainly includes the ability to move in the realm of the unconscious.

This much time has been devoted to these matters since they relate closely to the difficulty of the texts as we have them. The radical obscurity of our texts is that on the simplest level of composition there was a chasm between the experience which the prophet had and this experience *as he was able to relate it*. There are subsequent serious problems of transmission, but this original one is serious enough to cause major problems.

At the risk of some oversimplification, it may be helpful to note the process by which the prophetic writings assumed the shape which they presently have. Obviously, the method of transmission varied considerably from one group of prophetic writings to another. Still, in the judgment of some, there is a common denominator which may be helpful to us. The common denominator will serve to explain the complexity of the process of transmission. From such complexity, genuine contradictions in the text could easily arise.

The first problem in transmission has already been pointed out. There is a natural chasm between the ineffable experience which the prophet had and his efforts to relate it. In this matter, prophet doubtless differed from prophet in skill or lack of it. The best of them fell far short. One of the salient features of Lindblom's *Prophecy in Ancient Israel* is his large selection of quotations from medieval mystics—mostly Scandinavians. In his selections, it becomes clear that the most educated of the medieval mystics had extreme difficulty in putting into words what had actually happened to them. And this in a tradition of several centuries of mystical experience. The Hebrew prophets on the other hand were compelled to describe a road which, so far as they knew, no man had ever trod.

So, despite the handicap that their experience far transcended their ability to relate it, the prophets strove to do so. This was only the first step in the process. The prophets explained their experience and its resultant message more than once. They explained it more than once because their audience did not understand it. Or they explained it to various audiences. As most of us would be aware (and teachers more than anybody) members of the audience understood the explanation in varying degrees. Most of them were moved, though, by what they had heard and they went on to relate the message to others, attempting to relate exactly what they had heard. Naturally, in this transmission, there was another gap, between the message (even so far as they understood it) and their ability to relate that message. Then, their hearers related the message to others, laboring under the same handicap.

When finally a disciple (or "school") of the prophet came to gather his teachings into written form, lest they be lost, he had to reassemble these teachings from those who had heard the man or heard about him. The men involved in this step were doubtless motivated by a desire to be as accurate as possible. The question at this juncture might well be just how much accuracy *was* possible.

In some cases then, either before or after this stage, the teachings of the prophet became part of a "cultic" situation. This would make demands of its own. While it is true that cult of its nature is highly conservative, it is conservative only of what is already cultic. Writings assumed into the cult would take on a new shape more suited to the cultic formulas. For this reason, one cannot argue, as some have done, that the "Holy, holy, holy" formula in Isaiah 6,3 was part of the Temple worship and then absorbed into Isaiah. (Commentators who hold such views argue from the "clearly cultic" nature of the formula.) It could have happened the other way around. A formula of the prophet Isaiah was written or rewritten to suit later cultic usage.

So far have we come from the original prophetic experience! In light of the Semitic attitude toward contradictions noted in the previous chapter (contradictory views are placed side by side without commentary), there is little surprise that we find contradictions in the prophetic writings. This is a singular tribute to the honesty of the transmitters. That a totally coherent work should emerge from such a process would seem almost impossible.

One of Amos' major themes rests on an understanding of economics which is somewhat simplistic, but his sincerity is in no way diminished by this. Amos saw in the land poverty in the midst of plenty. He did not stop to ask how this was possible, but preached simply that it was "unacceptable." Amos here stood apart from the world in which he lived. The ancient world did not so much teach "rugged individualism" as it lived it, especially in economic matters. A person was entitled to support only if he contributed some economic good to society. (That parents supported their children gratuitously stood only slightly apart from this. In the ancient Near East, as in any simple society, children fairly soon become economic assets—in normal times.) If the person does not contribute to the economic good of society, that society is simply not going to be concerned with his welfare. This point is worth underlining. With all that is wrong in our treatment of the modern poor, it is generally conceded that man has a basic right not to starve to death. In the ancient world, this would have been a new idea. The terms "widow and orphan" mean far more in the bible than they do in our world. It is not simply that the widow and orphan are weak and unskilled in the ways of the world, as might be true in any society. In the ancient world, they are eminently in danger of starvation. They have no services to offer society; the ancient world offered survival only in return for services. In Hector's great speech in the *Iliad*, his basic fear for his young son is not that the enemy will murder him, after Hector's death, but that no one will feed him. In a few pathetic phrases, Hector contrasts the present delicacies of the boy's diet (rich bone marrow!) with the unsuccessful begging that will be his lot should Hector be slain.

The sufferings of the poor in Amos' time were considerably increased by the age-old import/export problem of what was then an "emerging nation." The nation was undergoing profound economic changes and, as is always the case in such changes, the poor were suffering very badly as a simple society was becoming highly complex. We noted, when treating of Solomon, the problems which the nation faced in efforts to import. Israel's national industries at this time were much better off and there is archaeological evidence that the nation had materials to export other than the rawstuffs of an earlier age (woven and dyed materials for example). But the demands of importing were also far greater. The chariot, originally quite a simple machine, had now become enormously complicated. A chariot of this period would be put together from materials of fifteen to twenty different kinds. Most of these materials were imported. Since the effort to build better chariots involved a constant struggle between swiftness (which demanded lightness) and resistance to enemy weapons (which demanded heaviness), the introduction of a single material hitherto unused in chariotry could threaten to upset the military balance of power. One would have to be sympathetic with the nation's desire to have military weapons as good as any that opposed them. Still, the ultimate result of this was enormous inflation at home. And the burden of that inflation fell, as always, most heavily on the poor.

Of some of these factors, Amos was probably not aware. Still, he did know that, in a nation which was supposed to constitute a single family, there were persons of enormous wealth and citizens of the direst poverty. This, Amos thundered, the Lord would not abide. There was only one inevitable result he concluded: "Israel. Prepare to meet your God!" (Am 4,12).

This sentence carries a double force. The more obvious meaning is that the nation will indeed be punished. Perhaps less obvious to the modern reader is the idea that this punishment will involve a meeting, a direct contact of some kind, with the Divinity. So the threat of punishment is not a threat of unmitigated pain. As one commentator has put it, the punishment will involve tragedy, but it will be a *meaningful* tragedy. If the God of the Old Testament comes to punish Israel, it remains nonetheless true that *he comes*. Israel will experience from this punishment a new closeness to the Divinity which could not arise from simple forgiveness. This is one of the great themes of the Old Testament. The Lord can love with a gentle warmth (as we shall see exquisitely portrayed in Hosea) or in a raging fire. These notions are conflicting, but it is one powerful love that is described. The wisdom of the notion that truth can be found in apparent contradictions is perhaps most easily seen here. Jahweh's love is too vast always to show itself in a single way. There is a time and a place for violently different manifestations of what is essentially one and the same love.

Finally, Amos calls his people to repentance. (Although he truly believes that the repentance will follow the punishment and not precede it.) The Hebrew word he uses is from the root *shub*. The word means to turn around and go back, to retrace one's steps. (It is the word used today in Israel for a return ticket on a train or bus.) Amos' cry to repentance then is positive and not negative. He urges the nation not to a negative act, but to something really positive. He wants the nation to turn around, to retrace its steps and go back to where it once was—to a fidelity which made it eminently beloved of the Lord himself.

HOSEA

The book of Hosea is difficult reading in its present form. One would judge that it has been much rewritten. Basically, the book tells of a relatively simple story. A man marries a woman who subsequently abandons him and runs away with another. Her new lover rejects her and the first husband learns of this. He goes out after her, prevents her efforts to rejoin her lover and finally takes her once again to himself. In the course of the narration, it becomes clear that Hosea is speaking not only of some personal experience of his own, but is presenting a figure of the relationship between Jahweh and the nation of Israel.

There are many problems in establishing the story as told above. Once again the question arises of whether this is fact or fiction. There is nothing to add here to what has been said in previous discussion of the fact/fiction problem. There is some question of whether Hosea's wife was a temple prostitute or whether she is described as a prostitute simply in light of her abandonment of a faithful spouse. There is also some question of the temporal relationship between the life experience of Hosea (if it was a life experience) and his use of the experience as prophecy. Lindblom, in the work already mentioned, gives quite analogous examples from lives of later prophets. Simple events in the life of Nicholas of Suso found their way into his prophecies. There is perhaps also an analogy to what seems a "retroactive effect" of external stimuli on the dreaming subject. The alarm clock fits into a rather complicated dream which seems, at least to the awakened dreamer, to have been in process before the alarm went off. This is not a perfect example, but the only point being made here is that prophecy belongs to an area of human life somewhat independent of time. For that reason, it may have seemed to the prophet that the Lord did indeed order him to marry a prostitute, from which action the prophecy then flowed, when, in fact, the time order had been different.

In any event, the basic lesson of the book is extremely moving. So warm is the relationship between man and wife, such is the love between Jahweh and the people of Israel. But more than that. When Israel fails and runs after another, as a wife sometimes pursues another man, what will the reaction of the lover be? In human terms, the reaction of the husband is generally fierce. It is one of the strongest evidences for the dictum of folk-psychology that love and hate are separated by the finest of lines. The offense of the wife is certainly grave. In traditional Roman Catholic teaching, the crime of adultery gives to the injured party the right to seek legal separation. For the injured party simply to forgive the other and to accept the spouse back is considered beyond the normal demands of Christian marriage and an act of extraordinary virtue. So, however, does Hosea (and Jahweh) act. Not only is the injuring party taken back, but the injured spouse goes out and looks for her. He "blocks her way with thorns" (*Hos* 2,6) that she may not return to the lover who has abandoned her, but will be forced to return to her husband.

The whole of chapter two is written with extreme delicacy; it describes the resolution of the injured husband to seek out his fallen wife. At some point early in the chapter, it seems fairly clear that the speaker is Hosea himself, talking in human terms as a badly wounded husband. At the end of the chapter, it is clear that the Lord himself is speaking. Yet, the most careful reader will find it difficult to pinpoint the exact place in the monologue where the identity of the speaker shifts. The dramatic effect of this is considerable. The reader (or hearer) is totally aware of the deep human feelings in the passage, until finally he realizes that the speaker who is talking in such injured terms is the Lord Jahweh himself. It is the Lord who will take the beloved again to himself "as in her youth." This is perhaps the boldest figure in the entire passage. God is portrayed not only as a betrayed lover, but as an *aging* betrayed lover whose wife has abandoned him. It is difficult to overestimate the effect of this passage on an audience that was hearing it for the first time. The audience would realize, slowly perhaps, that much of the language was figurative and then would begin to grasp even more slowly what the figures signified. The Hebrew audience would finally come to grasp that the betrayer in the story was themselves and the betrayed lover, the One of Sinai.

This is of course an important point in the story. The God of Israel is not only the powerful and majestic figure elsewhere described in the Old Testament (and Hosea denies neither the power nor the majesty); he is also a figure of infinite warmth. Some psychologists teach that the normal human personality fluctuates between the two poles of *strength* and *tenderness*. Insofar as a human approaches a happy midpoint between the two, he enjoys good mental health. This midpoint is not easily reached, as the two characteristics are frequently set up in opposition to one another; to yield to one of them is to deny the other. The Old Testament frequently presents such a majestic picture of the *strength* of the Lord, that his tenderness is sometimes missed by casual readers. This has led to the appalling view, common among many Christians with a superficial grasp of the Old Testament, that the Old Testament deals with a powerful but wrathful God, and that only with the New Testament do we find the God of mercy. Hosea, among other Old Testament authors, gives the lie to that judgment. It is true that the power and majesty of the Lord is more clearly portrayed in the Old Testament than in the New Testament (leading to the danger of a New Testament spirituality which can be sentimental if it is not colored by the Old Testament), but the tenderness of the Divinity is eminently present there.

The figure of speech used throughout Hosea is certainly a powerful one, seen simply in terms of the deep human affections which are involved. Attributing these affections to the Divinity is anthropomorphism, but it is bold anthropomorphism. But the figure of speech used goes beyond mere affection and involves the use of frank sexual imagery. To some, this is a puzzling idea, that the relationship between God and man on any level be described in openly sexual terms. This type of image (common throughout the Old Testament, but perhaps more explicit here than elsewhere) is explained by Eliade in *Images and Symbols*. He criticizes Freud incisively but without rancor for having misunderstood the multidimensional being of the sexual act.

> Freud could never bring himself to see that sexuality has never been "pure" [i.e. nothing but sexuality]. That everywhere and always it is a polyvalent function whose primary and perhaps supreme valency is the cosmological function: so that to translate a psychic situation into sexual terms is by no means to belittle it; for, except in the modern world, sexuality has everywhere and always been a hierophany [manifestation of the sacred] and the sexual act an integral action [action of the whole man] and therefore also a means to knowledge.

This is a difficult paragraph. We have added the bracketed phrases in an effort to make the whole more intelligible. For Eliade, it is not surprising that much scriptural imagery is sexual. The sexual, he says, lies so close to the sacred in the common human psyche that to touch on one is to be very close to touching the other. This Freud never understood. His Hebrew forebears understood it very well. It is one of the clearest lessons of the Old Testament.

PRIESTHOOD IN THE OLD TESTAMENT 11

Most of the chapters in this book have a certain limited historical perspective. They deal with the work of a given man or with the growth of a given idea in a limited chronological context. Unfortunately, within the framework of a single book, it is not possible to treat certain Old Testament ideas with the chronological perspective they deserve. The notion of priesthood began very early in the Old Testament (or pre-Old Testament) period and continued to develop (into further refinements of the notions of religious personnel) well into the intertestamental period. An entire book would be required to explain with precision the contributions of each age of Hebrew history to this growing notion. We admit that our approach in this chapter admits of a certain lack of precision; the reader should keep this in mind.

The term "biblical theology" means different things to different people. Insofar as it means an effort to present the theology which the bible offers, obviously no one can have much objection to it. In the not too distant past, however, some in the Roman church have tended to use this phrase as a kind of shorthand for something else. They have felt there was nothing adverse to distilling a kind of perennial theology from the Old Testament (or even the New Testament) while prescinding from vital questions of authorship and historical problems pressing on a particular composer. This is unwise in the extreme. This chapter and subsequent ones on such notions as "Messianism" and "Covenant" may place insufficient stress on the precisions of historical growth. This is not because of any lack of esteem for such a scholarly method. It is simply a concession to the limit of space. Moreover, the history of Old Testament priesthood is presently not at all clear. Anyone writing on the subject, even in a format more scholarly than this book, would have to make some hard choices among probabilities.

If we accept that the basic Old Testament priestly acts were those of blessing, teaching and sacrifice, which seems to be the case, it soon becomes clear that the idea of priesthood is little more than the professionalizing of certain functions of the head of the family or clan. We can document the acts of blessing and sacrifice easily enough for the Old Testament head of a clan; the notion of teaching is certainly natural to the head of a family. That these roles did become professionalized and part of the priestly function is also clear. Precisely how and why this happened is

115

another matter. Some sociologists may feel that there is a kind of professionalizing dynamic in certain roles. These roles tend, almost of their very
nature, to become gradually more and more complicated. Ultimately, the
complication demands their full-time exercise by a professional. This is easy
enough to see in the matter of the teacher. It is not so patent in the role of
the person who sacrifices or blesses. Once again we must distinguish between the fact *that* something happens and the speculation on *why* or *how*
it happens. It is quite clear that what we might call cultic roles do tend to
professionalize. (The Old Testament cultic functions continued further to
specialize among the Jews after New Testament times. To be a member of a
priestly family, long after the priesthood had ceased to have an actual function, was to be disqualified from filling the post of *rabbi*—a much later development.)

The idea that the priest took on the cultic functions of the father of a
family or clan is most interesting in the light of some further developments.
In a passage from Judges which has already been cited in another context
(*Jgs* 17,10) a cultic figure hears the plea that he ought to stay and "be a
priest and father" to the man making the plea. The psychological connection between fatherliness and priestliness in this primitive world is certainly
not based on historical knowledge and the awareness that the priest has
come to exercise the role formerly held by the father of the family. Rather it
is, for good or ill, that the priest is seen as a father figure. What then are
some of the notions associated with the father figure of this period?

The answer to this question is not easily found. Still, since there are those
who see the present-day uneducated Palestinian Arabs as a fairly accurate
source for some ancient Semitic attitudes, certain nuances of the attitude
toward fatherhood among them may be illuminating. First of all, fatherhood is considered among the very best of this world's pleasures. Their puzzlement at the esteem of celibacy in certain Christian circles arises not simply from their high esteem of sexual pleasure but from their total inability
to understand a man's willingness to sacrifice the possibility of being a father. For this reason, some religious groups working among Arabs take to
themselves the title "Father" for all their members, even those who would
use some other religious title in another culture. With this constant use of
title, there is the possibility that the Arab might come to see celibacy as a
step toward a wider and broader fatherhood. This he could perhaps appreciate. That a man would willingly reject the possibility of being a "father"
under any formality, this the Arab could not begin to understand. An indication of Semitic esteem of fatherhood is the temporary change which
such an Arab may make in his own name, after the birth of a son. For
serious cultural (and legal) reasons, the Arab is known through most of his

life as "*ibn* so-and-so, the son of . . . ." Sometimes after the birth of a son and always after the birth of a first son, the Palestinian Arab will delight in the name " *'ab*, the father of . . . ." He will so introduce himself to strangers and will expect so to be addressed for some time after the birth. Then he will revert to his original name. The force of this custom can be properly esteemed only if one understands how important is *ibn* in the man's original and real name. Any change in the name could come about only under great emotional pressure. Such pressure is effected by the act of being a father.

The carrying of infants is a universal in any culture. What one notices in the modern East among the uneducated Arabs is the carrying of children by the father, long after the age when the child is capable of toddling along by himself. Part of this is of course pragmatic. A healthy thirty-year-old father can carry a five-year-old son longer than the son can walk by himself. But there is apparently more here. That the father enjoys the physical sensation of carrying the son is quite clear to the observer. The emotional effect on the growing son himself must be immense. If the fondling of a small infant plays a vital role in his psychological growth—and this is clearly proved—such affectionate physical contact with a much older child, with more developed perception and memory adds something else. This memory certainly colors the Arab's notion of what it is to be a father.

Those affectionate and strong hands occasionally play a role in the disciplining of the child. Unlike that of more formal societies, the chastisement of the Arab child is neither restrained nor cool. It is infrequent (since the Palestinian Arab parent is quite permissive), short-lived and explosive. Again, to the most casual observer, it seems that the child's memory of those strong powerful affectionate hands that carry him (as Jahweh did Israel) is tinged with a certain touch of awe. In any event, all of these emotions form a collage which serves as background to the development of some of the notions of priesthood in the Old Testament.

The Old Testament priest is also a *sacristan*. His care of the sacred vessels and the shrine (spelled out in some detail in Leviticus) comes from a long history of such a role. This is somewhat different from Western attitudes toward the functions of religious personnel. Generally in the West, the sacristan is a rather minor religious functionary, even in the most cultic of religions. In the Hebrew cult (and perhaps also in the pre-Hebraic), the role of sacristan is clearly priestly. In the final development of the various religious roles, that of sacristan becomes associated with a special class of priest. In the earlier stages, the highest in any "hierarchy" of priests is also a sacristan. What does this mean? It may serve to underline a close connection between priesthood and the Old Testament notion of "holy." For the reader who studies the Old Testament in English, this is a difficult word.

Qadosh or "holy" in the Old Testament is really something quite different from the "holiness" of Christianity. For the Christian, holiness is something subjective. It is perhaps the extent to which the Spirit dwells in an individual. Or at least this is one definition which would be acceptable to many members of the Roman church. For this reason, the idea of *sanctifying grace*, as it is understood in the Roman church, has been developed. It is an effort to explain how it may be possible for holiness to admit of degrees. The Old Testament idea of "holy" means something quite different.

For the Old Testament, holiness consists in being separated, set apart, other. It has been suggested that the notion of *qadosh* in the Old Testament, at least as applied to the Divinity, means the "wholly other." To a certain extent, the priest, because he stands in a special relationship to the Divinity, is in the Old Testament also, "holy," i.e., set apart, different, separated. While something like the later notion of subjective holiness may well exist in the Old Testament's idea of the priest, it is certainly not stressed. The notion of *separateness* is. By an extension of this, all articles which have to do with worship are "holy" and therefore must be touched only by "holy" persons. We have here another example of the thinking which later produced the notion of the "hedge around the law." The nation strove through a series of steadily widening prescriptions to protect the core of the legislation. Somewhat as a cautious driver might drive 50 miles an hour in a 55 mile zone, "just to be sure." Here it is really the Divinity whose "holiness" or separateness must be protected. So, under most conditions he is to be approached only by the priest who is, at least highly analogously, also "holy." The sacred vessels and other religious articles are also "holy" and therefore can be touched only by religious personnel. Both priest and vessels are "set apart" for the things of God.

The Old Testament certainly nowhere teaches that the priest is "better" than other men by reason of his office. It may seem to stress this because of its insistence that the priest be "holy"; however, we have explained now the meaning of that. The Eastern Christian church, to the present day, has an attitude toward the need for "holiness" in its priests which is, at least, interesting. Eastern Christians, at least those who have been educated in some isolation from influence of the West, are tolerant of a good many faults in their clergy which would be judged harshly in other cultures. In fact, it is not much of an overstatement to say that they seem willing to tolerate almost anything in their priests—provided that they seem devout in their performance of the cultic ceremonies. One may, if one wishes, deplore this. Still, it does seem closer to the Old Testament idea of the holiness of the cultic figure. Apart from the cult, the priest is viewed as are other men.

(In fact, as has been noted, this runs counter to a human dynamic that tends to glorify the cultic figure.)

THE PRIEST AS FORTUNETELLER

This notion is easily lost sight of, since it had little influence on later theological developments, in and outside the Old Testament. Still, it is clear that the one of the more original ideas of priesthood involved some ability to foretell the future. The Hebrew *KoHeN*, one of the basic roots for priest, seems surely to be related to the Arabic *KaHiN*, "seer" or "sooth-sayer." This idea perhaps was not esteemed by later editors of the Old Testament. For this reason, it is not clearly described to us. The strange articles of *ephod, urim* and *thummin* seem to have a fortunetelling function. The latter two are more clearly part of this function than is the first. The latter frequently seem to be something like lots for casting or dice. One scholar has soberly suggested that the latter were thrown into the air and then somehow caught in the (pockets?) of the *ephod* (which is clearly at times an article of clothing). The explanation is a bit ingenious, perhaps, but not to be dismissed altogether. In any event, doubtless for the same sort of reasons which caused the casting of lots eventually to fall into disfavor among the early Christians, this particular role of the priest seemed to die out fairly early. But it did exist and cannot be ignored in any overall survey of Old Testament priesthood.

TEACHER

It could even be said that this was the principal role of the Old Testament priest. Certainly, with the passage of time, this seems to be the role which was stressed. This may have been indicated in a number of ways. The connection between the priest and *Torah* is certainly clear enough, even to the reader in translation. What might *not* be clear is a certain force of the word *Torah*. While the word means "law" in the widest sense of the word, this sense also includes a very strong notion of "instruction." In many chapters of this book, we have taken positions which may seem to be ambivalent on the question of how valid our perceptions are of the "flavor" of particular words or phrases in foreign languages. That ambivalence reflects the ambivalence prevalent among linguists of the present day. It may be said in favor of the position which seeks to establish the special nuances inherent in foreign words that the translator does not so much seek to translate foreign *words* as foreign *meanings*. These meanings may or may not exist in his own tongue. (A simple example would be the *martinet* mentioned in an earlier chapter. This word has no precise English correspondence. Another favorite example of this among linguists is the fact that

Russian has no precise word for son-in-law as opposed to brother-in-law. The two categories are fused.) Analogously, *Torah* is built up from the same root as the commonest Hebrew word for *teacher*. Although this argument from the Hebrew *root* is not very strong in itself, still, the connection between the act of teaching and *Torah* is mentioned often enough to help establish the meaning "instruction" for the word. When the prophet Micah chastises the failure of priests, it is precisely for their failure to teach (*Mi* 3,11). This, joined with our linguistic suggestions above, would seem to indicate the important role in the Old Testament of the priest *as teacher*. This idea is frequently missed since the much later development of the role of *rabbi* places teaching precisely in his hands. But the priest was the teacher for a long time before the rise of the function of rabbi. Part of this dynamic is obvious. In a simpler society, the leader is leader in everything. Cult and learning would be two of the great activities of the natural leader. Moreover, it may be that there is an inner dynamic which resists entrusting the care of the "sacred books" to any layman. Whether that inner dynamic can be proved or not is one thing; still, a researcher would be hard-pressed to prove the existence of a society where the care of the "sacred books" was not generally in the hands of some clerical class.

But there is a special reason for the Old Testament priest as teacher. This arises from an idea which we might only note here as it will come up again in chapter seventeen, "The Wisdom Literature." The distinction between "wordly wisdom" and "other-wordly wisdom," if we may use the phrase here, does not really exist in the Old Testament. Wisdom is a gift of God, whatever the kind of wisdom. Training in the pursuit of wisdom is a "religious" pastime and belongs, in a special way, in the hands of the professionally religious personnel. Instruction was originally, according to this theory, placed in the hands of the priest, since it was too prestigious for other hands. With the passage of time, since the priest had acquired cultural status from other sources, the fact that instruction was in his hands enhanced the dignity of instruction. From these cultural dynamics, the modern Western Jew, according to sociologists, came to the technological age with a tremendous advantage. Modern Jewish culture in the West (as did American immigrants of Japanese and Chinese ancestry) brought to the modern world a *reverence for study* which many Western cultures developed only after the rise of technology made evident the need for a large learned class. For this reason in modern American society descendants of these three cultures have achieved success quite out of proportion to their numbers. Descendants of other cultures have lost some generations of time after the technology explosion while they developed some *analogous* notions of respect for study. But their attitudes are so far only analogously respectful of study as a human occupation.

The above is a disgression, but only to some extent. The perdurance of this reverence for study down to modern times among descendants of the ancient Hebrews indicates another dimension of the role of the Old Testament priest as teacher. Whatever this thrust toward study may have been apart from its development in the hands of the priest, it is clear that it did not diminish in the centuries when the priest was principally teacher.

MEDIATOR

The word is used here only with the meaning of "one who offers sacrifice." English offers no precise word for this priestly office. We noted at the beginning of the chapter that this role belonged originally to a nonpriestly class. The great sociologist of religion, Joachim Wach, states that the exercise of this role by the nonpriestly class would belong only to "primitive" societies. He feels that the inner cogency which drove toward the establishment of priesthood as a separate class was not, as we have suggested, a simple drive toward professionalism as the cultic role became more complicated. Rather, he attributes it to the "overflow" effect of cult which we have previously discussed. The priest for Wach stands in such a peculiar relationship to the Divinity that there is pressure on him to stand apart from the rest of mankind. The existence of the priesthood as a professional class, according to Wach, arises from the same mentality which finds it fitting that the priest should be celibate (although physically capable of the sexual act). Thus he is marked by his professional restraint as different, apart from the rest of men. This satisfies in one way the need of the nonpriest in such societies that this priest be "apart" as the Divinity is "apart." The Old Testament priest, of course, was generally not celibate. Still, there may be a trace of this attitude in the regulation that even involuntary sexual activity makes the priest temporarily unfit for performing certain cultic acts. As has been much stressed in these chapters, the Old Testament certainly does not find sexual activity "unseemly." Consequently, this regulation must flow from the basic desire that the participants in the cult be "apart." (The awkwardness of our use of "apart" in these remarks may point up the special flavor of the Hebrew word "holy." *qadosh* could be inserted in any of these sentences, were we writing in biblical Hebrew, and the whole would make perfect sense.)

The priest then is the one who is the *mediator* or who offers the sacrifice. By no means does this remove the layman from the sacrificial act. The sacrifice of an animal, for example, may be said to begin with the selection of the animal. This is made by the layman. In most cases, the animal is executed before he is handed over for sacrifice. This execution is sometimes performed by the layman. Both the selection and the killing of the animal are done according to carefully prescribed rules, thus does the layman closely participate in his own act of sacrifice. The methods of killing the animal are carefully prescribed. They were more carefully expounded by much later Jewish writing. Still, even from the beginning, many of them seem designed with one end in view: That the animal might die as painlessly as possible. In this matter, Hebrew (and later Jewish legislation) was far ahead of all its contemporaries.

The Old Testament sacrifices admitted of a wide variety which shall not be discussed here. Wach, in a bit of a departure from his usual practice of not making value judgments on the societies under study, writes that a society is "magical" or not insofar as its sacrifices were designed to control the god and to wrest blessings from him or if they were designed to praise the god and to express the submission of a given society to that divinity's power. Early in Old Testament development, the sacrifices had moved far, far away from magic. They then were offered with one principal end in view: To make the Divinity, for the moment, somehow more present, although it was of his nature to be "wholly apart." To the extent that the priest succeeded in doing this for any individual or tribe he earned for himself an immense amount of personal kudos which, through the generations, accrued to the office of priesthood itself.

PRIEST AND LEVITE

Those who remember much of the Old Testament at all from Sunday School days, remember one verse about the Levites. When they complain about having no share of the land which was divided after the conquest of Israel, they are told "The Lord Himself is their inheritance!" (Jos 13,33). This is a beautiful verse and one which has consoled many a modern cleric as he has compared his paycheck with the financial demands that are made on him. The verse is certainly there in scripture and the force of its teaching is very real. However, since the verse is found in a source of scripture which some commentators tend to take as very "late" there are doubts that it is a precisely historical account of the rise of the Levites as a class.

Most Old Testament scholars accept as fact that the Levites did not own any real estate in the Promised Land. They vary considerably on how this state of affairs came about. One school says that the Levites were marauders who were eventually subdued by the Israelites. These were then admitted to a kind of second-class citizenship and given secondary chores in the national worship. While this is speculative, as are most of these theories, there is a certain plausibility to it. The Levites are almost always described as kind of a priesthood second-class. Since the nation was a society which admitted of great upward social mobility, this continued second-class existence of the Levites is difficult to explain. Under the circumstances of upward social mobility of the nation as a whole (especially in its earlier periods) and the advantages of proximity to the cultural and educational center of the nation, the general failure of the Levites to emerge-in equality or superiority to the rest of the priesthood is difficult to explain, unless there was some good reason for "keeping them in their place."

An analogous theory says that the Levites were not marauders but exiled Canaanites. They were thrust out from their own land, thus were deprived of a means of livelihood, and were brought into religious worship as servants. This theory accounts for the upward social mobility of the lower classes in the nation. A group who began to work as servants in worship (and who were allowed to live as a convenient manner of getting this work done) eventually developed themselves into a class of priesthood.

It should be noted here that all scholars agree that the notion of "twelve tribes" is a later simplification. In fact, if all the names given in the Old Testament accounting for the tribes are added up, one finds a sum of more than twelve. The "twelve tribes" were certainly a convenient method of handling the national division. The division into tribes surely had good foundations in various periods, but it is most unlikely that the division was ever as neat as the Old Testament seems to describe it.

Another explanation for the existence of the Levites as a class of priests moves back to something we have previously discussed: David's gathering of small-shrine priests around the new cultic center in Jerusalem. The small-shrine priest would over the years have forfeited any land (if they ever had any), since they had an income flowing from their cultic activity. This was one reason why the transfer of these priests to Jerusalem was of benefit both to David and the priests. To David, as we have mentioned, since this gave him a religious class which (as the Jebusite priests in the conquered city) had every reason to be loyal to him. Apart from him they were nothing. It was of advantage to the priests, because so long as they remained loyal to David, they had a far greater measure of economic security than they would now have if they remained at their small shrines. (Prior to the Davidic centralization of national economic authority in Jerusalem, their local positions were probably fairly lucrative.)

There is one major difficulty with this last explanation. It would account for the development of the Levites as a class, but only very late in the history of Israel. The Old Testament teaches rather clearly that the Levites were a group from the beginning and one is very reluctant to dismiss this idea totally as simple "retrojection" (the attribution of later details to an earlier period). It is perhaps more acceptable that David's attraction of these small-shrine priests was inserted into the framework of a preexisting Levitical class. David's action then would grant a new impetus to the development of this class.

For some years, those who wished to defend the existence of a Levitical priestly class of real antiquity thought they could argue from a cognate word for Levite in an ancient inscription. They were handicapped by the difficulty in dating the inscription with any real certainty. Still, some were willing to date this Minaean inscription as of, roughly, 900 B.C. If this date were vaguely correct, the inscription would have been helpful. There are two ways of using a word in a text. One may use the word and then promptly explain what one means (as one would have used the word *astronaut* some fifteen years ago) or one may use it casually without explanation (as one would use the word *astronaut* today). In the latter case, a later reader could conclude that the word had been in use for many years before the writer had employed it, since the writer employed it as a *common word* which anyone would be able to understand without footnoting. So was the word *lw'* used in the Minaean inscription. Since the slow-moving world of the Old Testament introduced new words at a far more sluggish rate than does our media-dominated society, the use of *lw'* in this inscription could point to a very ancient existence of the word *lw'* in Semitic languages. Alas for the simplicity of such explanations and proofs! The dating of the Minaean inscription is today hotly disputed. Moreover, current philological opinion doubts that the word *lw'* in this context really means priest!

ZADOK

The Old Testament account of priests and their work gives a rather prominent place to a man named Zadok. Some of the Old Testament accounts of this man give him a Levitical ancestry (1 *Ch* 6,4-8; 24,1-3). However, there are enough difficulties with this, in terms of other Old Testament evidences that most historians, including J. Bright and R. de Vaux are willing to admit that the genealogy of Zadok is unknown. R. de Vaux sums up his position: "The genealogies of Chronicles are artificial and Zadok cannot possibly have been a descendant of Eli as 2 *Sam* 8,17 would seem to have it, since his appointment is presented as the fulfillment of the curse pronounced against the house of Eli." Consequently a number of theories has been offered to explain who this man was and whence he came. The most probable is that he was a major Jebusite priest of the pre-Davidic city of Jerusalem. One can reach this conclusion from two directions. First, Zadok seems to come into prominence only after the Davidic conquest of Jerusalem. Then there is the matter of his name. ZaDoK. (Here again, the capitals represent the Semitic *root*.) The name is reminiscent of MelchiZe-

DeK ("my king is ZeDeK") and AdoniZeDeK ("my Lord is ZeDeK"). Both names are prominent in the ancient history of Jerusalem. ZaDoK is of course from this root. The precise meaning of the name however is unknown. ZDK in general in Semitic languages means "justice."

At times the argumentation which Old Testament scholars use from names seems tortuous to the layman; it may seem a bit too ingenious or clever to be true. Of course, Old Testament scholars are as open to the temptation to manipulate in favor of their prejudices as are any other scholars. Still, the reader who is not conversant with Semitic languages should bear one possibility in mind. Both the nature of Semitic languages in general and the socio-linguistic stage at which biblical Hebrew stands, conspired to make the force of names in the Old Testament something for which our modern languages have almost no parallel. In cases where one's own society has no parallel, the scholar must be even more careful in his efforts to detect the nuance of something which a foreign society has. So then with the relationship between proper names in the Old Testament and one's function in Old Testament society. If the argumentation is correct here (and it is at least plausible), then by the time of David we have a major priest, arising from non-Hebrew origins, who comes to play an important role in Hebrew cult. Later editors were distressed by this idea and gave an eminently prestigious Hebrew background to Zadok, complete with Levitical ancestry. This is the type of mentality, perhaps, which rinsed out the idea that the pre-Hebraic cult had truly influenced the development of Hebrew worship—an idea which was introduced in an earlier chapter.

In any book, a great deal of selectivity is thrust upon the author. There are several topics which will never appear in this book. Why then did we devote a chapter to Old Testament priesthood? There were two basic reasons. First of all, the notions of priesthood which developed in some later Christian traditions were certainly much affected by the priesthood of the Old Testament. (The general theological relationship between Old and New Testaments will be treated, to some extent, in the following chapter.) But there was another reason for singling this out. Prior to the twentieth century, there was really very little work done in Old Testament studies (with a few notable exceptions) among Roman Catholics. The world of Old Testament studies was almost completely (and very competently) in the hands of Protestant scholars. Among them the relationship of cult (and priesthood) to prophecy and the broad world of Old Testament religion was hotly disputed. To some extent we shall return to this in chapter fifteen, "The World of the Psalms." For the moment, let us note that one school saw cult as a most inferior kind of religion. Members of this school admitted that cult had attractions for the common people, but saw it as a distraction from a higher and more spiritual kind of religion. The role of the prophets, according to this school, was to bring the people again and again back from the attractive world of cult to the more sober, spiritual and enlightened religion which was pure Jahwism.

A second school (among Protestant scholars) denies this view of affairs. They insist that the cult represents a very high degree of religious fervor and worship. What the prophets inveighed against, this second school insists, is the perversion of cult into magic, the development of the idea that the effect of cult is "automatic" and "guaranteed." To a certain extent, since no scholar writes from a "pure position of total abstraction," the members of these schools can be fairly neatly divided by the role of cult in their own Protestant affiliations. Protestants who esteem cult in Protestantism tend to esteem it in the Old Testament. Those who see it as a less-than-perfect in modern Christianity, tend to esteem it less when they find it in the Old Testament. There are exceptions, of course. H.H. Rowley points out rather hotly in one footnote that no one belongs to a less cultic form of Protestantism than he does and he esteems the cultic forms of the Old Testament. In any event, prescinding from the nature of nineteenth-century Protestant controversy, the question of the precise nature of cult and priesthood in the Old Testament remains a very open one. At this juncture in the volume, it is to be hoped that the reader will be not only tolerant of finding that there are differences of opinion, but will be eager to resolve some of these differences (at least for himself) through his own further reading.

OLD TESTAMENT AND NEW 12

Attitudes which Christians have taken toward the Old Testament vary across a wide spectrum. So do their attitudes vary toward the *relationship* between the Old and New Testaments. One group tends to read the Old Testament as a kind of detective story. They feel that the Old Testament is studded with clues. The well-intentioned reader is led by these clues with an inexorable logic toward reading the New Testament in such a manner as to find there the Divinity of the Lord Christ. Whatever any "official teaching" of the Roman church may have offered on the subject, this is the attitude which many members of the Roman church, certainly in the "over-thirty" bracket, imbibed in their earliest years from a host of "unofficial" influences. There are many difficulties with such a position, of course. Among other things, it makes the finding of Christ a rather simple Pelagian exercise for the "well-intentioned" reader.

Another band on the spectrum of Christian believers prefers to shift the idea, slightly but really, and states that the Old Testament presents a *promise* of which the New Testament is the *fulfillment*. There is much to be said for this view. A mentality which sees the two testaments as *prophecy* and *answer* is mechanical and limited. It is not fair to either testament. Certainly for many Christians, the special glory of the New Testament is that it exceeds the "prediction" of the Old Testament. Yet the content of the New ought somehow to be in the Old; Christian tradition is rather firm on that. For some scholars, the rubric of *promise* and *fulfillment* seems helpful. A promise may be vague in its details and clearly understood only after it is fulfilled. A vague and unspecified promise may be fulfilled by something greater than was originally understood. Only after one is in possession of the greater good, does he realize that this is fulfillment of the original promise—previously not comprehended.

But Christians have generally not been satisfied with a simple global description of the relationship between the two testaments. Faced with the large bulk of material which the Old Testament presents, they wish to apply it toward a better understanding of the New. The Christian instinct which tells us that we ought somehow to do this is a very sound one. In the experience of many, a New Testament spirituality which is not colored by the backdrop of what the Old Testament teaches tends to be somewhat sentimental. Still, when a Christian comes to making "Christian" applications of Old Testament specifics, he faces some very real problems. J. L. McKenzie has noted that it does not work, that our thought categories have simply changed too much to make applications of Old Testament specifics possible. The "spiritual exegetes" bear almost equal testimony to how difficult it is. Their insistence on allegory and on a certain flight from reality is really saying obliquely what McKenzie says directly.

But the preaching of the primitive church as recorded in the New Testament insists on this: Christ is the *Fullness of Israel*. Therefore, whatever is good in the Old Testament, in Israel, in its history and its thought, this must be found—and more perfectly—in the person of Christ. Therefore, to understand more clearly what Israel is all about is steadily to grow in appreciation of what the New Testament is preaching. From one aspect, it is that simple.

Still, apart from this view of the promised Christ, the Old Testament is a source of living theology for the modern Christian. In the dealings of God with man, to which we alluded in the introductory chapter, the Divinity comes through clearly as a *person*. In fact, this is perhaps the most lucid theme which runs through the entire Old Testament—the Divinity as person. (There are other theological themes which we have noted that vary considerably from book to book; this is not so with the personality of the Divinity.) What is meant by the Divinity as person would be most easily grasped by reading some of the contemporary Near Eastern theological literatures. In the most skilled of them, the Divinity is a personification; in the least skilled he is a caricature or sometimes a smudged reflection of the currently reigning king. The Divinity of the Old Testament is as different from this as a single real college freshman is different from the TV stereotype of a "situation-family-comedy." The actions of the latter are perfectly predictable far in advance. He is the least common-denominator of a class, a Xerox copy. The real live college freshman is not predictable, because he is a person; he is unique. So also is the God of the Old Testament. Because of this dimension of uniqueness—nowhere else so clearly shown—the wise Christian refuses to look on the Old Testament as a book whose time has come—and gone.

It is against the above that one other message of the Old Testament takes on a fuller meaning: Man is like God. So man is not like some abstraction or pale sketch of something. Man is like the Divinity who has been richly described. There is one tension in this. Man is certainly weak; he is prone toward evil. The Old Testament never retreats from this position (or any other, for that matter). Nonetheless, he is also like God.

Why is it that the Christian has so frequently had difficulty in esteeming the Old Testament? This is puzzling if for no other reason than that the Lord Christ himself so obviously esteemed it. We shall return to this in chapter eighteen, "The Old Testament and the Law." But for now, this should suffice: The New Testament fairly often deals with the Old Testament in the perspective of Pharisaism. Pharisaism is a religious tradition of ancient beauty and deep religious insight. It esteemed the law as God's greatest gift to the Hebrew people. Pharisaism so loved the law that it wished to protect it and to see the law observed in perfection. For that reason, the Pharisees surrounded the law with a host of small prescriptions —correctly judging that the true believer would never be satisfied to observe the law *in globo* if it were somehow possible to observe it in fuller detail and thus fulfill the Divine will more perfectly in this life. The twentieth-century reader has extreme difficulty in understanding this mentality. He is frequently unsympathetic both with notions of the law as a thing of beauty and with the asceticism which the Pharisaic tradition demands. (An asceticism not unlike that of the Cistercian tradition which has been highly regarded in Roman Christianity until our own lifetime.) But prescinding for the moment from these difficulties to which we shall return in a later chapter, almost universally the Christian has difficulty in understanding the beauty of Pharisaism, because of the perspective of the New Testament on this question.

The New Testament is not presenting an historical study of Pharisaism. It is treating with the Pharisees of an extremely limited time span. It describes a small band of men, prominent in Pharisaism in the short years of the Lord's public life or contemporary with the writing of the New Testament. From the evidence of the New Testament, in comparison with our other sources on Pharisaism, it seems clear that this genre of Pharisaism was an aberration. The motivation of a joyous love had been obscured. (To this day, one of the most frolicsome of Jewish festivals is the "Feast of the Joy of the Law.") Moreover, the Pharisaism of Jesus' time had moved closer to one aspect of magic than at almost any point in the history of Jewish religion. The Pharisees believed that if for one day the law were to be kept perfectly in all Israel, the Messiah would come. The line between this belief and the belief that they could so *cause* the Messiah to come was fine indeed. It was from this movement toward magic that an aspect of Pharisaism developed which many of us find its least attractive feature. The Pharisees believed themselves to be responsible not only for their own keeping of the law; they judged themselves called to assure that all other members of the Hebrew nation should keep it also—willing or not.

Even in the above, there is one basic idea which is worthy of the greatest of religions: Man ought to be fulfilling the will of God at all times and in detail to whatever extent that this is possible. The New Testament does not stress this aspect of Pharisaism, because it is dealing with something else—the Pharisaic opposition to Jesus. Since the New Testament does not purport to present an historical study of Pharisaism, it feels no obligation to footnote that the Pharisaism with which it deals is an aberration of the genuine article. For many Christians, the New Testament treatment of Pharisaism has proved an insurmountable obstacle to appreciating the Old Testament.

In fairness to Christian scholars and teachers, it should be noted that there are three levels of "intellectual" influence on the thought of any Christian. The first is what the New Testament teaches; the second is what many theologians judge the New Testament to teach; the third is the New Testament as it is popularly interpreted in those circles in which a given Christian moves. Frequently, even for the best educated Christian, the third circle may prove to be the most influential. The word "Pharisee" has come to have a meaning in certain circles as "hypocritical," "insincere," as, doubtless some Pharisees of Jesus' time were (as are many Christians of the present day). The scripturally naive have come to equate Pharisaism with a stern, demanding religion, tinged with much hypocrisy, and the Old Testament with Pharisaism. But once having made this judgment, such Christians, understandably, have little further to do with the Old Testament.

The Pharisaic view of the Old Testament, more benignly understood, stresses one aspect of Old Testament religion—the demands of the law—to the exclusion of many other deep religious values. But this is part of the human lot. Man cannot embrace all his values at once. For example, many educators today are properly stressing the value of "joy in learning" for the ghetto schools. They judge correctly that this is a help in getting culturally deprived children to be able to read and write. On the other hand, stress on "joy in learning" is building a real limitation into how much learning the brightest of these children will ever acquire. Serious learning, long before the Ph.D. level, involves some stretches of boredom and real pain. If a child has been brought up to expect nothing but "joy in learning" and to judge all schools in comparison with "Sesame Street," he will find the boredom and the pain even more difficult than the rest of us. Still, many educators are willing to choose the first good, at the risk of the second, but with the realization that it is humanly impossible frequently to have two conflicting goods. If the Pharisees lost some of the warmth which the Old Testament offers in stressing the primacy of law, they avoided the smooth sentimentality of some later New Testament genres of religion.

In recent years in Roman circles, the idea of the "emerging messianic consciousness of Christ" has come to a position of some respectability even in popular (as opposed to more scholarly) circles. This idea, in treating some of the theological problems involved in Christology states simply that Christ as "true man" groped for knowledge as do the rest of us. Most precisely, he groped for the knowledge of who he was and only gradually came to an awareness of his messianic role. Properly understood there is nothing threatening in this idea and it is accepted by the more moderate Roman theologians and exegetes (Raymond Brown, for example, in *Jesus, God and Man*). The idea is singularly attractive for many reasons.

To examine this idea in any detail would take us far afield. In order to use it in our work, two points might be noted. First, while the idea has not gained universal acceptance among Christians (in or outside the Roman church) it does not contradict any basic Christian notion. While it stresses the humanity of Christ, it seems in no way to compromise his divinity. Secondly, if the idea is true, many conclusions flow from it which add their own richness to Christianity. (Of course, these conclusions are hardly proofs that the idea *is* correct.) Father Brown concludes his work:

> Unless we understand that Jesus was truly human we cannot comprehend the depth of God's love. And if theologians should ultimately come to accept the limitations of Jesus' knowledge that we have seen reflected *prima facie* in the biblical evidence, then how much the more shall we understand that God so loved us that he subjected himself to our most agonizing infirmities. . . . A Jesus for whom the future was as much a mystery, a dread and a hope as it is for us and yet, at the same time, a Jesus who would say, "Not my will but yours"—this is a Jesus who could effectively teach us how to live . . . for we would know that he laid down his life with all the agony with which we lay it down. We would know that for him the loss of life was, as it is for us, the loss of a great possession that is out-ranked only by love.   (*pp. 104-105*)

If the view is correct, it does add another dimension to our reading of the Old Testament. The Old Testament was the "sacred scripture" which Jesus of Nazareth read and loved, even in childhood. Largely through his reading of the scriptures, then, did he come to a steadily growing awareness of his messianic role. For us who read the Old Testament today, our reading can be an effort to recapture the prayerful throught processes of the truly human Jesus.

The New Testament tells us very little about the education of Jesus, child and man. The little that it does tell us leads us to believe that he had the kind of education, available even in the first century, to gifted Jewish boys. He had available to himself that education which was in the process of developing into the classical rabbinic training. Even Prat's *Life of Christ*, considered ultraconservative by today's standards, offers some support for this view. (Prat's work first appeared in French in 1930). He points out that the finding of the child Jesus in the temple (*Lk* 2,48) which the New Testament has somewhat dramatized, may be understood more simply. The "amazement" of the teachers at his questions, was the kind of wonder aroused in an enthusiastic teacher by a truly gifted student. If one allows one's imagination to wander here and to see the child Jesus confounding his adversaries at this juncture as a first century, twelve-year-old F. Lee Bailey, he makes the mistake that the apocryphal gospels made. They thought the incarnation was best dramatized by attributing various spectacular acts even to the infant Christ. Ignatius Loyola's spiritual instincts were more sound. He observes that the great lesson of the incarnation is the manner in which "the Divinity conceals itself." It concealed itself in the guise of a person who had to learn by studying. What he studied first and foremost were the Jewish scriptures. For this reason, if for no other, many of us never tire of Old Testament studies.

J. L. McKenzie notes that it is the history of Israel which sets Jesus apart. From this history grew all his cultural values. Future historians in studying the influence of Pope John XXIII and Nikita Khrushchev on our century will surely devote much time to researching the mores of the Italian and Russian peasants. It is impossible to understand either man without understanding his cultural background. (This is perhaps more clearly illustrated by a comparison of Pius XII and John XXIII. Chronologically, they are separated by a decade or so. Culturally, a chasm separates. Pius came from a poor but quite aristocratic Roman family, John was the peasant son of a long, long peasant line.)

The early church understood the importance of Christ's cultural background very well. There is evidence that one of the first books which the early church put into the hands of the first non-Jewish converts was the Septuagint—the Greek translation of the Old Testament. True, this may have been for a number of reasons. The early church had an identity problem of her own; it took her some time to realize that she was not Judaism. (This then offers us another motive for reading the Old Testament, that we may relive with the early church the discovery of her identity.) The early church, of course, had another thing in mind for her catechumens. She wanted them certainly to understand the cultural background of the Lord Christ, but principally she intended something else. The church wanted to begin where the catechumens were. Jewish converts had an extraordinary advantage over the other catechumens in those early days. They were already well on the road to Christianity. By steeping her non-Jewish catechumens in the Septuagint, the church hoped to bring them to the point the Jews had already attained.

What was that point? The charge has often been made against Christianity that it obstructs present progress by concentrating on the *eschata*. Certainly in the long history of Christianity, that charge may sometimes be reasonably made. On the other hand, it is difficult to convict the early church on this charge, if we may judge from her preaching as represented in the New Testament. The New Testament does not offer "pie in the sky" as a substitute for solutions to present problems. It is not interested in present problems. Christ, the immediate apostles, and Paul do not seem much interested in reforming social structure. This is *not* to say that the twentieth-century Christian is not called to reform social structures in light of what Christ *did* preach. In cold fact, however, Christ himself did not become engaged in such reform. He tolerated slavery, for example, as Christianity did for centuries after him. Later species of Christianity may have told the poor and oppressed, "If you will but accept Christianity, we shall alleviate your poverty and oppression"; Christ, Paul and the early Christians told the poor and oppressed no such thing. When they mentioned poverty at all, it was not in the framework of social reform, but to note that freedom from material concern could be an asset in the Kingdom. Generally, though, the poor and oppressed were addressed as though their poverty and oppression were as nonessential to their Christianity as their racial or national origins. Despite this, the poor and oppressed listened intently and accepted Christianity. How was this possible?

If a preacher (or a salesman or a politician) addresses a man who is poor and oppressed, ignores both of these facts, and still manages to capture and keep the man's attention, there can only be one explanation. He is offering to his hearer the solution to something which bothers him more than his poverty and oppression. Any speaker addressing a hearer both poor and oppressed can ignore these data *if the hearer is in deep pain* which the speaker shows himself able to alleviate. Thus (and in no other way) can the speaker succeed in these circumstances.

What was the nature of the pain which the audience of the early Christian preachers felt (and the Jews more keenly than any others) and which the apostolic preachers promised to ease? It was the conviction that man stood somehow convicted under divine judgment and that there was no available escape. Non-Jews and Jews felt this in two different ways. The Gentile felt it as many in the modern world feel it today. He sensed only that he was in extreme pain and less surely felt somehow guilty and unable to ease that pain himself. If the Gentile believed in God at all, he believed himself to be estranged hopelessly from that God. The Jew understood the state of affairs more precisely. He knew that there was a primeval separation of man from God and that he somehow shared it. He may not have understood with precision how it was that he shared it; the manner in which man "ratifies" some primeval sin through his own personal ill conduct was left to the discussions of future theologians. But the Jew, or at least the pious Jew reading the Old Testament, knew that he stood somehow or another convicted and estranged from the God of Sinai.

This was the point where the primitive church met him. She did not deny his innermost feelings; the consciousness of the church shared them. She did assure him that she had an answer to his problem in the person of the redeeming Christ. Since, thus, the church offered the prospective convert a solution to the one thing which bothered him more than living in an occupied country and being without financial resources, the convert came to the side of the early church. From this, the church saw the wisdom of placing the Septuagint in the hands of prospective Gentile converts. It was not a sufficient propaedeutic that they be vaguely unhappy and dimly aware of some kind of estrangement from a personal God. They had to learn something of the nature of that estrangement and that God. They had also to learn how in Old Testament times the Divinity had not been satisfied to let the estrangement rest, but had thrust himself again and again into the affairs of men.

But as the church taught, so also did she learn. Sharing with her catechumens what she had learned from the Old Testament, she came to learn something else. She resolved, for a time, her own identity crisis learning that she was not merely a latter-day Judaism. It may be that part of the church's modern day identity crisis comes from a reading of the New Testament devoid of its Old Testament backdrop. For an individual Christian, such a reading can give birth to a personal Christianity that can be thin and sentimental. For the church or any given church, such a reading can produce an analogously lacking Christianity. If it is true that the Roman church is today overstressing individualism, it may well be that deeper reading of the community-centered religion of the Old Testament might serve as a corrective.

Religion, as most other human activities, admits of fads, styles, shifting emphases. There have been periods in the history of Western Christianity when the Old Testament was extremely popular among theologians and laymen; there have been others when it was almost totally ignored. It may be that the pivotal factor for a given age in determining the popularity of the Old Testament is the nature of world crisis. Some have remarked that when the world is relatively untroubled, the Old Testament is easily forgotten. When the mood of a given age is crisis-laden, the Old Testament becomes once again popular. This may well be, although it must be admitted that perhaps only in retrospect does any period of world history ever look free of crisis. To the citizens of what we might now regard as a golden age, the age may well have been something else. We could perhaps phrase it differently. A Christianity free of the Old Testament borders so on the sentimental that it is a religion which is helpful to the wealthy, the intellectually gifted, the emotionally untroubled. Such a religion ignores the large majority of mankind. A Christianity which rests solidly on the reality of the Old Testament with its firm demands on men, with its insistence that God is to be worshiped, whether or not rewards seem to flow from that worship in this life or in any other, with its insistence that there is a good and evil, that there are good spirits and bad, that there are good *men* and evil *men* with a powerful Divinity ruling over all, such a Christianity may have something to say to the twentieth century. Such a Christianity, of course, can come forth only if the modern church resolves her own identity crisis. This may come about as did the resolutions of the early catechumen and the early church in an atmosphere of meditative reading of the Old Testament.

At the beginning of our work, we took as an operating definition of myth and cult as they appear in the Old Testament, the "recital and reenactment of the saving event." The particular nature of the event was left unspecified for a host of reasons. We shall leave it unspecified still, for the event varied throughout the whole history of the Old Testament. This would have to be so, since the Divinity always begins where man is, in a given historical period.

What did Abraham really want, when first he confronted the Divinity? His needs were rather simple, the product of his environment, he wanted land, children and flocks like any other bedouin sheik. These would guarantee him some modest comfort in his own life and a species of "immortality" after his death. And what did the Lord grant him? "Count the stars in the sky, if you can, such shall your descendants be" (*Gen* 15,5).

And what did the Hebrew clan really want? Not very much. Land, water, freedom from adversaries. And what were they then promised? "Land from the Nile to the Euphrates" (*Gen* 15,18; *Dt* 1,7). (The translation Nile is disputed here. Sufficient to our purpose they were offered land reaching from "the river to Egypt" to the boundary of the other great known civilization of the day.) The Divinity's plans for Israel, as his plans for Abraham, far exceeded man's power to imagine.

And the people who met Christ while he lived among us or met him in his church after the Resurrection, what did they generally want? Again, their needs were very simple. They wanted release from pain, but from pain of a particular nature. They wanted surcease from the vague, troubling thought that something had gone badly awry, long before their lifetimes, and they could not set it straight. They wanted, in some cases, release from the feeling that the Divinity was angry with them—doubtless for a reason—and they could not restore an important, now shattered, relationship. And Christ in his church tells them, not that this state of enmity can be brought to a close, but that they can somehow be made sharers of the divine life. Whatever that power is in virtue of which the Divinity is and acts, that power can dwell in them.

The saving event can mean a variety of things to the Christian reader of the Old Testament insofar as his own life is concerned. Some Christians may seem to place a greater stress on the event as something that happens once-and-for-all. Others stress it as more of an ongoing process. For all Christians, one's subjective saving event is an experience which seems to admit of fuller and fuller amplification. It is in light of this rubric that reading of the Old Testament is most helpful. In studying the saving event of Israel through history, one comes better to understand the nature of one's own. It was because of their understanding of the ways in which the Divinity moves to shape the saving event that the transmitters of the Old Testament handed the work on as they did. They handed on not only the "beautiful" parts—as our aesthetic sense judges them—but they transmitted the dull and the tedious and the "disedifying." In his reading then, the wise Christian ponders all these parts together. While the Old Testament has much to teach any individual reader, one lesson seems available to all who study the Old Testament as the *promise* of which the New Testament, the church and our daily lives are the *fulfillment.* It is this: The saving event we ask for is not always the one we receive. The Divinity, relentlessly pursuing man through history, seems again and again to teach in the Old Testament that he has a tendency to give to man more than man dares to seek.

NOTIONS OF COVENANT 13

The problem of *translation* asserts itself not only in the movement of words from one language to another, but also in the movement of symbols from one cultural world to another. Problems of connotation arise also—the emotional cluster of feelings which surround a word in one language and do not move with the word when the word is found in some other tongue. The native English speaker has difficulty in using the word *Bauer* in German. This word, at least in its core meaning, somewhat approximates the English word "peasant." In many English usages, "peasant" conveys unfavorable, even contemptuous connotations, totally absent from *Bauer* but quite present to the native English speaker who is conversing in German. (For long after such a speaker has learned to think in the German language, he continues to think in English culture patterns.) Interestingly enough, if such a speaker remains long enough in a German culture, the pattern almost reverses itself when he returns home. He will rarely find himself failing to find the proper English word when he speaks, but he will frequently use a word without regard for its British or American connotations.

If the above is true (and it is) in matters of two cultures so closely related as modern American and modern German cultures are, the reader can begin to understand the depth of the problem if he allows himself to read Old Testament words in English translation without a real effort to cross, somehow or another, the "culture barrier."

The example given is a poor one in one respect: *Bauer* is a word of major importance in modern German culture. It would probably occur among the first five hundred words in most word-frequency lists. *Peasant* on the other hand is of minor importance in English. The theme under discussion in this chapter is the word *berith* in Hebrew. This word, of major importance in ancient Eastern cultures, has some correspondence to the English word *contract*—which word is also of major importance in the English-speaking traditions. The connotations of these two words, as we shall see, are poles apart.

To fail to understand the word *berith* is to miss what is perhaps the central theme of the Old Testament relation of the Divinity to the children of Israel. Unfortunately for the modern reader, the Old Testament uses few universal themes to describe the relationship of God to man. God is described as a wounded lover (Hosea), and as a raging bear, bereft of her cubs (Amos). These are probably universal enough. Most of the other themes though involve us very deeply in the culture of another world. For some Old Testament authors, for example, the Divinity is the *goel* of the nation Israel. This figure, only remotely present in modern cultures (although perhaps present in some modern Jewish and Italian notions of family), was apparently a common personage in the Old Testament world. The *goel* was the most powerful member of the clan. He was *obligated* to come to the rescue of the lesser, weaker members of the clan. This obligation extended even to his being required to buy them back, should penury force them into slavery. (It is this aspect of the *goel's* role that the Vulgate translates as *redemptor*, "buyer-back," whence the English word *redeemer*.) Obviously, if one does not have some grasp of the notion of *goel*, one cannot appreciate the touching condescension of the Divinity who acts as *goel* to a nation. He is in this sense a member of the family, albeit the most powerful and distant member.

Still, for the reader of the Old Testament, the above idea is not a misleading notion. When he comes on the word *goel* in translation he frequently finds the word *kinsman*. The alert reader realizes that, whatever that word means, it must have some connotation different from that of the English word. So he does not deceive himself. But it is possible for the English reader to come on the word *berith* translated as "covenant" or "contract" and think that he has some understanding of what the word means in the Old Testament. That would be a most serious mistake, a mistake that has in fact been made frequently right up to our own lifetime.

The mistake was one of major proportions. (Although perfectly understandable in light of the absence of evidence.) Old Testament scholars continued to examine *berith* as some kind of testament or contract. The centrality of the issue here is evidenced by the usage of the terms Old and New Testament to describe the two religious literatures. Why is it so distressing to use the word "contract" in this context?

The word contract is distressing as a translation of *berith* since contracts, in the world of Anglo-Saxon law, involve at least two layers of equality. The persons involved in making the contract are to some extent equals (at least in the making of this contract). Moreover, the goods exchanged in the contract must be of equal value if the contract is to be a just one. Certainly, the Old Testament scholars of fifty years ago did not think that the Old Testament *berith* was a contract between equals. It is sometimes less clear that they saw the total inequality of the goods rendered by the sharers in the Old Testament *berith*: The Divinity himself and the children of Israel. Most simply presented, the sharers in the Old Testament *berith* promised loyalty and service to the Divinity in return for his love and protection. But there is no exchange here. The Divinity does not need the loyalty and service of anyone. Moreover, when this loyalty and service is represented in detail (as in fidelity to the commandments) service is for the good of the server. As we have previously remarked, morality is for the sake of man, not for the sake of God.

It is precisely this inequality between the two members of the Old Testament covenant and the inequality of the goods exchanged which excited researchers some years ago as they examined a collection of ancient documents from the land of the Hittites. This people occupied the site of modern-day Turkey and seem to have had considerable influence (notably through trade) with the ancient world of the bible. Among all the Hittite documents, the ones which touch our problem is a collection of texts which have come to be called *Hittite Suzerainty* (or Sovereignty) *Treaties*.

These treaties are very real contracts. Both parties, as the language of the texts clearly indicates, feel themselves *bound* to fulfill the precepts of the treaty. Still, neither party is under any delusions that the contract is between equals or that the goods under discussion are equal. (In fact, in many of the cases, this last point may be a fiction. Presumably, in many of the texts, the exchange of goods was equal or there would have been no contract. Altruism in governmental dealings was not conspicuously more present in the ancient world than in our own. Still the fiction of nonequality of goods was much insisted on by the more powerful of the two participants in the treaty.)

The two partners in these treaties were always a greater power and a lesser power. In some cases, the greater power was a nation, a powerful tribe, or a great Lord. The lesser power was a weaker tribe, clan or an individual. The language of these treaties is often redolent of expressions found in Old Testament covenantal language. But the striking resemblance between the Hittite material and much of the Old Testament is found in more than a few phrases. Even the basic structure of these treaties is much like familiar Old Testament patterns.

Scholars generally divide the Hittite treaties into the following divisions:

1. The preamble   The great power begins the treaty by stating: "I am the Lord so-and-so." He frequently describes himself with a variety of epithets. If the lesser power is mentioned at all in the preamble, it is to make clear that he is really not of much importance.

2. Historical prologue   This frequently follows the preamble. It is a recitation of the great events in which the Lord has been involved for the good of the lesser power. It is a recitation of past favors. The precise difference between the preamble and prologue is that in the former, the great power is defined independently of his relationship to the lesser power. Here it is exactly their relation (in the past) which is discussed. While it is made clear here that the lesser power is just that, still this section of the treaties begins the "I-Thou" relationship of the covenant. In the preamble, the lesser power is generally ignored. Here, while his inferior status is never overlooked, still he is addressed as a *person*.

3. Stipulations Here are spelled out in some detail the exchange of promises. The great power is to offer protection of some kind or other in return for a variety of services. The language of the treaties tries at times to create the impression that this protection is an act of sheer largesse; the services offered in exchange are little or nothing.

In the Old Testament of course, these correspond most clearly to the expressions of the decalogue or ten commandments. There are two full expressions of the decalogue in the Old Testament (*Ex* 20,1-17 and *Dt* 5,6-21). Some of the individual commandments are brief in the extreme; others are quite lengthy. Some have concluded from this (and other evidence) to a long history ·of transmission. Moreover, there is evidence of cultic and perhaps even rubrical origin for some of the commandments which later developed into precepts of far broader scope. As rubrical and cultic precepts, the decalogue would fit even more exactly the pattern of the stipulations in the Suzerainty treaties. Some scholars see connections between precepts which occur in other places and more developed notions of them which appear in one of the two great collections of the decalogue. The great Old Testament concern for the shedding of blood manifests itself in the forbidding of murder. It also manifests itself in the detailed care which is to be taken in offering sacrifice that the blood of the victim not be spilled carelessly. Perhaps to the modern mind, the connection between these two might not be so evident in an ethical code. Still, for the ancient Hebrew, both of them flowed from a deep and abiding reverence for life. In all its manifestations, this reverence for life has continued to be one of the hallmarks of the evolving Judeo-Christian tradition down to the present day. It may well be true, as certain polemicists insist, that modern Christian opposition to abortion arises partly from a perverted ethic which exaggerates the evil of sexual sin. It is at least equally true that such opposition flows easily from an ethical tradition which insisted that even in the necessary slaughter of animals, care and reverence be shown for the victim's blood, since that blood (according to the ancient dictum) was the abode of life.

Among the other stipulations made in the Hittite treaties are some which are interesting in light of later Judeo-Christian development. Enmity with other lesser powers is sternly forbidden, for example. The greater power will not tolerate a servant who is faithful to him, but not cooperative with other lesser powers engaged in the same service. On the other hand, the lesser powers may never grant asylum to enemies of the great lord. In light of the liturgical developments among the Hebrews, the "annual appearance" before the great lord is also worth noting. These stipulations are common; many others are contingent on conditions suited to a particular time and place.

4. Public reading   Then provision was made for the public reading of the treaty. At least one scholar has made the observation that the role of *laws* can be seriously exaggerated in any effort to reconstruct the culture of an ancient period, since so few people were capable of reading! But it is precisely for this reason that these treaties included provision for depositing the laws in a public shrine. There on the occasion of the greater feasts, they would be read aloud to the populace. Over the course of the years, even an illiterate people would come to know much of the law by heart. (Even as the literate Roman Catholic congregation of past decades came to know much of the gospels from the rather limited selection of readings which took place during the liturgical year.)

5. Gods as witnesses   Then the gods are called to witness all that has been agreed on. This too is probably for a variety of reasons. Certainly it is a very basic human conviction that a promise is solemnized by the presence of any witnesses, even human ones. Invoking even the abstract to witness ("our sacred honor") can be a protest that should the pledge fail, life will never again be the same for the man who made the oath. Too, there is a conviction that God will be sorely offended if the oath is violated, that a god invoked falsely will take his own retribution. Perhaps there is something more. Men in the ancient world, even more than man in the twentieth century, lived in stark terror of isolation. In our lifetime, a man's need for people is largely a psychological need, conditioned by a variety of unconscious factors. These needs vary considerably among men. It is true that the urban civilized man has need for the *services* of a large number of other men, but he lives removed from much personal contact with the men who offer those services. Not so in the cruel world of the ancient Near East. Man lived in immediate contact with the men whose services made continuation of his life possible (as his life made theirs possible). If after generations this produced strong bonds of family and clan which were psychologically rooted, more proximately this felt need of other men was rooted in actual need of union with them for personal survival. From this flowed a deep fear of isolation. To offend the gods, as by swearing falsely in this treaty, was to enter into even a worse isolation. No man wishes to be a friend of the Divinity's enemy (something made fairly clear in the Psalms, especially in the Dahood translation). To be isolated from both the Divinity and from other men was a pain beyond bearing. Thus a man would be *alone* in a hostile environment. Faced with this sanction, signers of the treaty had almost no need of the next method of treaty enforcement.

6. Blessings and curses Most of these treaties conclude with a list of both. If the lesser power is faithful to his obligations, may all manner of good things come his way, but if he should fail . . .! The genre of cursing was raised to a high standard by the Hittite authors of these treaties. Their curses are best left uncited. Perhaps though, one observation should be made. The cruel and abusive nature of the curses, the hope that nature and the Divinity might turn on a faithless signer had at least two effects. For the signer who genuinely believed in the power of the invoked deity, fear alone might bring him some actual harm. Always unspoken but always present was another idea. If the great power in a treaty regarded violation as worthy of such curses and punishments (to be administered by the gods) what kind of punishment would he bring himself to inflict? The mind of the lesser power could lead him here into an imagination's world of terror without limit.

Since the suggestion was made that there was a parallel between the Hittite Suzerainty Treaties and the Covenant of the Old Testament, scholars have busied themselves in finding the biblical parallels. In light of remarks we have made about the nature of biblical composition and because the Hittite documents are so ancient (from the viewpoint of Old Testament composition) it is no surprise that we do not have parallels in the Old Testament where the six divisions described above are matched line for line. Still, it is rather easy to find fairly convincing parallels to the individual portions strewn through much of the Old Testament literature. If a single parallel is not convincing, for many scholars the congeries of all parallels together is rather so. Still, in one passage, Joshua 24, one finds an introductory formula and an historical prologue (with the I-Thou formulation spelled out). There is the stipulation that other gods be rejected. Provision is made for the writing down of the covenant and its being placed in the shrine.

Understandably, most scholars have not been distressed by the difficulty of finding passages where lesser deities are called to witness. Joshua 24,22, for example, states that "You yourselves are the witnesses!" In light of the Old Testament's ultimate stern monotheism, one would not expect minor gods to be called to witness. Still, in Deuteronomy 30,19, we read that Moses called heaven and earth to witness. It is most unlikely that this represents any shaky monotheism on the part of later editors (and uncertain that we have here a *verbum ipsissimum* of Moses). Rather it may be an indication of the Hittite Suzerainty influence on literary development; the use of the term as a cliche, whose vital force is no longer meant by the speaker (as Nikita Khrushchev in his public utterances made frequent use of "God forbid!" and "Thank God!" thus witnessing that his peasant upbringing was with him yet in rubric if not reality).

In addition to Joshua 24, most of the elements of the Hittite formula are found strewn throughout the Pentateuch. Historical recitation of Jahweh's great works is common (as in *Ex* 19,4 and 20,2). The decalogue is probably the core of the stipulations demanded in the Hebrew covenant. The tribes are commanded to cooperate with one another as were the vassals in the Hittite treaty. The great annual festivals of the Hebrews involved a pilgrimage to Jerusalem which certainly corresponds to appearance before the great lord. 1 Kings 8,9 relates a tradition that the stone tablets of the law were preserved in the Ark of the Covenant.

One does not find in the Old Testament express command that the law be read publicly. Still, at least one scholar has suggested that Deuteronomy 27 was an annual and not an isolated event. (This chapter has Moses summing up all the requirements of the covenant in a homiletic form.) Again, Josiah's reaction in 2 Kings 23,3, where he reads the "rediscovered" Torah out loud, may well indicate a preexistent tradition of such reading.

To many, it seems strange that we do not have a clearly documented Old Testament festival of "Covenant Renewal." Some scholars have cited various fragments throughout the Old Testament in contention that such a festival did in fact exist. Why then is the festival not clearly recorded? If all that we have said up to now is true, this is a puzzle. Perhaps part of the solution is to be found in later confusion on the notion of covenant. This confusion asserts itself in some of the treatment of notions of covenant in the prophetic literature where covenant seems not highly regarded by the prophets. For this reason, a generation of scholars taught that the prophets did not esteem covenant but saw it as an earlier and more primitive stage in the development of the religion of Israel.

Today, most would agree that this judgment is not correct. The confusion arises from this: There are at least two major divisions of covenant in the world of the Old Testament, the Sinaitic and the Davidic. In the Covenant of Sinai, the stern demands made on the people of Israel were quite clear. Prescinding from any later confusion on whether or not the Divinity *needed* the services of his people, the Covenant of Sinai makes it quite clear that his continued goodwill rests on the faithful performance of those services. If the people of Israel are faithful in their performance of them, he will continue to be faithful to them. But if they should fail . . . Whatever else may be amiss with the religion of Sinai, it permitted little room for the development of quietism among the tribes of Israel. The refrain, "If you obey, then you shall prosper" recurs, with variation in formula, in a happy monotony throughout the Pentateuch. It is strongly emphasized in Deuteronomy.

But as the nation reflected on David's relationship to the Divinity, the idea of covenant underwent a vital shift. We have noted in an earlier chapter the eternal love affair of the nation of Israel with King David. Denying none of his weaknesses, the nation looked on them with indulgent love. Partially from this starting point, a theology developed which saw David as a special favorite of the Divinity. Perhaps the reasoning was: If we love David this much, then how much more must the Divinity love him! This attitude is fairly clearly developed in 2 Samuel 7 where the Divinity is quoted as making a number of remarkable promises to David. One of the promises touches on an Old Testament theme which we have previously noted in discussing Amos. When David errs, God will assuredly punish him. Forgiveness prior to punishment is not characteristic of the Old Testament. But he will punish him "as a father punishes a son" (7,14). Then it is said that David's throne is established forever. His sons, when they err, may feel the rod of God's wrath, but the kingdom will never be taken away from the Davidic family, as it was taken from Saul. This theme returns again and again in the Old Testament. Moreover, the theme grows in its implications beyond mere preservation of the house of David.

As the theme grew, later ages came to see the promises made to David as a setting up of a kind of covenant, in some opposition to the Covenant of Sinai. The Covenant of Sinai was *conditioned*. God's fidelity to his people rested on their continued fidelity to him. The Davidic covenant was *unconditioned*. No matter what happened, no matter how sorely Israel sinned, the Lord would never abandon her. And this for the sake of David. In 1 Kings 11,13, the promise is modified somewhat, doubtless in light of later developments. It may be that a king will be separated from many tribes. But *one tribe will always remain*. This is perhaps the starting point of a much later "remnant theology." According to this theology, in any given age the ranks of the Jewish people may be sorely decimated. Still, the nation will never be extinguished. A "remnant" will always remain from which the nation can rise again. In light of the awful events of the Second World War and the subsequent rebirth of the nation of Israel, modern Jewish theology has been much preoccupied with notions of the "remnant."

Long before the rise of "remnant theology" the Davidic Covenant was open to much misunderstanding on the part of the simple believing Hebrew. The fact that David's descendants were promised the chastisement of a stern but loving father, should they misbehave, was soon forgotten. The fact that David's kingdom would never be taken away from him was much exaggerated. From this grew a popular theology, quite superstitious in nature, which taught that Israel was the beloved of God without conditions or without demands on her moral posture. The stern voices of the Prophets here were raised and they had the two choices which any teacher faces. They could have attempted with some subtlety to refine the views which the people held. Such pedagogy runs a considerable risk of becoming wasted effort. Or they could thunder against "covenant," leaving to later ages the task of distinguishing between the good and the bad in popular appraisals of the Davidic Covenant in the history of Israel's religion. Wisely they chose the latter course.

Surely, the prophets could not have preached against covenant with any other intention. As we have seen, the notion is central to the Old Testament. Like many other great religious ideas, covenant admits of misinterpretation. (Many pious members of the Roman church are distressed by superstitious attitudes toward the papacy prevalent in the city of Rome itself.) Most religious movements stand in need of constant correction. The prophetic indictments were a corrective of a lofty idea. To read them as much more is to make a serious mistake.

The question is often asked how the Hittite formulations came to play such a large role in the literary substratum of Old Testament theology. The most precise and honest answer is that we do not know. Still, one may speculate. As a result of Hittite influence on Hebrew culture, their treaties were known among the Hebrews from the earliest years. As the early Hebrew theologians developed some of their own ideas on the relationship of Israel to Jahweh—his greatness, remoteness and freedom from them and their absolute dependence on him—the Hittite formulation must have struck them as fitting—condign, as a later age of theology would have expressed it. Did the Hittite formulation serve only as the external format into which the Hebrews set a preexisting theology or did some of its ideas (some precise stipulations?) influence the emerging Hebraic theology? We do not know. Still, we may confidently assert that theology, here as always, developed not as something totally foreign to a given culture but as something that flowed from the culture, gracefully and easily, under the divine hand.

TWO VIEWS OF MESSIANISM 14

Most of us have extreme difficulty in resisting the prejudices acquired from the first source where we have learned something. In an age not terribly distant from our own, all Jesuit schoolboys were fairly well read in the Greek of Homer and the Latin of Vergil. Someone once remarked that it was almost impossible for them to read Homer without prejudice. In the Jesuit curriculum, for good reason and bad, Vergil preceded Homer. Students came to their second account of the same war with an ineradicable prejudice from their first reading. Schoolboys are not always broadminded and this made it most difficult for teachers of Homer.

Most of us have some analogous problems in reading much of the Old Testament. Unlike the early Christian converts from Judaism, it is the New Testament which we read first. In light of New Testament teaching or even in light of further Christian development of New Testament teaching, we turn to reading the Old Testament. It is no wonder that most of us find real difficulty in *reading the Old Testament on its own terms*. The New Testament, with some justification as we shall note, judged itself as capable of reading and *interpreting* the Old Testament. Still, if we are to read the Old Testament *in se* we must divorce ourselves to some extent from this interpretation.

A theological insight of fairly recent vintage may be of some help here. This insight teaches that scripture contains a *sensus plenior* ("fuller sense") as well as its ordinary sense. The *sensus plenior* contains something which might not have been clear to the human authors who wrote. Still, one may argue to this meaning as truly present in the passage as that passage comes more fully to be understood *in the light of further scriptural treatment or further revelation*. This is of extreme importance. Scholars who hold for the existence of a *sensus plenior* are quite modest in their application of the term. One example may suffice. In Hebrews 11,9 and 14, the author makes a reference to Abraham as a sojourner, pilgrim, nomad upon the earth. Most scholars agree that he is alluding to Genesis 23,4 for the words of his description. In fact, the context there is much simpler. Abraham is not speaking of himself as a pilgrim on his way to some heavenly city, but tells some Hittites with whom he wishes to do business that he is a "stranger and passerby." Moreover, in light of some Hittite tax documents which we

146

have, there is reason to believe that Abraham is making a frank appeal to avoid getting caught in a situation where he will have to pay land taxes. Hittite documents state that the taxes must be paid by any man who owns an entire tract of land "with trees upon it." Abraham is attempting to purchase only a small cave. But the Hittites, after much polite conversation on both sides, insist that Abraham must buy the entire tract of land "with the trees thereon." Sojourner or no, he is now in a situation under Hittite law where he must pay taxes. But the author of Hebrews saw this text as teaching something else. He would insist that the revealing God knew that Abraham was a "pilgrim" whether or not he (and the human authors who relate the story) knew it. For the scholars who feel sympathetic to the *sensus plenior*, this might be an acceptable example, since the example *is developed in further scripture.*

This is an important point—the limited use which must be made of the *sensus plenior*. So many competent scholars support this rather limited use of the *sensus plenior* that some students wonder at the seriousness of the opposition which the idea has aroused. One good reason for the opposition, at least in Roman circles, is that we have been some time coming to a full appreciation of the literal sense and scholars are frightened by anything which might seem to compromise that appreciation. If any use of scripture is permitted which is remotely allegorical and which does not have some built-in restraints, subjectivity may run riot. A famous medieval defense of ecclessiastical use of the temporal sword concluded its argument with the suggestion that the Apostle had himself said, "Lord, here are two swords" (*Lk* 22,38). This is an extreme example and we would certainly not contend that this is a use of scripture common among those who depart from insistence on stern controls of all nonliteral use of texts.

All the above may bring the question to some minds, "Why is it possible for the New Testament authors to indulge in this type of exegesis and it is not permitted to the rest of us?" One answer we have already proposed elsewhere: Even in the composition of the New Testament (and assuredly in the preachings of the fathers) we do not have the entire amount of the emerging work but only those portions *which came to be accepted by the Christian community.* Others advance the argument, common in many religions, that the "primitive period" had special gifts not given to later Christians. Finally, we may suggest that there remains today a slight possibility for the rise of a latter-day Paul or Matthew who will see Christianity in a brilliant new light. Still, such a person (and the validity of his teachings) will be recognized only some time after his intimate personal sharing in the passion of Christ. Moreover, it does not seem consonant with Christianity to hold that creative theological insights (of the stature which Paul

had) are common events among Christians. Again, when theological geniuses do arise, their insights are subject to the ultimate criterion of acceptance by the Christian community.

The New Testament is not the Old Testament all over again. Even
though the New Testament authors may seem to insist that much of what
they present is already in the Old Testament, the reader must be careful to
note the *manner* in which this New Testament material is present in the
Old Testament. The manner is rarely spelled out, since little of the New
Testament is a work of speculative theology. Still, the serious reader of
scripture will want to understand something about the manner in which
the earlier work contains material present in the later. If he does not, his
reading will not be fair to either work.

Messiah, as most readers doubtless know, is derived from an Aramaic
word (*Christos* in Greek) meaning "anointed." The symbolism involved in
the word is fairly clear. Kings and priests are anointed in a near-universal
symbolism. Anointing in the ancient world (as to some extent in our own)
was taken also as a means of restoring health. Possibly, although this need
not be accepted, the Messiah himself was seen as somehow restored to
health as part of his messianic activity.

In speaking of messianism in the Old Testament, it is more accurate to
say that the Old Testament does not so much contain an implicit theory of
messianism as to say that it presents a plurality of messiahs. Moreover,
there is some clear evidence that for most pre-Christian readers of the Old
Testament, there was little effort expended to identify one of these many
messianic figures with any other. For a student with some reading in Christian literature, this is a difficult idea to grasp. An evolving Christian theology has so completely identified the plurality of messianic figures with the
one person of Christ that it is difficult to realize that it was not ever thus.
Moreover, some scholars feel that the notion of "suffering" is not clearly
identified in the Old Testament with any messianic figure (although, this
can be disputed). Still, the fact that there is reason for dispute on the *possibility* of a suffering Messiah, shows the difficulty of easy identification of
the views of the nature of messianism represented in the two great religious
literatures.

The "suffering servant" passages in the Old Testament (*Is* 49,1-6; 50,4-
9; 52,13-53,12) have become a portion of the Christian view of the Messiah.
It seems at least probable that this suffering servant was not, in pre-Christian times, clearly identified with the Messiah. These passages in the
prophet Isaiah deal clearly with a beloved of the Lord who was a totally innocent figure. Despite this, he suffered severely and some of the passages
reflect on the meaning of his punishment. Jewish theology has interpreted

this variously. Some Jewish theologians see the servant as a personification of the children of Israel whose role it is innocently to suffer in this world. Their suffering, somehow or another, is for the good of all mankind. Another school of Jewish theologians says that an individual or group of individuals lives in the world at all times, whose role it is to suffer, although blameless. This group, too, somehow or another averts the wrath of an angry God from a sinful world.

On the occasion of President Kennedy's assassination, an ecumenical mourning service was nationally televised. In it were representatives of the major American faiths. Some spoke with great eloquence. Others were less successful in articulating the nation's grief. For many viewers, the most striking moment was the appearance of Rabbi Abraham Heschel. Possessed of striking patriarchal appearance with flowing white beard, he read simply for a few minutes from the passage which includes the words:

> By this chastisement we are healed . . .
> the Lord laid on him the guilt of us all.
>
> Isaiah 53,5-6

In the best manner of a preacher using parables, the Rabbi explained nothing, but read slowly and quietly and then sat down. He left his audience to ponder the idea that, through some mysterious way, this awful death was a working toward some good for the sake of men.

It is certainly no surprise, in the light of the Christian message, that Christians early seized upon the "suffering servant" as an image of the suffering and innocent Jesus who would take away the sins of the world. Still, there is little clear evidence that any reader of the Old Testament prior to Christian times has read these passages as messianic in content.

There is one line of reasoning which might make the "suffering servant" stand more clearly in the line of messianic texts. (Although it is by no means clear that this line of reasoning was followed by any pre-Christian readers of the Old Testament.) This connection is introduced by one of the clearer differences between the theology of Old Testament and New. Beyond the proclamation of the divinity of Christ which many readers find in the New Testament, there are few clear differences. Such differences which exist have been frequently exaggerated.

One clear difference may be found in the two attitudes toward "sin and forgiveness." Most certainly forgiveness to the sinner is always clearly available in the mainstream of Old Testament thought. Almost without exception, though, *forgiveness follows punishment*. We have just noted that David and his descendants will be forgiven by the Lord after he chastises them, paternally but vigorously. One other striking text comes to mind. Hosea, treated in chapter ten, is one of the clearest Old Testament proclamations that sin may be forgiven. The graciousness and total forgiveness shown by the image of the wounded lover are difficult to match in any other religious literature. Still, there may be some indication of the general Old Testament idea that punishment ought to precede forgiveness. A difficult line (*Hos* 2,13) in the Hebrew text may carry the meaning, "I shall punish her for her pagan past." In a work which is such a striking example of gracious forgiveness, this is very meaningful. If it truly belongs to the earlier edition of the work, it means that the earliest authors were totally in the mainstream of the Old Testament thought that forgiveness follows punishment. If this line was added in a fairly late stage of redaction, it shows that the Old Testament idea of forgiveness after punishment was so strong, that some later editors had difficulty in accepting the Hosea story and somewhat modified it.

In either event, the above may show some function of the "suffering servant" in a history of Old Testament ideas. If Israel was to be forgiven in the messianic age, everything in the Old Testament taught that punishment must first come. The "suffering servant," innocent though he is, receives punishment for the good of others and perhaps then, although not himself the Messiah, makes possible the coming of the messianic age. This idea is never clearly spelled out. Still, apart from later Christian development of the idea, this connection seems too logical easily to be dismissed.

The notion of *goel*, cited previously, certainly has some messianic connotations. Even as the punishment of a sinning world is laid on the shoulders of the just "servant of God" and sinners are somehow spared, the *goel* too is involved in delivering men from their slavery. Frequently the nature of this slavery is not spelled out. Presumably, most pre-Christian readers of the Old Testament saw the *goel* as bringing about some very concrete kind of *redemption* (even as the Divinity himself had been a *goel* in the movement from Egypt). The notion of *Son of Man* covers an enormously long history in Old Testament and post-Old Testament literatures, and the notion fluctuates considerably. From the viewpoint of messianism, perhaps the most important idea in the Son of Man concept is that this personage has a relationship of special intimacy with the Divinity. There is a massive gap between this idea and the "Son, eternally begotten of the Father." Still, the Son of Man is closer to the Divinity than are any other of the sons of men. The New Testament itself has a certain ambivalence in the use of this term. At times for example it seems to use it in the simplest sense which the Aramaic sense bears, "a true human being." Jesus is quoted as so describing himself when he observes that he has no place to lay his head (*Mt* 8,20;

Lk 9,58) and when he notes that he is said to come eating and drinking (*Mt* 11,19; *Lk* 7,34).

If one were to seek a focal point for the idea of Old Testament messianism, one could do far worse than to focus on the personality of David. A very basic aspect of the Old Testament messianism is the royal messiah— the great personality who will come as a King and thus deliver Israel. With all that we have said about David in reality and legend, the reader can easily see the ease with which the Messiah would be described in Davidic terms. What would the royal messiah be like? Of course he would be like David! At some points in history, the theologians of the Hebrew nation might stress that the royal messiah would be a "larger-than-life" image of David. In other periods, so great had the image of David grown, that the simple Hebrew faithful might well have asked: "A messiah who is greater than David? Is this possible?"

As long as the memory of David remained fresh along with the glory of his reign and the glory of his immediate successors, a rather simple theory of messianism was possible. The messiah would simply step into the succession of Davidic kings and begin a slightly more glorious reign than any Davidic king had ever enjoyed. But this simple theory ran into difficulties. Writings from the eighth century had to deal with the fact that kings had arisen, reigned and died who lacked any semblance of the Davidic stature. The pious faithful had extreme difficulty in believing that a royal messiah could simply step into such a succession. Some of these kings were inept; some of them morally reprehensible. None of them seemed a likely candidate to be an immediate predecessor of a royal messiah.

In consequence of this state of affairs, another view of messianism began to emerge. This view explained that the royal messiah would appear only at the end of time. With all the vagueness that *eschatology* possessed for the peoples of the Old Testament, a view of messianism arose which saw it as something *eschatological*. This is not to say that the writers who developed this latter view attempted to stamp out or supplant the earlier view that the Messiah would be in the normal succession of Davidic kings. The two views continued to grow side by side. This is characteristic of the honest theology of the Old Testament authors. They are not frightened by apparent contradictions such as temporal/eschatological. These *two* ideas were allowed to grow and this fact alone would support the view that it is erroneous to speak of a "messiah" in the Old Testament where there is really a plurality of messiahs.

In the history of ideas, this tension described above is highly analogous to one in the development of Christianity. Certainly in the early days of the church, the notion of the attainment of perfection by the church was viewed as something historical. At a definite moment in time, the visible and imperfect church would become a perfect one. As early decades passed and there was little evidence for movement in this direction, another idea arose, that the church would attain perfection only with the coming of the *eschata*. Until very recent years, most of us have lived in a period of theological synthesis, certainly in a given tradition and to some extent between traditions. The emergence of the dichotomy between historical/eschatological messiahs (and the analogous problem in ecclesiology) reminds us that many great theological ages tolerated the coexistence of contradictory notions, since each seemed valid and no means of synthesis was yet available.

Nor was the temporal/eschatological the only dichotomy in the Old Testament notion of messiah. Notions of messiah as king and messiah as priest were to flourish until the intertestamental period when (notably at Qumran, site of the "Dead Sea Scrolls") the notion hardened that two clear and distinct messiahs were to be awaited. The ultimate background for this notion reaches perhaps into the pre-Hebraic world. Through another natural dynamic, the roles of king and priest tended now to merge, now to separate. In many early societies, the principal cultic roles were acted by the king or political leader. As the cultic role became more complicated, it tended to professionalize and to become separated from kingship. On the other hand, as we have previously noted, the role of cultic leader tends to take to itself a large measure of authority outside the cultic sphere. This real tension in the real, historical world tends to flow into the world of speculative thought. The "priestly" source of the Old Testament composition, for example, tends to present a different picture of Aaron the "high priest" and brother of Moses. In some Old Testament sources, however, Aaron is a minor figure. In the priestly source, he is bold and dramatic; in some cases, he succeeds in upstaging even the unique Moses. In some measure, the tension in the world of thought between these two figures of royal and priestly messiah may well flow from historical tension between them. Still, it may be that even removed from historical specifics, there is an essential conflict between these two roles. Each tends of its very nature to usurp the position of the other. Christianity could peacefully unite the two roles in one person without conflict only because it asserted that the person was divine.

The original idea of the Messiah was doubtless a very simple one. He would simply be "an anointed one" from among the people who would then lead his people, under the divine hand, to the "saving event." This idea grew more complicated and perhaps elevated through a dual urgency. The idea tended to grow of itself, and it also came under the influence of other cultures with which the Hebrews lived. Whatever the most important source of the "divine adoption" motif in ancient Israel, it came to have considerable significance in shaping notions of messianism.

The Roman liturgy for Christmas begins with the entrance song, "Thou art my son; this day I have *begotten* thee" (*Ps* 2,7). Christian worshipers are sometimes puzzled by this phrasing and wonder at its suitability for a Christmas text. They sometimes assume that it refers to the eternal begetting of the Son by the Father. (Perhaps defenders of *sensus plenior* might so accept this interpretation as now made clearer in light of subsequent revelation.) But in fact there is a simpler explanation for the suitability of this text. The Hebrew language (and perhaps New Testament Greek in imitation of it) does not carefully distinguish at all times between the act of begetting and the mother's act of being delivered of a child. Perhaps the implicit poetry here is more accurate than our own; both actions are seen as bestowing the gift of life. The psalm itself in genuine historical context means this: It is a reference to the *divine adoption* of a king on the occasion of his ascending the throne. This idea, of considerable significance in the ancient world around Israel, meant that from henceforth the king had a special relationship to the Divinity and would act in his stead. With the rise of ineffectual (and even morally corrupt) kings, this notion continued to live in Israel only with difficulty. It was accordingly transposed into another key. The line (and others like it) was seen as referring *par excellence* to the Messiah who would be the "Son of God." He would be specially adopted and would truly reign in God's stead. He would fulfill, even more perfectly the role of divine sonship which the Divinity had always intended for Israel's rulers. Again, in connection with this notion, the idea of the king's cultic role comes to the fore. Who could perform cultic rites with more confidence than the expressly adopted Son of the Divinity himself? For reasons like this, it is perhaps remarkable that the royal role in cult came to be diminished as it did. Perhaps a partial explanation is that the custody of the sacred books (in Israel as in most religions) came into the hands of the priestly class. This left them with unique opportunities to reinterpret (if not to rewrite) the cultic history of Israel. They sometimes exploited those opportunities.

The priestly class had another advantage too, of course, to which we have elsewhere alluded. The notion of priesthood arises, to some extent, from the common fear that men have in approaching the Divinity. It is comforting to men in many religions to judge that the Divinity has chosen a group of men and set them apart expressly to approach him in the name of their fellows. In historical periods where the divine adoption of the ruling king was not taken with the utmost seriousness, the king would be to some extent handicapped as priest, simply because he was also king. His dual role would

resist the professionalizing dynamic which makes priesthood a specialty
and contradict also the Old Testament desire that the priest be something
totally apart.

If one consults a concordance of the Greek Old Testament, the Septuagint, and checks the entries under *Christos,* "anointed," one makes an
interesting discovery which points up fairly clearly the role between Old
Testament and New Testament on this issue. A fairly frequent occurrence
is the expression, *Christos Kuriou,* "the anointed of the Lord" (since
Kuriou is genitive case). The expression shows up in a variety of contexts
and it is not always clear to the reader that one may distinguish (in an individual context) between the eschatological and/or historical Messiah. This
much *is* clear, that the person under discussion, whether a presently described historical figure, a proposed figure of the historical future or an
eschatological image, is certainly the "anointed of the Lord." (It is perhaps
also worth noting here that *Kurios* is generally used by the Septuagint to
translate *Jahweh.*) Then we come to the delightful Christmas sermon recorded in Luke 2,11. The marvelous birth is a source of joy, the angels relate, since one is born who is *Christos—Kurios!* The Anointed—the Lord!
The nominative case is used, not the genitive in an expression which
would have startled some of the early converts, with their easy familiarity
with the Septuagint's text. Properly to appreciate *Christos—Kurios* one
must have been brought up on *Christos—Kuriou.* Properly to understand
the condescension of the divine *goel,* one must have been brought up to
expect that the Divinity would send a special messenger and then be
startled to find, as the New Testament text has it, that the Divinity came
himself.

It should be noted that the philogical argument in the above passage
may not be outside the reach of refutation. What did *Kurios* mean in the
first century? Was the New Testament author affected by that connotation more than by the Old Testament Septuagint connotation? Was the interpretation given in the preceding paragraph visible only to the eyes of
faith? In any event, perhaps as much as any other passage, the passage in
Luke points up the futility of certain types of Old Testament exegesis
which strive to find there the specifics of the New Testament message.
Such exegesis is not fair to either Testament. Moreover, even as the development of the notions of Messiah in the Old Testament showed, the scriptures are not intended as magic books explaining the future in such detail
to the devout that the devout need not fear the future. Within the Old
Testament itself, one could not use scriptural passages to "predict" how

the notion of Messiah would develop, much less could one use the Old Testament to "predict" specifics of the New Testament. If a great religion gives its members confidence to face the future, it does not do so by explaining that future in such detail that the hiddenness of the future evanesces. To face the future with fear and awe and wonder is very human. Here as always, the Judeo-Christian tradition does nothing to undermine the human lot.

THE WORLD
OF THE PSALMS 15

In Fitzroy McLean's rather remarkable memoirs of his long career as a British diplomat, he tells of attending the famed "Moscow Trials" of the thirties. In these trials, some of the Communist heroes of the earliest years of the Revolution—now fallen into disfavor—found themselves on trial for their lives. Almost without exception, they were quickly found guilty and summarily shot. In a moment of high drama at the trial, Andrei Vishinsky (later to become internationally prominent as Soviet Foreign Minister, and then the special prosecutor at the trial) confronted one of the hapless victims. He presented to him a piece of brown wrapping paper with some writing on it. He announced that the paper had been found in the victim's pocket and he proceeded to read from it aloud:

> Let God arise and let his enemies be scattered: let them also that hate
> him, flee before him.
> Like as the smoke vanisheth, so shalt thou drive them away: and like as
> wax that melteth at the fire, so let the ungodly perish at the presence
> of God . . .
> Whoso dwelleth under the defense of the most High: shall abide under
> the shadow of the Almighty.
> I will say unto the Lord, Thou art my hope and my stronghold: my God,
> in him will I trust.
> For he shall deliver thee from the snare of the hunter: and from the
> noisome pestilence.
> He shall defend thee under his wings and thou shalt be safe under his
> feathers: his faithfulness and truth shall be thy shield and thy
> buckler.
> Thou shalt not be afraid for any terror by night: nor for the arrow that
> flieth by day;
> For the pestilence that walketh in darkness; nor for the sickness that des-
> troyeth in the noon-day.

These selections from the sixty-eighth and ninety-first psalms had been written out in longhand and placed in the victim's pocket by his wife. Alas for the drama of the moment! Rosengolts, the man on trial, did not share his wife's faith. When asked to explain the presence of the paper in his pocket, he said he had permitted his wife to put it there, "as a talisman." Vishinsky repeated this phrase, McLean relates, with a broad wink at the hand-picked crowd in the courtroom and the result was general merriment.

Still, McLean was moved by the experience. The victim, confronted by his adversary, had found a real parallel in words used by the psalmist some three millennia before the Moscow trials. This powerful example points up something which should be noted as we begin to treat of the psalms. They are moving. They are so moving in various translations that (sometimes with considerable editing) they have come to be reverenced throughout the whole literate world. McLean's work cited the psalms as they appear in English in the book of common prayer. He did not discuss the Russian version read aloud and which he easily understood.

The psalms, more so perhaps than any other form of religious literature in the West, have come to have a place of their own in translation and without historical explanation. They are like certain of the religious shrines of Europe. With the passage of enough time, it no longer matters whether the Divinity or the Blessed Virgin truly appeared there (as many of the faithful believe). The prayers of those very faithful have brought a special holiness to the spot in question. This is not to deny the possibility that the Divinity has hallowed these spots. In any event, the prayers of the faithful have made them holy. Some scholars do not understand this. Consequently, they are distressed when they find editions of the psalms which bind them and the New Testament together, making the psalms but a Christian prayerbook. Certainly, the psalms have a dimension that is totally other than that of Christian prayerbook. Yet, centuries of use have made it that also. For the reader who cherishes the psalms as Christian prayer, no amount of study should distract him from that aspect of them.

This is not to say that some historical appreciation does not add another dimension occasionally (but not always). For example, a good deal of time and energy have been wasted in efforts to explain the last verse of Psalm 137. It begins beautifully enough:

> By the rivers of Babylon we sat down and wept
> when we remembered Zion

and then concludes with an angry imprecation at the enemy, Babylon,

> Happy is the man who shall seize your children
> and dash them against the rock!

The Christian who reads the psalm in a prayerful mood has only a few choices at this juncture. First, he can simply skip the verse. This solution has a great deal to be said for it. First of all, it is honest. It is certainly infinitely preferable to attempting some kind of smooth and harmonious exegesis which will undermine the power of the line. A second solution is just such an exegesis. The reader attempts to explain the line as "a powerful figure" without actual intent, a vivid means of expressing the hope that the enemy will suffer badly.

And then there is a third solution—an effort to read that line in the mood in which it was written, an effort to get some feel for another world whose emotions we do not totally share. The powerful world of medieval Scandinavia has already been mentioned as an example of some of the kinds of thought and emotional patterns common in much of the world of the Old Testament. We cited Sigrid Undset's *Kristin Lavransdatter* as a novel of a world much like the world of Judges. Bergmann's film classic *The Virgin Spring* also affords some insights into such a world. True, like *Kristin Lavransdatter* it is a world that has been Christianized, but only to some extent. (The movie opens with a deeply moving invocation of a pagan deity by a maidservant.)

The precise point of comparison between Bergmann's film and the world of the psalms comes at the highpoint of the film. The stern father of the maiden who has been violated and murdered finds that her assailants, unwittingly, have taken refuge for the night in his house. They are two strong, young adults and are accompanied by a small male child. After first locking them in their chamber, he begins an act of obvious ritual washing, cleansing himself, as it were, for the sacrifice. Then he boldly confronts the two of them. In a brief scene of great violence, he brings death to both of the murderers.

And then he faces the small child who accompanies them. The modern, Western, Christianized film audience pleads silently for the child's life. But again, with incredible swiftness, the father lifts the child in his arms, flings him the length of the great hall and the child falls dead to the floor.

In fact, the avenger soon comes to regret his action. In atonement largely for this excess of violence, he plans to build a shrine (at which shrine miraculously, there flows the "virgin spring"). Still, there may be something in this violently punitive act, in a world not totally Christianized, that is reminiscent and explanatory of the lines cited from Psalm 137.

How is evil to be removed from the world? This is a problem with which every great religion has had to cope. This is not precisely the "Problem of Evil" (why does the just man suffer?). Rather, when an evil man or group of men has perpetrated evil, has somehow or another increased the amount of evil living in the world, how is that to be cleansed? In many societies, there is much to be said for the view that this evil must be literally blotted out. The evildoers, and all associated with them, must be removed from the world. Certainly in a world like that of the Old Testament with its limited views of immortality, death of one's children was the direst of punishments since it took all "immortality" away from the bereaved parents. But that is only part of the reason for such death (since, in other contexts in the Old Testament, brothers, sisters, wives of the evildoers meet the same fate).

In a pre-Christian, or faintly Christian world, death and destruction of all associated with the evil is the only method of blotting out this new excrescence of evil. With the fullness of the Christian teaching, the Act of the Redeeming Christ is seen as the only method of removing evil from the world. Certainly in a very Christian world, the act of the evildoer must sometimes be punished (if only through medicinal punishment), but evil is no longer something which continues to grow after the commission of an evil act. The work of Christ is seen as limiting chaos in this regard. In the pre-Christian world, chaos is seen as somehow unleashed again by the performance of any evil action and it must be rechained. Some may find this explanation somewhat speculative. At any event, it may serve to remind the Christian reader of the psalms that they truly represent a wholly different world from the one in which he lives.

In another context, we have already made mention of the difficulties which some Protestant scholars had with the notion of "cultic" vs. "noncultic" prayer. They tended for a variety of reasons to see only the latter as truly worthy of the name prayer; many of them tended to see "cult" as a poor kind of substitute for genuine prayer. Nowhere did this notion handicap some of these great scholars more than it did in their study of the psalms.

If cult may be defined as "reenactment of the saving event," there are other dimensions to be stressed in a fuller definition. It is of its nature a *public* reenactment. It is a prayer of the *community*. Many of the periphera attached to cultic worship such as special clothing, gestures, even the use of candles and incense, may be explained as flowing from the public and communal nature of the worship. These periphera are required that the chief cultic figure, the priest (and his ritual actions), may be seen at a distance so that the entire community may participate in the act of worship.

Some nineteenth-century Protestant scholarship was handicapped in its grasp of the cultic origin of the psalms because it equated cultic worship with an inferior kind of religion. This was a perfectly understandable mistake. Still, what is at stake here is rather not what cult means to Christians, in the reform tradition or outside of it, and certainly not the question of whether cultic religion is *per se* more perfect than noncultic (can such a question be answered?), but rather what did cult mean to the early Hebrews?

Since cultic prayer is the chief prayer of the *community*, it is hard to overestimate its role in the world of the Old Testament. If Second Isaiah began to move toward the realization that "all men are brothers," certainly the entire Old Testament is permeated with the idea that "all Hebrews are brothers." In one's relationship to the Divinity, Hebrew notions of brotherhood cut two ways. Certainly the sin of an individual Hebrew falls on the entire nation. On the other hand, the virtue of an individual Hebrew affects the entire nation also. Nowhere is this clearer than in the psalms.

One of the most puzzling aspects of the psalms for the modern reader is the psalmist's frequent protestation: I am innocent! Hear my prayer! Most of us feel that in making a prayer on that basis, we are not dealing with the Divinity from a position of strength. Almost any plea would be stronger than telling the Divinity that he ought to answer our prayer because we are so innocent. This plea, strange to our ears, can be explained in two ways, both of them related to Hebrew notions of cult.

First of all if the psalms are of cultic origin (something we are presently presuming rather than proving), even the "I" of the psalms is reflective of choral recitation. When the psalmist says "I" he is singing in a group. It may be that even thus does he mean "we." This is one of the peculiar strengths of community worship. The worshiper feels that he is presenting to the Divinity, not his peculiar innocence, but the innocence of the worshiping community. The Roman liturgy makes this explicit: "Look not on our sins, but on the faith of your church!" So the psalmist says, "Hear my prayer; I belong to the community of your beloved Hebrews, so, in this sense, I am innocent." But someone might object that the Hebrews saw themselves as a "backsliding, stiffnecked" people. Membership in such a group could hardly afford confidence in making any plea to the Divinity! Certainly, the Hebrew mind never lost sight of the nation's weakness and infidelity in response to the love of Jahweh. On the other hand, as Augustine has noted, "God is the only Lover who can love to the extent of making the object of his affections lovable." The Hebrews never lost sight of that either. As a family, they were a most special object of God's love. So the Psalmist may have prayed, "Hear my prayer; I am a member of your best loved family."

But "innocence" (*zedekah*) to the psalmist may be something else. In certain places in the Old Testament it clearly means *fidelity to cultic prescriptions,* and it may mean that also in the psalms. The psalmist's confidence in himself, by reason of his cultic fidelity, can be wrongly understood. This is not necessarily a world of magic; the psalmist does not feel that cultic fidelity can substitute for moral integrity. Rather, he esteems cultic fidelity as it has been esteemed in many other religious traditions since.

Cultic fidelity is something that is *measurable;* moral integrity can be measured only with difficulty because it brings us to the world of human motivation. (And the murkiness of human motivation was something known long before Freud, though much more clearly since his work.) But one can honestly answer the questions: Have I fasted? Have I performed the ritual ablutions? Have I brought only ritually pure animals to the sacrifice? If the honest answers are also affirmative, the questioner can then face Infinite Holiness with that modicum of human confidence which is the best that any worshiper ever has in the presence of the Divinity. (In this connection, it may now be noted that the attitude of the Eastern faithful toward cultic performance as a criterion for the "holiness" of their priests may not be so magical as it first seemed.)

Are the psalms largely of cultic origin? Since the work of Mowinckel, there can be little doubt that a large number of the psalms originated or grew in a cultic setting. One of the arguments may be very briefly put: The "atmosphere" of much of the psalms is cultic. They are preoccupied with song; they are a veritable catalogue of musical instruments; they speak of processions.

> We are seeing thy processions, O God,
> The processions of my God and my King in the sanctuary,
> Singers in front, musicians behind
> Between them girls with tambourines.   *Ps.* (68,25)

Even to the scholar, the amount of wrangling which went on over the question of cultic vs. noncultic origin seems now rather tedious. Certainly a rehearsal of the arguments, pro and con, is beyond the scope of this book. It may be that both sides overstated their cases somewhat, in light of the evidence. One side insisted adamantly that the psalms were of cultic origin, virtually without exception; the other side that they were almost exclusively of "private origin."

Both of these are overstatements in light of what we know about the transmission of poetry in the ancient world. "Private" poetry might be in large manner publicly composed, as we have previously noted. On the other hand, if the public poetry was truly esteemed, would there not be occasional private recitation of the same? Then, in light of what we know about poetry in Ugarit, it is most likely that the period of composition of the psalms covers nearly one thousand years. Is it even theoretically possible over such a span that beloved poetry would not move back and forth between the two worlds?

Do some go back as far as 1300 B.C. and are some of them of pre-Hebraic origin? The state of the evidence does not yet admit of a firm answer without possibility of error. Still, the overwhelming probability is that the psalms are in fairly large measure influenced by the most ancient of poetry in the Canaanite world. Some of the argumentation is rather difficult. One noted scholar in this area prefers to speak of the Ugaritic literature as a means of "elucidation" of the psalms rather than as a source that "influenced" them. By this he steps around the presently impossible question of documenting a strict chain of evidence which will connect large numbers of the psalms with an original Ugaritic source. On the other hand, as a language scholar, he feels too overwhelmed by the number of linguistic parallels to dismiss them simply by saying that the songs of Ugarit and the psalms belong to the same general milieu. (The connection must be more than that; it was only with the material from Ugarit that we came to understand a large number of linguistic problems in our present edition of the psalms.)

There is some historical evidence too. The Ugaritic material makes reference to the existence of "guild singers," professional religious composers. Such professions were "boundary-free," these religious personnel were welcomed wherever it went. (That the guild singers were principally engaged in religious composition is totally clear.) It is inconsistent with all that we know about the high esteem both of the skill of public composition and the skill of professional participation in public worship to suggest that the guild singers would not regularly find themselves moving across borders and selling their wares. Moreover, because of the sacredness of tradition in the ancient world, these guild singers would certainly bring with them a stock of a common repertoire. This is evidenced by certain expressions, puzzling in the psalms and made clear in the Ugaritic texts. Jahweh is *rokeb ba 'araboth* in the psalms. This was regularly translated as "rider of the clouds," an image which was somewhat puzzling in the Hebrew world. In the Ugaritic material, the same epithet is applied to *Baal*, a great deity, and the context makes another translation clear: "mounter (impregnator) of the clouds." Here it is evident that the epithet was one of immense significance in a fertility religion. The deity impregnates the clouds whose life-giving rain then brings life to the earth. Jahweh's participation in the fertilization of the earth was something which was less clear to later and more sophisticated Hebrews, but they handed down the ancient title, received from the people of Ugarit, even though they no longer understood it.

The title cited in the above paragraph is now virtually a cliche among biblical scholars. In fact, however, there are many, many more Ugaritic titles in the psalms. These are becoming clear only in the most recent scholarship, since these titles were largely misunderstood by the Massoretes who changed the vowels of the words to turn them into something intelligible in their lifetime and thereby made them unintelligible as what they really were—fine Canaanite titles. Moreover, in addition to these titles, a large number of myths came into the Hebrew world directly from the intellectual world of Ugarit. Previously, scholars had tried to explain the presence of these myths as flowing from Mesopotamian influence (which is not impossible). Still, with the Ugaritic material, a simpler solution is at hand.

Nor is the time gap between the Ugaritic material and biblical poetry very large. The most ancient biblical poetry is from 1250-1100 B.C.; a large number of the psalms from 1000-550. Since our Ugaritic texts date from 1375-1195 B.C., we are virtually in the same world. Moreover, what is the alternative to concluding that a strong influence existed between one set of these compositions and the other? Only that the Hebrew psalms grew up out of nothing. This is not only contrary to the normal literary dynamic, but resists, as we have noted, the Semitic reverence for tradition.

It is hard to understand why there has been so much resistance to the idea that the psalms were composed under large—direct or indirect—pagan influence. Granting the force of a kind of pious chauvinism, the obvious power of genius to transcend religious boundaries seems too well-known to be denied. In the heat of Christian religious reform, great musical patrons hired the most talented religious genius, be he Lutheran or Roman, to compose religious music. Twentieth-century America dedicated a National Center for the Performing Arts with a Mass—written by a Jewish genius. It is precisely the gift of genius to express clearly the thoughts and emotions of other men the way they would wish to express them, had they the gifts of verbal or musical articulateness. Despite much innate emotional resistance to the idea, the preponderance of evidence seems to indicate that the psalms owe much to a band of nameless geniuses in pre-Hebraic times. These men played the role of Bernstein in our own culture—and Bach and Pindar in other times and other cultures. For a price, they sold their genius to the celebration of a tradition which they did not always share. Not only are individuals of genius hired for such purposes, but an entire profession may be so employed. (In our world this is so accepted that the same commentators who noted Bernstein's religion in writing of his Mass, never commented on the religion of the soloists and principal musicians engaged in interpreting the work.) It is clear that David so employed a non-Hebraic priesthood of many classes. It is only slightly less clear that among this religious personnel were guild singers of the class that flourished in Ugarit. In almost every aspect of this matter, we seem to be dealing with a convergence of probabilities which is too powerful easily to be dismissed.

A generation or so ago, it was common to call the Psalter, the "Hymnbook of the Second Temple." The judgment of many who used the phrase was that the psalms were composed very late and precisely for usage in the Second Temple (ca. 500 B.C.). Such an opinion is no longer acceptable without some refinement. However, the enduring genius of the Psalter is such that it may well, some centuries after its substantial composition, have come to play the role of hymnbook in the Second Temple. The world of the Second Temple was surely a much different one from the world of the First. However, cultic worship in the Christian tradition, Roman and other, is totally different from either, and the Psalter has found an abiding place there. This is characteristic of great religious poetry: It can, with some adaptation, live on in another culture long after its mother culture has passed away.

A fairly large number of psalms carry the title *le Dawid,* sometimes translated, "of David." If the translation is correct, we may have here another example of authorship by attribution. (That all of the psalms so named could not possibly be written by David is quite clear. Linguistic evidence would make it impossible for at least some of them.) But there are other problems. The nature of the particle *le* is particularly obscure; its obscurity is evidenced by the Ugaritic texts where, among other things, it can mean "to" and "from." Then there are difficulties with the word *dawid.* It certainly can mean David, but then what does David mean? David is certainly a proper name, but does it belong to an individual? Some have suggested that David was a throne-name for the great king who had been previously called *Elhanan.* If this is so, a second theory is quite plausible: It came to be a subsequent title for the reigning king (thus Caesar in Latin, living on to the death of the last Kaiser.) Some evidence for this is perhaps derived from the core meaning of the name. The root *dwd* in Hebrew means "beloved." It is the word used for the loved one in the Canticle. It lived on in medieval Hebrew (and in the modern) as "Uncle," "Aunt," or the title of affection which children would use toward some adult who was a close member of the family circle, but neither father nor mother. Using Barr's argument on the force of a word's *subsequent* history, this development gives some credence that the title *David* was given to the king by a grateful and enamored Israel and handed on by him to his descendants, worthy and unworthy of the appellation. At any rate, the history of the word somewhat weakens the possibility (destroyed by other argumentation) that these psalms are to be seen strictly as David's compositions.

While there are references in the psalms to many festivals, otherwise largely undescribed in the Old Testament, we may cite only one group of them. Psalms 47, 93, 96 and 97 all contain references to a festival, the "Enthronement of Jahweh." In these psalms, the joyous shout occurs, "Jahweh has become King!" and this phrase needs some explanation. (Some translations persist in rendering this as "the lord reigns," but it means more than that.) Once again, we are in the world of sacramental representation. No pious Hebrew believed that in this annual festival the Divinity assumed kingship for the first time (nor did any pious Babylonian so think at the annual festival of the Kingship of Marduk). Rather he believed that some great primeval event, when Jahweh assumed rightful kingship over the whole world (after a struggle?) was now being made present again. The capabilities of the human mind and psyche being as limited as they are, the worshiper tends to feel that it has somehow happened "again." So in Christian Easter liturgies, the language of the liturgical texts may be somewhat restrained: "He is truly risen!", but the popular hymn phrases it differently: "He is risen *today!*" and the Christian worshiper at the Easter vigil, on hearing organ and bells, loses somewhat his firm grasp of space and time and tells himself, "He is risen *again*—even as he promised."

So powerful are the psalms, that even the man who misunderstands their origin can read them with deep profit. Still, the reader who understands that these powerful lines were not written for quiet contemplation in one's room but for boisterous proclamation in a cultic situation sees them for what they truly were: Prayer which was written to appeal to the whole man.

Anything then that we know about the origin of the psalms only tends to heighten their mystery. If some of them do go back to a professional and even pre-Hebrew authorship, does it lessen their grandeur? Rather it enhances it, that these powerful religious songs move men now, after millennia, whether they are on trial for their lives, waiting in a hospital bed or corridor or standing at an open grave. If we do not understand that this history adds rather than detracts, it is because we have lost some feel for the beauty of tradition and intellectual inheritance. Not so the geniuses among us. James Joyce, in *A Portrait of the Artist as a Young Man,* when he wished to write of the Christian's view of Hell, did not compose an original sermon. Rather he revised the standard, cliche-laden sermon of the Redemptorists of his contemporary Ireland. Perhaps this was with some polemical intent. Still, Thomas Merton has observed that the artist in Joyce rose superior here to the polemicist. The resultant sermon, according to Merton, presented a powerful picture of the transcendent God which Catholicism preached and was a great influence in bringing Merton to the Roman church.

(If the reader's curiosity is piqued enough now to go back and reread that sermon on Hell, Merton's insight may be lost on him. In this case perhaps he should conclude, as did the writer of this book, that Merton's literary sensitivities were a bit better than those possessed by the rest of us.)

Still, the use of a "traditional sermon" in rewriting a religious situation may be part of an ancient pattern. This may involve one of the factors connected with social composition. The human experience, especially when it touches on man's relationship to the Divinity, is simply too complex for a single man to express, unless he succeeds somehow in inserting himself into the long chain of men's efforts to describe the human experience. Today's reader of the psalms places himself in a world of religious values which has absorbed the best which Canaanite, Hebrew and Christian tradition has to offer. Thus, he never prays alone.

THE LITERATURE OF ISAIAH 16

The thrust of this chapter will be more an effort to describe the *mood* of the biblical work than an attempt to write a commentary. Writing a commentary within such a short space would be impossible. Moreover, a new reader of the Old Testament is best served when he begins specific books by some awareness of the mood or atmosphere of the books in question.

In the literature of Isaiah, the mood is of particular importance and interest. It is largely the difference in atmosphere which led some biblical scholars, after centuries of a contrary opinion, to suspect that the bulk of chapters 1-39 came from one particular source and 40-55 from another. There are other reasons, too, for such a view. The chronological span of the activities in these two works varies considerably, as does the geography. It is certainly not impossible that the Divinity should have transposed the prophet from one time and place to another far removed. (Although that would run counter to what we have seen to be the Divinity's easy and graceful movement in the midst of history, cooperating with the normal human pattern of events.) But the personalities of the two works seem considerably different.

Chapters 1-39 which scholars generally call "First Isaiah" are chapters largely of threats, thundering denunciations, powerful imprecations. "Second Isaiah" (or Deutero-Isaiah) is a collection of comforting and consoling literature, "the book of the consolation of Israel," as it is sometimes called. One general reason for this difference is quite simple and does not argue to the necessity of dual authorship. The first collection threatens Israel with disaster if there is not radical repentance. The second work flows from the period after the disaster. No need for threats now from any religious leader. The disaster is already past. What is needed now is pastoral assistance in meeting the disaster and making it "meaningful tragedy" rather than wasted pain. Some have compared the two works, somewhat sentimentally perhaps, to the attitude of a parent with an adventuresome child. The child may be threatened and scolded about the dangers to life and limb in some reckless bit of play. Should the recklessness, however, result in personal injury, the parent changes roles and becomes the comforter as the child mends. Perhaps even this sentimental figure shows the difficulty in an easy assumption that the two works are of different origin.

Earliest analyses of the two works attempted to discover identity or plurality of authorship by comparing the "style" of the two works. Most recent efforts in linguistic scholarship have pointed up the difficulties of this procedure. First of all, questions of "style" are measured with extreme subjectivity. It is the reader who decides, for example, that beginning a sentence with a word that is not usual in the first position tends to *emphasize* the meaning of that word. But did the author feel this emphasis? Quickly to affirm that he did, is to assume that notions of style are universal—and they are not.

Moreover, if certain aspects of style are near-universal (let us grant this for the moment), may not an author vary his style for any number of reasons? An interesting example of this is the extreme variation in vocabulary in the sundry works which Kierkegaard published under a host of pseudonyms. Granting that Kierkegaard was deliberately trying to conceal his identity, the apparent ease with which he wrote in a variety of different "styles" should make us reluctant to assume that difference in style means *per se* difference in authorship.

Still, from the late eighteenth century until a few decades ago, a consensus had emerged from among scholars to a near-universal judgment that the works were of two different origins. The reader is here reminded of our much earlier comments on the origin of prophetic literatures. While it is quite possible that these works stem ultimately from two different *individuals*, it is perhaps more accurate to say that they flow from two different *schools,* so complex has been the handling of this literature from its beginning to its final written form. Roman Catholic agreement with this broad consensus of dual authorship was slowed down a bit by a cautionary decree of the Biblical Commission in 1908, part of a general queasiness over "Modernism." By the time that this decree had lost any binding force, Roman Catholics returned to the question to find the consensus solid and the case closed.

In very recent years, a doctoral dissertation at Hebrew University of Jerusalem opened the case to some extent. There are really only two successful ways of writing a doctoral dissertation. One must either prove something that has never been proved, or prove it in a way that has never been previously employed. A student of the noted Hebrew grammarian, Chaim Rabin, undertook to use a computer to examine the question of plurality of authorship for the book of Isaiah. Early excitement over the possibility that the computer could easily solve all manner of biblical problems has given way recently to a more sober reappraisal. It is notably in the area of *style* that the computer has so far proved somewhat of a disappointment, since the programming of stylistic questions admits the same problems of subjectivity that have hindered all previous stylistic analyses. However, this dissertation circumvented many of these problems in a clever way. Principally, the study occupied itself with pragmatic and pedestrian questions, i.e., the average number of syllables per word in one work or the other. Unlike the question of simple study of vocabulary, this sort of thing would seem to be under an author's control only with extreme difficulty. (After all, we have no reason to surmise that any group of authors had reason deliberately to write the Isaian literature in such fashion as to delude later readers.) The type of thing analyzed in this dissertation and the clear statistical differences in the occurrence of one phenomenon or another in First Isaiah, but not in Second and *vice versa,* have quite put to rout any possibility of return to the theory of a united authorship.

This much time has been devoted to the question of single *versus* plural authorship in Isaiah for a good reason. Acknowledging plurality of authorship makes much of Isaiah intelligible on a level that would be otherwise almost totally unintelligible.

In light of its long and complicated transmission, the work of Isaiah obviously cannot be read with the easy assurance that one chapter will follow exactly from the one that preceded it. It is by no means necessary (perhaps not even profitable) to attempt to write the book over again in an order which is more "intelligible" to the reader. On the other hand, the reader ought to be aware in reading any given chapter that what immediately precedes or follows it may not be especially helpful in understanding that one portion.

Almost all readers are in agreement on the importance of chapter six in Isaiah where the prophet is seen as describing the great event of his life, the special manifestation of the Divinity to him. The precise question on this chapter is the timing of the event which it describes. Was this the beginning of the prophet's career? Or was it, as one scholar has described it, the "turning point?" This scholar sees the oracles which precede the chapter as totally different in tone from those which follow. Only in the great event described in chapter six did the prophet come to realize the intention which the Lord had in bringing his terrible punishment on the beloved nation. After the great events of the chapter, the prophet turned to speaking of the "remnant" and became possessed of a kind of messianic vision. This may be a remarkable insight. On the other hand, many readers find oracles occurring long after chapter six which seem similar in tone to those which precede the chapter.

In the great verse of this chapter:

Holy, holy, holy Lord, God of Hosts

The Filling of Earth is his glory!

there is a striking dichotomy. Holiness, we have earlier remarked, is something which belongs to the Lord. Anything else in the Old Testament
which is "holy" is so only in some relationship to the Lord, but all holiness,
other than his, is a drastically inferior kind of holiness. Holy is his name,
rather "Holiness is his name." This verse which has been used in many
Christian liturgies to introduce the most sacred portion of the mass is perhaps most accurately reproduced in one of the Syriac liturgies which
renders the phrase, with its own special accent:

qaddish, qaddish, qaddishATT

or in English:

holy, holy, holy art THOU!

That is one half of the dichotomy. Holiness is something which belongs really to God alone. And the essence of holiness, at least in the Old Testament, is to be other, apart, totally distant. And yet this remarkable verse
continues: That act which fills the earth is his glory (*kavodh*).

Kavodh, here as always in the Old Testament, does not admit of easy English translation. Most scholars would agree with a most awkward paraphrase as a fairly accurate translation: "The essence of God insofar as it can
be manifested." Note then the dichotomy which struck Isaiah in his great
vision. It is of God's very essence to be holy, that is, apart. Still, that holiness overflows and that essence which is his alone somehow or another fills
the earth. Perhaps nowhere in the Old Testament is the value of using parallel contradictions to teach about God more clearly shown than here. God's
essence is to be remote and apart; it is also his very essence, somehow or
other, which fills the earth. No explanation is given to tie these two ideas
together; no totally satisfactory explanation is possible. The New Testament will introduce the notion of *charis* (grace) and the later theologians
in the Christian church will attempt modifications of this idea as an attempt
at "speculative" explanation. The Old Testament, short of speculation here
as always, rests content with the flat assertions of the two different ideas.

Paddy Chayevsky in *Gideon* quotes his hero in a moment of depression
saying, "Who can love God—except a god!" In fact, of course, this idea was
echoed by speculative theologians after the Old Testament period (and is
asked by them still). Perhaps Chayevsky knew (although this is unlikely)
that his question really was phrased in a manner which the Greek Fathers

of the Christian church would have found relatively easy to answer. They spoke of *charis* in the New Testament as something that brought about the "divinization" of the Christian and thus made it possible for him to love God on God's own terms, so to speak. For them this in no way diminished the majesty of the Divinity, since this divinization was always his own gift.

It is beyond the scope of this chapter (and this book) to look deeply into the history of *kavodh* previous to Isaiah's use of the word and after his usage. Still the word is so important in Judeo-Christian theology that this brief mention of its stature had to be made. Though Isaiah did not (as some Christians would see the problem) resolve the difficulty of God's distance and immanence, still in the one passage in chapter six, he helped further to point up the problem. With the majesty of the vision which he saw in the Temple, the awesomeness of the seraphim, their fear in the Divine Presence (they "covered their face and feet") he left little doubt on what the *kavodh* was: God himself to the extent that he could be manifested. He left to later theologians the question of how God's life could be shared.

The egocentrism of the Old Testament's view of history is perhaps nowhere more clear than in Isaiah, as for example in 10,5-34 where the role of Assyria in world history is discussed. To understand how Assyria is downgraded in this passage, one must first have some view of Assyria in world history. In its various phases, Assyria was one of the most terrifying of the ancient military powers. If the nation lacked some of the terrors which modern military forces have had at their disposal through the "advances of technology," she compensated by an even greater savagery. It is a commonplace in the "Annals" of the Assyrian Kings that the account of a battle ends rather complacently: "Then so many thousand of the inhabitants I impaled outside the walls of their city and left them to die." Considering the fate of the captives in a city, the wonder is that any city ever did surrender to the Assyrians.

Nor is the military technology of the Assyrians to be underestimated. Until their arrival on the world scene, the defensive possibilities of a great city largely outweighed the offensive power of an advancing army. (It is for this reason that ruse and betrayal play such a large role in ancient military annals.) The Assyrians did not totally turn this around, but the ancient Assyrian reliefs show a steadily increasing role in the use of relatively simple but devastating machines in their assaults on the foe.

And there may be added to their savagery and technological superiority the sheer weight of numbers. The ancient world had never seen any adversary quite so horrible as the Assyrian, bringing slaughter and deportation to entire nations.

But how does Isaiah view Assyria? God's "rod of anger and staff of

wrath" (10,5). Once again, due to the majestic poetry of the English translation (and we would not change it) some of the emotional overtones of the
original expression are lost. It is true that "rod and staff" in tandem can
mean simply "authority" or "strength" as in Psalm 23. But there is at least
one other possibility. The "rod" here may well be that of Proverbs 13,24
and 22,15 (among other places in the bible). Again the Victorian overtones
of the "rod" of English translation ("He who spares the rod, hates his son"
and "Evil is bound up in the heart of the child and the rod of discipline [or
the teacher] drives it away") gives these passages a dignity which the original does not have. The rod is a switch used to chastise an errant small child;
it is nothing more! When the chastisement is over, the switch is destroyed
and the child is loved more than ever. "Do not fear the rod of the Assyrian
though he strikes you . . . for a brief moment and then it is over and him
will I utterly destroy!" (Is 10,24-25). For later and more sensitive thinkers,
it is distressing that one nation could serve such a function, that it might be
used only as an instrument of punishment and then cast away. But for a nation who had felt (or who had reason to believe that it would feel) the awful
punishment of the Assyrian armies, this view of the Assyrian might as nothing but a stick in the hand of a loving but chastising God was great consolation.

IMMANUEL

"Behold a maiden will bear a child and will call his name, God-with-us"
(Is 7,14). In light of the Christian teaching of the Incarnation in which God
became man and was born of a virgin, this line has assumed enormous importance. Once again, though, in fairness to both testaments, we would like
to take a look at the verse while prescinding from the later Christian teaching. The verse is certainly an intriguing puzzle.

It can be understood fairly simply (perhaps) on one level of interpretation in its Old Testament context, but even in that same context a host of
problems will arise. A direct prediction about the near future is being
made, and the prophet says something like this: "A young lady presently
pregnant will give birth. Before her child is five years old (and can thus dis-
cern good and evil) this prediction will come to pass." Yet in light of all that
we have said in this book about the assembling of prophetic literature, this
simple meaning would most unlikely be enough to keep this passage handed on through generations of the prophetic "School of Isaiah."

Moreover, what is virtually the same verse of scripture is found in the
Ugaritic material. "Behold a maiden will bear a child." (Text 77.7 in the
accepted enumeration). The operative word *almah* which we have translated as "maiden" is an interesting one. It is generally translated, "Be-

hold a virgin will conceive . . ." as Matthew 1,23 interprets it. But the Hebrew is not quite that simple. Scholars make a good case for the fact that
almah is rarely (probably never) used by itself in the Old Testament to
express the meaning of *virgo intacta*. Hebrew does have such a word: *betulah*. If *almah* is used, the writer generally spells out the fact that the
almah in question is without sexual experience. (But some qualification is
occasionally used even with *betulah,* which in *Gn* 24,16 occurs thus: "A virgin which no man had known"). The Septuagint translates *almah* as *parthenos*. If it is true that *parthenos* clearly means "virgin" by New Testament times (and this is perhaps open to dispute), it by no means clear
that the word has this meaning clearly and without cavil in the Septuagint.

None of the above ought to be terribly distressing to the believing Christian who holds firmly to the doctrine of the virgin birth. That view of the
text is certainly clearly held by centuries of Christian interpretation. The
only question being raised here arises from strictly linguistic considerations.

But even on strictly "scientific" grounds, Mowinckel in *He That Cometh*
offers an observation which makes far more difficult the swift dismissal of
"virgin" as a translation for *almah*. He points out that the Ugaritic occurrence of the verse is in a cultic context. There "virgin" could be used of a
woman (as it was in fact used in many other cultic rituals after Ugarit in the
ancient world) who is presently known to be a mother but who becomes
"ever virgin again" in the course of the recurring liturgical year. With typical scholarly caution, Mowinckel stresses that this does not *prove* that
almah means virgin in the Hebrew context. While the verse is clearly cultic
in the Ugaritic and may well have had a subsequent history of cultic transmission, there is little evidence that Isaiah 7,14 in its present form is cultic. On the other hand, Greek speaking Jews in the world of the Septuagint (where Greek and Latin mythology preserved this idea) would have
had a rather clear notion of the "mother becoming virgin ever again"
and it was in this milieu that *almah* was translated *parthenos*.

> Be comforted, O my People, be comforted
> . . . it is the voice of your God
> Speak tenderly to Jerusalem
> And tell her . . . that her punishment is over
> she has received from the Lord full measure
> for all her sins.
>
> (*Is* 40,1-2)

Thus the great work of Deutero-Isaiah begins, and it involves once again
a notion, largely foreign to much Christian thought—if that thought is not

modified by contemplation of the Old Testament truths. The idea here is perhaps in some opposition to an idea which receives great prominence in the New Testament (and in many subsequent Christian theologies). Yet each of the two somewhat opposed ideas is beautiful. The Christian to some extent looks for forgiveness without punishment, judging that the person of Christ has in some mysterious fashion taken all punishment on himself. This notion is largely foreign to the Old Testament (although it may be involved in the suffering servant as previously noted.)

The Old Testament tells the believer that forgiveness follows punishment. This is not an inferior idea to the Christian notion, merely different. The well-loved child knows that after punishment he is loved in a different way and perhaps more deeply than ever. Cardinal Newman, writing of the Roman position of the "particular judgment" notes that when the Christian hears his sentence from the Supreme Judge he will rejoice in hearing the Divine voice "though it speak but to chide." Part of this joy, of course, is that punishment involves some kind of particular attention of the judge to the culprit.

But there may be far more joy in Deutero-Isaiah's proclamation than this. In the few verses immediately following those cited above, he assures Israel that "the glory of the Lord will appear and that all mankind will see it." If all we have said about the glory (*kavodh*) of the Lord is understood, the joy of this proclamation may be easily grasped. God himself will become strikingly present. Not in fearful form (as in the many previous manifestations of the *kavodh*), but in some manner which would be inspiring of joy and comfort. Any other interpretation would violate the context of this passage. The Old Testament student must be very restrained in his exegesis of this passage, yet it is easy to be sympathetic here with the Christians of the early church who judged Deutero-Isaiah to be far wiser here than he knew, and saw in this verse a clear proclamation of the coming Incarnation.

Deutero-Isaiah is deeply human. He speaks of a God who is truly creator of the whole world, but singles out touching details. While it is mentioned that his understanding cannot be fathomed, it is mentioned also that "He grows neither weary nor faint" (*Is* 40,28), and that he gives of that same strength to those who are weary, exhausted, stumbling and falling. In the cruel seasons of the ancient Near East (mitigated to some extent now by modern buildings and technology) the prospect of a Divinity who did not tire (*Ps* 121,4) and could even give of that energy to weary mortals, must have been deeply comforting.

CREATION AND A NEW EXODUS

One of the great theological themes of Deutero-Isaiah is his treatment of creation. Scholars frequently observe that the meaning of the Hebrew *bara'* (with the possible overtone "create out of nothing") is much clearer in Deutero-Isaiah than in Genesis. This may be, but once again it should be noted that creation is not treated as an isolated theological theme. Nor is it demythologized. The prophet makes references to an ancient battle with a dragon and a struggle against the waters of the deep (*Is* 51,9b-11). Moreover, the notion of creation is treated in connection with the promise of a "new exodus." Nor is this surprising. The exodus was of such emotional importance in the history of Israel that (as we have seen earlier in the book) the entire history of the nation pivoted about it. Thus, the greatest promises of the future, including the new presence of the divine *kavodh*, struck the author as the glories of the exodus all over again. He doubtless felt that nothing could be a greater divine gift than that.

In chapters forty through fifty-one, the prophet deals with creation, redemption and the new exodus (with some hearkening back to the exodus of old). These themes are not treated separately, but are, to use one of Anderson's favorite figures, "woven together like a Bach fugue." It is important to realize this. While the literature of Isaiah is a great sourcebook for the modern writer of Old Testament theology, he must be very careful in his use of it. The demands of pedagogy may require that he isolate notions of creation *or* redemption *or* exodus. But the man who does the isolating must ever be aware that the theology which results may be more his than Isaiah's thought. The dissection of the thought of Isaiah, while it may sometimes be necessary, may result (as the dissection of flowers and love poems) in the creation of a new reality and not a deeper understanding of the reality which one had set out to study.

IDOLATRY

In a rather humorous passage, Deutero-Isaiah takes on the subject of idolatry (44,12-20). The context is serious enough. The prophet is speaking of the uniqueness of Israel's God and then he begins to make comparisons with other gods. He speaks of one worshiper who cuts a log in half, uses one half of it to light a warming fire and carves the other into a kind of figure. Before this then he bows down and adores! He gives another figure or two of this kind of worship and says to his reading (or listening?) audience: This is idolatry!

This passage, and others like it, must be examined carefully. It may well be, of course, that this is what the prophet believed idolatry to be. (Centuries later, St. Francis Xavier seemed so to understand idolatry in the Far East.) Or it may be that the prophet was faced with a pedagogical problem analogous to the one we discussed under the rubric of "covenant" in

chapter thirteen. Confronting an audience which had notions on the subject which were seriously awry, the teacher had only two alternatives: He
could subtly and with considerable nuance point out what was right and
what was wrong with the positions that they held (a device successfully
used by skilled teachers with very good classes) or he could reject totally
their present position with a view toward eventually reteaching the whole
business himself—a goal which he might or might not attain.

The reason why the above is important is that idolatry does admit of a
benign interpretation. It is certainly possible that in certain cultures a man
carves a log and calls it the divinity, believing himself to have brought that
divinity into existence. But there is another possibility. A devout worshiper,
with firm belief in a preexisting divinity, carves a log or casts an image and
then calls on the divinity to come and to inhabit that image. In fact, how
much different is this from building a temple and then calling on the
divinity to be present to that temple in a special way? This is exactly what
Solomon does, of course, while protesting his awareness that even the heavens and the earth cannot contain the Lord (*1 Kgs* 8,27).

The poor view of idolatry in Deutero-Isaiah has been not without influence in many studies of early Hebrew religion. Even as later editors of the
sacred texts tend to read back later views into earlier writings, so modern
Old Testament theologians (until very recent times) had found in themselves the same tendency. Certain religious activities of the patriarchs have
been misread or underestimated. For example, due to the fidelity of the
early Hebrew editors in recording the text, we read in Genesis 31,13 that
Jacob once anointed a sacred pillar in honor of his god. A student of Babylonian religion described such a phenomenon in a chapter which he entitled, "The Care and Feeding of the Gods." The devout worshiper would
oil carefully the wooden image, giving it a rubdown, as it were, and making the divinity feel good! Thus the divinity would be disposed to hearing
the worshiper's prayer. What was the shape and nature of this "cultic
pillar" (*massebah*)? We have little evidence, *pro* or *con*. Still, the Babylonian parallel is strong enough to cast doubt on the statement, often confidently made, that there are no images of God in the worship of Israel.

The possibility that the patriarchs did use images detracts little or nothing from the glory of Hebrew religious thought. First of all, as discussed
above, there is nothing wrong with the idea of images in divine worship.
Secondly, it was in Israel's eventual movement toward the description of
the *Divine Personality* that she transcended her neighbor's religious contributions. In religion, the difference between Israel and her neighbors did
not rest in simple external differences, but in the heart of the matter.

But what Deutero-Isaiah has to say about idolatry represents about the only negative thoughts which he has to offer. And of course, they were negative only from the viewpoint of the idolater. The pious Hebrew would find this condemnation rather positive! Moreover, the humor in the description of the one log which became both fuel and god may have been as pleasant to the Hebrew as it is to us. If so, the humor in this passage makes it fittingly a part of the gospel of the consolation of Israel.

Deutero-Isaiah is comforting and kindly. His comfort is not sentimental; it does not deny the reality of the present pain. It contemplates the present in light of the best of the past and concludes to the coming of a truly comforting future. If First Isaiah was thrilled by the vision in the Temple which assured him that God's *kavodh* filled the earth, Deutero-Isaiah is possessed of a vision which assured him (and his readers or hearers) that God's *kavodh* would some day be seen by the whole world in a manner which would convey comfort, strength and assurance. This is the joy of the Christian, of course; he believes that he has lived to see that day.

THE WISDOM LITERATURE 17

Included in this category of Hebrew writings are the books of Proverbs, Ecclesiastes and Job. Some religious traditions among Christians also include later books called the Wisdom of Ben Sira and the Wisdom of Solomon. These last works were probably written around the second and first centuries B.C. In the preecumenical age, various religious traditions devoted much vigor to disputes on whether these books were "canonical" or not. In our present, slightly wiser age, these disputes have died out, since the Christian traditions realize now that very little separates them on this issue. Protestant traditions which consider the latter books as "apocryphal" (which word they interpret less harshly than one might think) yield that the books are ancient and "edifying" and that they teach religious truths. It is questionable how much more the notion of "canonical" adds to this.

Part of the confusion in this dispute arose from the tendency of the differing traditions to use different words to express perhaps the same meaning. Roman Catholics used the word "deutero-canonical" for the books that some Protestants called "apocryphal." Catholics named "apocryphal" certain books (in the New Testament era) which arose at the same period as the canonical books but which were of extremely doubtful "apostolic" origin and which were characterized by rather unbridled imagination. As most Protestants went on to explain their use of the term "apocryphal" (at least in the matter of the Old Testament books), they seem to be talking about notions of "deutero-canonicity." Much energy and time was lost to scholarship (on both sides) during the years of these disputes.

Apart from the question of this quarrel among Christians, the wisdom literature does present an extremely interesting problem to the scholar. Even if the question is restricted to the three books (Proverbs, Ecclesiastes and Job) which all, Jew and Christian alike, now accept as canonical, the question must be asked: Exactly how did these books come to be accepted as canonical by Jewish thinkers? (Remember, as we have noted earlier, *canonical* here means belonging to the *canon*, the collection of most specially approved books believed to have their origin, in some fashion or other, from the Divinity himself.) Why does the question arise? The milieu and mood of the wisdom books is totally different from that of the other books in the Old Testament. To the casual reader, much that is in them is not "religious" but secular. Both Proverbs and Ecclesiastes and the later wisdom books may seem to be cynical. They offer "worldly" advice; they teach a man how to get ahead. They ignore much that is basic in the rest of Torah. How did these books, both canonical and deutero-canonical, come to be revered in the various religious traditions? This is the real question, as opposed to the false dispute mentioned earlier.

In order to get some perspective on this, it may be helpful to look at the broad milieu in the ancient Near East of what we may call the "World of Wisdom." Wisdom literature belongs to an international intellectual atmosphere which, in some respects, transcended any such atmosphere which the world has since known. In Egypt, Babylon and ancient Israel, there was a kind of "intellectuals' club" within the boundaries of any nation and crossing those boundaries easily, at least through the means of international correspondence. The "wisdom writings" of all the nations involved grew out of a common atmosphere. It is no surprise that the writings in the wisdom genre are so like one another in whatever nation they are found.

How did this class of intellectuals originate? Governments, then as now, had need of the assistance of a large body of "intellectuals." In fact, then as now, what the government wanted from these men was not profound thought but certain pragmatic skills. In the ancient world, the first of these skills was the ability to read and write for purposes of international correspondence. This skill was not a small one in a world where two of the major languages were non-alphabetic. In order to be able to write a single dialect of Assyro-Babylonian, one would have to memorize some three hundred or more symbols. To work in the archives (consequently to be involved in more than a single dialect) would mean the learning of two or three times as many symbols. To be involved in international correspondence would mean having a similar command of one other non-alphabetic language besides one's own; consequently, an intellectual way of life was required to be a successful scribe. Youngsters were taken from their homes at an early age and drilled in the rudiments of composition and reading. Thus, by early manhood, those who had made the grade were ready to devote their lives to some kind of intellectual activity.

The difficulties and awkwardness of correspondence in the ancient world cannot be overestimated. A serious scholar has suggested that the Assyro-Babylonian empire eventually collapsed under the weight—at least partially—of trying to carry on imperial correspondence in a cuneiform tongue. This may be an exaggeration, but it does point up the difficulties of the language. Therefore, someone who successfully made it through the scribal school system had proved himself possessed of at least some of the requisites for serious intellectual activity.

Their choices on finishing school were somewhat limited. One could devote one's entire life to assisting in the composition of royal letters or working in the royal archives, adding to the growing descriptions, frequently somewhat embroidered, of the marvelous victories that a particular king had won. Many scribes did so devote their lives. But some of them were not satisfied. In order to learn to read and write, they had spent hours in the best learning process of the day, copying previously written texts. A logical sequel of this activity was that the most gifted of the scribes on reading and copying a particular text thought to themselves: I can do better! And they began to write. Thus in the scribal schools each year was produced a steadily growing body of creative intellectuals.

This explains something which occasionally puzzles the reader of wisdom literature in the Old Testament or outside of it. Why did these "intellectuals" devote so much time to the composing of proverbs? This strikes the modern reader as being a rather low-level use of serious intellectual talents. But if a student has spent much of life in the copying of other men's proverbs, a fairly early intellectual ambition will be a desire to improve on this rather humble (from our viewpoint) literary form. The intellectual may eventually go on to create greater literary works, but he must first satisfy his earliest intellectual ambition, to write "better" proverbs, wittier and more lapidary, than those to whose copying he devoted hours of a somewhat stunted childhood and youth.

This same academic milieu explains the "internationalism" of the intellectual elite of this period, an internationalism which intellectuals have rarely attained since. It would be difficult for a scribe in Egypt or Babylon or Palestine to devote his young life to the copying of texts in his own and foreign tongues (with the realization that young foreign scribes were so spending their lives) without developing a real affinity for the international world of the scribes. When it came to writing, the scribes were as influenced by tradition as any person in the ancient world. However, their intellectual horizons were not limited to the traditions of their own nation and faith, but were limited only by the boundaries of the known world. This led to an internationalism in outlook which was probably superior to any since attained.

This also explains the "humanism" of the wisdom writings. What is central to their concern is man, not men of a particular time and place. Perhaps their views of a universal human psychology were somewhat exaggerated. (Remember how similar were the lives of the Palestinian, Egyptian and Babylonian scribes.) They tended to see all human existence as one, not realizing perhaps how similar was their own environment to that in which the scribes of other nations lived. They concluded, falsely perhaps, that all men were very much alike, independent of environment.

This may also explain the "sweet reasonableness" of existence as they saw it. Within the schools, life was rather simple. The moderately gifted scribe who worked hard from earliest years became a success. The unmotivated or untalented lad tended to pass out of the system. (One might seriously question the need of much self-motivation in the harsh pedagogical system of the ancient scribal schools. Still, the scribes, like most men, would like to attribute their success to their own endeavors.) Since the scribal school system was the only life the scribes knew for most of their formative years, they tended to equate it with life. In much of the mainstream of the wisdom tradition (in and outside of Palestine), the view grew that much of life was under man's control. Hence, the steadily growing collection of proverbs on the manner in which one could help to bring about one's own success. "Existence is reasonable!" taught the scribes, largely influenced by the fact that the microcosm of their own little world seemed, at least to those who succeeded in it, to have been eminently reasonable.

In the Jewish wisdom tradition, of course, this view does not go unattacked. Ecclesiastes challenges it and Job rejects it utterly. This is hardly surprising. The fact of the extreme unreasonableness of existence is much too clear to human experience. A view that existence is harmonious and reasonable could not long survive unchallenged. What is surprising is that the Jewish tradition permitted that the two views be handed on to further generations. Could this again be an indication of an idea which we have cited several times before: Jewish thought sees truth as complicated? The recitation of simultaneous contradictions teaches the truth and the idea of its complexity very clearly.

One is tempted to view the three books another way: Proverbs suggests that life is very much under control; Ecclesiastes notes that there *is* a control, but it is the control of seasons and rhythms whose inner workings man cannot know. Job protests that if there is any inner reason to life, it is known to God alone and admits of no human control at all. If this view of the three books is correct, one could perhaps see their having been canonized as representative samples of three major wisdom viewpoints.

CANONIZATION

The problem then is this: From our viewpoint most of the items which make other books of the Old Testament "holy" are largely missing from the wisdom literature. To a very large extent, the wisdom books ignore notions of covenant, cult and messiah. These ideas are of such great importance in Hebrew thought that it is difficult, at first glance, for us to see how any book could be "religious" for the Jewish people and ignore these ideas.

There is no satisfactory single focus for the explanation of the canonization of the wisdom books. Rather it seems that a *congeries* of forces conspired to thrust canonization eventually upon the books. Since we are dealing here with a collection of causes rather than one that is single and clear, the force of the argumentation may not be too satisfying.

One of the chief arguments for the canonization of the wisdom literature is that wisdom itself is seen so clearly as a gift of God. (1 *Kgs* 5,29-34). The modern distinction between secular and sacred wisdom would be quite wasted on the Hebrew mind. All wisdom comes from God and is his gift. Therefore, those books which are largely preoccupied with wisdom would be "religious" since they are dealing with one of God's gifts. And wisdom is a gift of God to *men*. One scholar has so explained the attribution of some of the wisdom literature to Solomon. The ancient Hebrews did not care for the idea that wisdom was some kind of abstraction having vague divine origin. Rather they saw it precisely as coming from God to men. By naming Solomon as the author of some of the wisdom literature, they made clear this contact of Divinity with the human. Again, canonization of the wisdom books would follow as a fairly logical sequela from this judgment.

Too, wisdom is largely associated with the priesthood (as we saw in chapter eleven, "Priesthood in the Old Testament"). In these ideas (and in the ones to follow) there is a kind of "innocence by association" of even the "secular wisdom" which is to be found in these books—i.e., a wisdom which is secular at least from our viewpoint. This type of wisdom came to be associated in the popular mind with wisdom as a gift of God and with wisdom which emanated from a priestly milieu. And therefore it followed that the wisdom books belonged in the canon of sacred writings.

For most scholars, the notion of immortality is something which is largely missing from the Old Testament books, short of the wisdom books. In fact, for most scholars, such notions of immortality are also missing in the books which are canonized by the Jewish authorities. Still, some scholars see evidences in Job, for example. If their judgment is correct, this would be another reason for "innocence by association."

Less controversial than the above would be the great religious dimension of Job and the possible influence which that would have on the canonization of these other books by the dynamic which we are discussing. All wisdom was seen as being in the same milieu as Job and would thus be suffused with a kind of reflected halo which would enable it to be canonized.

Some readers may find this a false problem. Does it matter *why* Jewish authorities admitted these books into the collection of inspired writings? Perhaps not. But for those of us who reverence tradition (and wish to understand it) the fact that Jewish authorities did something is sufficient cause to investigate their mode of thought. It remains sufficient cause even when (as in the present case) it becomes quite clear that we are not going to attain a thoroughly satisfactory answer.

Oddly enough, the latest of the Jewish wisdom writings, Ben Sira and the Wisdom of Solomon would seem in the judgment of certain Christian traditions to be more easily canonized. Their themes are surely more "religious" and more Jewish. They are more Jewish, since they insist on the strong superiority of the Jewish cultural heritage.

The Wisdom of Solomon is more "religious" at least for certain scholars, since it begins to treat of the notion of immortality. The notion helped to resolve problems of the "unreasonableness of human existence" and was of immense significance for later religious thought. Ben Sira is more "religious" than other books, preoccupied as it is with cult. Why were these books not canonized? It is possible that the religious tradition which dominated the Jewish process of canonization was prejudiced against the books, since they stressed one idea or another, (dominance of cult? immortality?) which a later Jewish mentality chose not to stress. Or it may simply be that the books were too recently written at the time of canonization. They lacked the aura of sacredness which only distance in space and time can give to a person or a work. Both of these works may lack the authority of tradition. (Certainly this is true of the Wisdom of Solomon which was written in Greek.)

PROVERBS

The book offers simple, practical advice. It is confident of its ability to teach a man "how to get ahead," since life is reasonable and under control. A man need only master a few simple rules of life-conduct and all will be well with him. His children can be offered an advantage in getting ahead, since they can be compelled to learn habits (which the adult has had to discover for himself) that will enable them to keep life under control.

In connection with our earlier remarks about the composing of proverbs, the origin of this little book (and its extremely limited viewpoint) is fairly easy to understand. But then a puzzle! Along with some chapters of simple, myopic and sometimes banal proverbs, we are given a chapter or two about wisdom as a personification. She is described as a creature, but the first of creatures, present at the rest of creation, "playing in the sight" of the creating Lord. She is to some extent his intermediary. Men who listen to her will not be disappointed.

It is difficult not to be sympathetic to the manner in which Christian Fathers treated these passages. They tended to see wisdom here as the Spirit (and were not overly distressed by the fact that wisdom was "created").

They lighted on identifications of wisdom and spirit to be found in Jewish thought: The rabbis taught that when the last prophets died, the Spirit of God left Israel. The Fathers saw this wisdom as a gift to men, as the Spirit would be clearly the gift of the Son to men. The Fathers saw the Old Testament here as teaching something expressly which the New Testament would make only a bit more clear.

But what did these two discourses of personified wisdom (1,20-33 and 8,1-36) mean to the authors of Proverbs? There is a possibility that the external literary form is influenced to some extent by Canaanite mythology. But what is its inner meaning? No answer is satisfactory. Does this personification serve only to place an intermediary between God and man, thus guaranteeing God's distance? Is wisdom personified to enhance the distance between God and man needed to safeguard the Divine transcendence? Or is the personification a poetic effort to express one idea: Wisdom is more than simply a gift of God to men, it is a way of sharing God's own activity and thus wisdom as a creature was the only way the ancients could express a divine *attribute,* seen as somehow distinct? Lacking a sophisticated mode of expression for this, and concerned to maintain the oneness of God, they make it a creature. Perhaps none of these explanations can be accepted to the exclusion of all the others.

ECCLESIASTES

The title in English may be a bit puzzling. It is an effort to reproduce some flavor of the Hebrew title: *qoheleth.* In fact, the meaning of the Hebrew is not clear. It certainly has some relationship to the Hebrew word, *qahal,* the religious assembly. Both Jerome (*concionator*) and Martin Luther (*Prediger*) and the King James Version (preacher) saw the work as that of a man who was addressing a religious assembly and setting it straight.

The three books of wisdom in the Jewish canon represent three different viewpoints. While there is a mainstream of wisdom literature, it is difficult to locate it in the Jewish canonical books. Proverbs, as already noted, is largely practical and stresses the reasonableness of human existence. Job stresses the deep religious dimension (and consequent unfathomability) of human existence. Ecclesiastes, without stressing the religious dimension, does underline the limitations of wisdom. All things are fleeting, even the gift of wisdom. The author of Proverbs takes himself very seriously, the author of Ecclesiastes insists that nothing is to be taken too seriously.

There is a rhythm in human affairs (if not a reason). There is a time to win and a time to lose and each moment will assert itself no matter what men do. Nothing is to be taken too seriously. Human effort cannot change the relentless tides.

The inclusion of this work in the books of wisdom admitted to the Jewish canon is quite significant. If wisdom is a gift of God, it is for Jewish thought only one of many gifts. The inclusion of Ecclesiastes serves as a restraint on the non-Jewish idea that wisdom is the greatest of all possible gifts and that he who has it and continues to grow in it can control existence. Not so, says Ecclesiastes; life has its moods and its rhythms. They assert themselves in their proper season. They are not controlled by men or even by gifts of God. They are controlled by God alone.

JOB

One is not even tempted, within the limitations of a page or so, to attempt a "commentary" on the book of Job. But a few gross errors can be corrected even in a paragraph. Job is not the model of the patient sufferer, the stoic. His deep rage at the distresses which assail him comes across (even in the poorest of translations) in a thundering majesty of rhetoric. His is a mighty rage. He asks angry questions and waits for an answer.

The book is not easy to understand. There is some evidence that it was not understood by some of those who helped write it. The prologue and even more the epilogue attempt to comment on the story and to explain its inner meaning. They fail miserably; they have not understood it. The epilogue gives a happy ending to the story and thereby ruins both its drama and its lesson. The lesson of the book of Job is this: Why does the just man suffer? *Do not ask the question!* The Divinity has tamed the primeval beast, attended the wild goat giving birth in hidden mountain crags, struggled with and overcome the forces of chaos. He will not entertain questions from men, just or otherwise.

If the above interpretation is correct, it solves another pseudo-problem. One work in cuneiform literature is close enough to the book that it has been called, rightly, *The Babylonian Job.* There are those who feel (out of that pious chauvinism which we have discussed earlier) that this somehow detracts from the greatness of revealed scripture. It does not, of course. First of all, it proves only that Job, as most of the great literary works of ancient times, was written with strong bonds to a tradition. More than that, to read the Babylonian version is to come up against a kind of nihilism. The just man suffers because this is the way life is. Job is written within the tradition of the speculative wisdom literature which the Babylonian version represents, but makes significant contributions to that genre. The description of the personality of the Divinity is considerably enriched by the pages of Job. Is Job angry? His rage is nothing in comparison with that of the confronted Divinity.

The core of the book's lesson is to be found in chapter thirty-eight. No one is to question the Divinity, now or ever. If the just man suffers, he ought not to lose what small claim he has to being just by daring to ask the Divinity impertinent questions. So far is that Divinity removed from man. Is this a book calculated to comfort the suffering just man? It is, to some extent; but it is a book suited to comfort only the strong. It is certainly some comfort to know that a Divinity as powerful as that of Job rules the entire universe. To get some small insight into the nature of that Divinity is to realize the futility of asking him the question: Why?

To later readers (and certainly to many Christians) the wisdom literature has many aspects which are not totally satisfactory. The modern reader finds it cynical where it perhaps could more benignly be viewed as urbane. The difference is that while the cynic and the urbane man alike understand human weakness (which the wisdom literature understands very well indeed), the man gifted with urbanity views human weakness with understanding and affection. The cynic despises it. In this dichotomy then, the wisdom literaure is urbane.

But this will still not satisfy many readers. Apart from the richly religious dimension of Job, much of the wisdom literature seems preoccupied with themes which are not sufficiently lofty to be "religious." The problem is not easily solved. We live in another world and view things quite differently than did the authors of the literature. Moreover, we also see life differently from the way it was viewed by the saintly scholars of Jamnia. They saw religion as something which affected the whole man in all dimensions of his life. Suggestions on how to get ahead, to please one's neighbors, to find the ideal wife, to discipline one's children, to garner wealth, to retain the wealth thus garnered—all this they saw as part of the "religious life." The reader who sees religion as something different from that must remind himself regularly in his reading of the wisdom literature that his views are not necessarily better or worse than those of the writers of the literature or the scholars at Jamnia. But they are surely different.

THE OLD TESTAMENT AND THE LAW 18

At an interfaith meeting one evening, one of the speakers became distracted from his main theme, which was Christianity, and began to explain some of the beauties of Islam and its religious work, the Koran. A Jewish lady in the audience was interested in the topic and asked only one question: "Are there then beautiful laws in the Koran?" With this question, the questioner showed herself to be squarely in the mainstream of Hebrew religious thought in the Old Testament period and since. Religion is to a very large extent simply law.

This is a point worth stressing. For a number of reasons, many non-Jewish students of the Old Testament have extreme difficulty in grasping the point. Christians have particular difficulty. Paul, for a variety of reasons, stressed one special viewpoint. The view he discussed and against which he reacted was that of a small group of Jewish religious leaders, limited in one time and place. It would be difficult to say that that view represented anything which we might call "mainstream Hebrew/Jewish thought." But the Pauline exaggeration of an adversary's position has had enormous influence on the difficulties which some Christians have had in reading the Old Testament.

And many of today's "modern Humanists" have their own difficulties with the notion of law. For a variety of reasons, some of these humanists have come to see law, any law, as enemy. In fact, their preoccupation is with civil Law, which they see as evil. When they come to the reading of the law-laden Old Testament, they bring to it the same mistrust. For a reader who largely mistrusts law as law, a paragraph or two is hardly sufficient rebuttal; but perhaps a paragraph will give him some pause.

One of the great lawyers of our times, Morris B. Ernst, wrote a rambling autobiography in his later years and entitled it *My Love Affair with the Law*. Perhaps he overstates his position. Still, the thrust of the book is that the study of the law is worth all a man's efforts. For Ernst the church has failed; most modern social structures have failed. Only man's creation, the law, has within itself the potential to enable man to save man, if enough men will but study it.

Some religionists will find that position offensive. They will see in it a deification of the law and will not accept it. On the other hand, some religious men have understood very well the power and the glory of law as law. At the beginning of his play *A Man for all Seasons,* Robert Bolt limns Thomas More as a good *man;* only much later in it does he describe him as a great Christian. In this earlier phase, More defends the "thickets of the law." He will not perform a certain action even though it is morally proper, because to do so would be to cut some of the legal brush down. He is afraid that to cut a little would be to start a precedent which would enable the laws to be chopped away one by one:

> And when the last law was down and the Devil turned round on you—where would you hide, Roper, the laws all being flat? This country is planted thick with laws from coast to coast—man's laws, not God's—and if you cut them down . . . do you really think you could stand upright in the winds that would blow then? Yes, I'd give the Devil the benefit of law for my own safety's sake . . . And whoever hunts for me, Roper, God or Devil, will find me hiding in the thicket of the law!

The reader who comes to the Old Testament handicapped by emotional difficulties with the very notion of law would do well to meditate on Ernst's book or on the passage from Bolt. It could make his reading of much of the Old Testament far more fruitful. In fact, if one cannot come to grips with the emotional problems which make impossible for him the acceptance of law as a thing of beauty, much of the Old Testament becomes totally unacceptable. But then much else of human life, history and culture will also remain unknowns for him.

We have noted many times before now the difficulty which one has in locating something in the "mainstream" of Old Testament thought. The mainstream is certainly there, but the Old Testament, like all long-lived bodies of religious knowledge, is possessed by numberless streams and currents. The mainstream of what the Old Testament teaches on a particular issue is not always easy to locate. A view presented in one time and place within the Old Testament literature may be contradicted by another view presented under another set of circumstances. Not so with the notion that law is godlike. The motivation for reverencing law in all its details, the form in which the law is presented, the fluctuation from oral presentation to rigid codification—all these may vary from time to time. What does *not* vary is that law is to be heeded always with respect.

THE DEUTERONOMIC HISTORIAN

Much of the work of the books of Deuteronomy, Joshua, Judges, the books of Samuel and Kings has been done by the rather firm hand of a rewriting editor, frequently called "The Deuteronomic Historian." The role of this man, generally believed to have been active as late as 550 B.C. must be precisely understood. On the one hand, he was not simply a compiler of the data of the past. He had a special viewpoint of his own. For example, he almost ignores the famed King Omri, while Assyrian sources came to call Israel the House of Omri! He is much preoccupied with affairs of temple, cult and covenant. The dealings of prophets with kings within the Hebrew framework occupy him much, but he ignores some international issues which later readers might think to be of far greater concern. Still, this is not to say that he was not an accurate historian. He was rather a creative one. He sought to interpret the data of history (cf. our remarks on Lincoln's second Inaugural in chapter two). If there was one difficulty with the basic viewpoint of the Deuteronomic Historian, it was that he was trying to present a *complex* and *nuanced* viewpoint. Most audiences tend eventually to muddle complexities and nuances. So did the audience or congregation of the Old Testament.

The historian's view was this: So long as the people of Israel were faithful to the Covenant and observed all its precepts (including a host of prescriptions which historically could not have been present at Sinai), the Divinity was faithful to his Covenant. When they were unfaithful, the Divinity withdrew his protecting hand. Indeed, he occasionally lifted it in anger and used his chastising rod. One could sum up the conclusion of the Deuteronomic Historian thus: When you were faithful, then did you prosper! It might not be inaccurate or unfaithful to his position to say that implicit in it was the view: While you observe, then will you prosper. What happened to the subtle and nuanced view which this religious editor was trying to present?

A later religious viewpoint concluded that there was a *causal* relationship of some sort between observance and prosperity. Moreover, they concluded then that the motivation of such observance was to guarantee prosperity. Some later religious thinkers (in the Old Testament and after it) became very confused on this issue. Finally, they lost sight of the fact that observance of law is for the sake of man, not for the sake of God.

Yet, even when the idea of the relationship between God's love for Israel and her fidelity to the covenantal prescriptions was most confused, at its core there rested a strong religious insight. This was the notion that in any love affair, divine or human, love is shown more in deeds than in words. Since the covenantal prescriptions gave Israel the possibility of showing her love for the Divinity, she hearkened, in some of her traditions, as much back to Sinai as to the exodus for her beginnings. We read in Deuteronomy 32,10 that the Lord found Israel in a desert land. Certainly one meaning of this "finding" of Israel in the wilderness meant that only in Sinai did the nation truly begin to be a nation. This tradition has had great influence on many modern scholars who refuse to speak of "Israel" before Sinai. There it was that she grew into a united whole. And the source of the unity? It was the law. This was God's gift to his people, a clear manifestation of his will. This is what the Hebrew people chose to accept, to enforce, to love.

When a later tradition encouraged the growth of the law of Sinai into a bewildering collection of over six hundred precepts, the motivation remained the same. It stemmed from the normal human desire to have a checklist against which one could compare one's progress. It served also to assuage one of the two secret fears of the lover, that he does not really love the beloved. With law, even with a rigidly codified checklist of prescriptions, the lover can console himself by comparing his actions with some established criterion.

Deuteronomy provides a theoretical framework. The subsequent historical books of the Deuteronomic history (which Jewish tradition lists as "the former prophets") offer the actual historical amplification of the theory exposed in Deuteronomy, "when you observe, then shall you prosper." The Deuteronomist attributes all of his teaching to Moses who preaches in Deuteronomy to the children of Israel. This attribution is like that of even later Jewish teachers who attributed their amplifications of the law to Moses himself. It is impossible at this point clearly to determine how old are the various strands of teaching in this book. While it is fairly clear that the Deuteronomist did some heavy-handed editing, it is most improbable that he could have succeeded in selling the adoption of a substantially new legal viewpoint. For this reason, most scholars are willing to admit that the Sinai experience is substantially historical. They accept that some dramatic event took place there and that the Hebrew law code truly finds its origin in that spectacular experience. The Deuteronomist rewrote, modified, reassembled; he did not create out of nothing.

One can perhaps (without doing historical violence to the subject matter) detect a number of major stages in the growth of Israel's love of law. Each stage involves its own special emphases. But there is a common denominator to all of them: Law is a gift of God; it is to be observed and loved. The old Roman *Rituale* for the wedding service contained the dictum: "Sacrifice is usually difficult and irksome; only love can make it easy and perfect love can make it a joy!" The law-observing Hebrew of any period would understand this view perfectly.

THE SINAI EXPERIENCE

One important amplification must be added here to what we have already said about Sinai. The law as revealed there is largely *apodictic* (and this term is opposed to *casuistic*). Casuistic or "case law" is common throughout the ancient Near East. "If a man's ox shall gore a neighbor, then . . ." In other words, the law governs disputes between men. If one man gives serious offense to the other, then he must do such and such in requital of the offense he has committed. Even in areas of casuistic law, the Hebrew experience is quite superior to all which preceded it. Most readers recognize "an eye for an eye and a tooth for a tooth" (*Dt* 19,21 *et alibi*) as stemming from the Old Testament. What they might not recognize is that such a dictum represents considerable progress. Previous law codes (and many subsequent ones) permitted restitution of four- and ten-fold or even death as the penalty for limited physical injury. The Hebrew principle is one of great mercy.

Still it is the apodictic law which represents a truly great leap forward. In such law, the lawgiver merely decrees "Thou shalt!" or "Thou shalt not!" There is no motivation offered for obeying. One is simply to do as one is told. Moreover, and this is perhaps a greater difference between the two, with casuistic law there is the hope offered that order can be restored after the offense. The offender loses an eye or a tooth and the world of justice is as it was before. No such hope is extended to the offender who violates apodictic law. Some irreparable damage has been done. This notion, of course, leads to a clearer image of the grandeur of the Divinity. It is however a painful and threatening idea. It may be in efforts to cope with the pain of this idea that later notions such as *Yom Kippur* (the Day of Atonement) developed.

THE TEMPLE PERIOD

The extent to which the Jerusalem Temple was an *innovation* is frequently a difficult idea for the Old Testament reader to grasp. The centralization of worship in Jerusalem was made possible only by the Davidic personality. The postponement of the building of the Temple for a generation may well have been a concession to the sensitivities of David's generation who saw Jerusalem worship as something new and different, and therefore threatening.

Yet, with the centralization of worship in Jerusalem and finally with the building of the Temple, law found itself a natural home. The human dynamic of which we have spoken began to operate. The basic core of the law code was amplified (in terms of cultic practice) so that the faithful had something against which they could measure themselves.

There was another reason why the temple period led to a growth in national esteem for law. The king was a major cultic figure himself. Since much of the Old Testament was rewritten in a later time, when cultic activity had been largely taken over by the priests, the king as cultic figure is not too clearly defined. But he was just that in the judgment of many contemporary scholars. That being the case, the temple period could only lead to an enhancement of the role of law in religion. The king was cultic leader; he was also the man who interpreted the law and decreed secondary laws of his own. The drama of cult, coupled with the king's role of lawgiver, could only serve to increase the dignity of the notion of religion as law.

Something else served to increase that idea, too. In the years immediately before the Temple and during the first years of the temple period, the Hebrews had as kings, Saul, David and Solomon. David's stature has been made eminently clear. Saul, after all, made enormous contributions toward eventual unity of the nation. Solomon, even if his role in wisdom is exaggerated by later tradition, made equally great contributions in guiding Israel on the world stage—at least it seemed so in his own lifetime. From this something human and understandable happened. The office of the king became identified with the greatness of these individual persons. This led eventually to a theological crisis. But during the years of their reigns, it was hard to overestimate the dignity which they brought to law, since they, the interpreters of primary law and the authors of some secondary law, were themselves men of such mighty stature.

FROM SOLOMON TO THE EXILE

One can with some justification look at this massive sweep of history and focus on a few theological shifts. The popular theology of the Solomonic period had come to focus on three major issues: 1. The greatness of the King; 2. The impregnability of Mount Zion; 3. Love of the Temple and a theology of *Shekina* (the Divine Presence). These three major theological tenets (at least of the popular mind) were all to crumble.

In Hebrew history, Solomon was to be followed by a number of undistinguished kings—incompetent, bumbling and sometimes corrupt. The equation of greatness with the office of king (and a consequent confident reliance on his protection) could not survive under these circumstances. The popular desire for a firm place on which to stand had to look somewhere else for satisfaction.

This popular desire took its focus then on the notion that Mount Zion was impregnable. The conquest of Zion was the key to David's taking of Jerusalem. Although the text is a bit garbled (2 *Sam* 5,8), it seems that David took the city only by ruse. The natural defensibility of the locale was perhaps the beginning of this theory that "Zion will never fall!", but it was only the beginning. Zion belonged to David. The popular mind saw this as part of the Davidic covenant that Zion would never fall.

In addition to this, the Temple was built in the area of Mount Zion. And the Lord dwelt, somehow or another, in the temple. The mode of his dwelling became the subject of the *Shekina* theology. The theologians of Israel were far too intelligent not to see the problems in stating simply that the Divinity dwelt in his Temple. They worked long and hard to describe that he was somehow present to the Temple in a special way. But their subtleties were wasted on the popular mind which concluded simply that the Lord dwelt on Zion. And therefore Zion would never fall.

Finally the Assyrian invasion of 701 B.C. had the mighty horses of the invaders within sight of the city walls. For a variety of reasons, they did not take the city. Possibly they concluded that the taking of it was not worth extended effort and satisfied themselves with a lesser degree of booty. Now the popular mind was convinced more than ever: Zion will never fall!

Then Zion fell.

THE EXILE

In light of the above, it should be fairly clear that the exile was a theological trauma without precedent in Israel. The dogmas which the people had accepted as strict tenets of faith were now stripped away. They had learned to live without kings of great stature; they saw their nation crumble on the world stage (after a very brief career there). They paid ransom to keep the city alive, while consoling themselves that it had not fallen. Finally, it fell and the nation was left to reconstruct a religion deprived of most of what the people had believed to be essential and basic.

The efforts of religious leaders to lead the adjustment were varied in nature. There was hearkening back now to the *demands* of Sinai and a reminder that the Lord's promises there were not unconditioned (as the people thought his promises to David had been). Then Jeremiah and Ezekiel reminded all that religious practice had always required a certain *inwardness*. This reminder of the requirements of interiority which had always been there have sometimes been misunderstood by students of the Old Testament. They see Jeremiah and Ezekiel as praising a religion of *individualism* in opposition to the older inferior cultic practices. This is not so. What they were reminding the nation was that an important constituent of the cultic practices now, remained, although their exterior manifestation would have to be different.

During the exile itself, law turned in another direction (and laid the way for a final shaping of its direction after the destruction of Jerusalem in A.D. 70). During the exile period, law came now to substitute largely for the cultic practices as *some external measure of a man's devotion.* The human need to exteriorize the very powerful strivings of the interior asserted itself in this way.

EZRA/NEHEMIAH
The books of Ezra and Nehemiah present a variety of problems in terms of time or origin, editing and their synchronization. With the rise of the mighty Cyrus on the world stage and his conquest of Babylon, the path was made smooth for the return of the Hebrews to Palestine. This was in keeping with Cyrus' basic policy of repopulating the lands which the Babylonian empire had devastated by allowing the descendants of the exiles to return. The national religious leaders of the Hebrews found though, that they were not really ready for return.

The natural terrors of the exile have been much overstated. It is true that the intellectual and leading class were largely deported. Still, a substantial population was left behind. (Bereft of the leading class, they developed many theological aberrations which were to plague the Hebrew religious leaders when the return took place some fifty years later.) Still, since it was an intellectual and ruling class which was deported, they were persons who could thrive in their new situation very well. There is some evidence that they fitted quickly into the Babylonian structure, since they had some of the necessary skills which a busy imperial center could always use. This too was to cause problems on the eventual return. Erstwhile pious Hebrews and their children seriously questioned the value of leaving their established positions in Babylon for rather vague possibilities of a more religious life in Israel. Israel must have seemed rustic indeed to a new generation which had lived at the heart of a mighty (though decaying) empire.

TEMPLE CULT AFTER THE EXILE
Understandably many of the exiled Hebrews in Babylon looked to *restoration* in Israel as a return to the past. Things would be again as they once were. In the matter of temple cult, as so frequently in the history of religions, a true return to the past proved impossible. First of all, temple worship seemed to demand a powerful role for the king. Enlightened though the Persians were, they were not *that* enlightened. Though a Davidic prince was very much at hand (Zerubbabel) and though he would cheerfully have taken on the royal role (including the cultic), the Persians were not about to permit that, and Zerubbabel mysteriously disappears from the accounts we have after then. Thus the cultic worship of the past was quite handicapped.

But a return to the past may have been impossible anyway. In the cult-deprived period of the exile, law had grown in stature. To some extent, it had replaced cultic exercise. Artificial decrees and fiats are generally ineffective in trying to reverse human tides. So was the case here. Law had emerged as a truly powerful national force. One could modify the law (and certainly amplify it). To attempt to cut it back and to replace it, even with the reestablished cultic worship, would have been psychologically impossible.

For the future history of Judaism, of course, this was a blessing. The steadily growing strength of law as the center of Jewish life was to serve the people well. With the ultimate destruction of Jerusalem and the subsequent cruel events, the historian could see little inner reason why the Jews as a people with a national identity should survive. But survive they did. And this in large measure because an expanding law code provided them with a criterion to measure the faithfulness of any man who proclaimed himself to be a Jew.

EXTERNAL CHANGE AND INNER PERMANENCY

While the external manifestation of Hebrew religious practice has been forced to change massively throughout a history of nearly four millennia, the inner heart of it all has remained largely the same. This can be illustrated perhaps through the vagaries of the religious celebration of *Yom Kippur* (Day of Atonement) or *Yom hakippurim* (Day of Expiations). If the festival is of monarchical or premonarchical origins (which many scholars would dispute) it allows of at least three major stages of development. If it is of later development than this, there are at least two major stages. In any of these stages, the inner core of the festival rested always on two pillars: Man's desire to be forgiven and the Divinity's unique power to forgive. The manifestations of these two themes varied considerably but the inner core of them remained always there.

If there was a monarchical role in the *Yom Kippur* (which we cannot prove), presumably his role was that of the priest in a slightly later stage. He placed himself somehow or another in the special presence of the Divinity (as the high priest was later to enter the holy of holies). In some kind of contact with the Divinity, he received some assurance that the sins of the people were forgiven and conveyed this assurance to them. In the priestly period, the high priest entered the holy of holies carrying a basin of blood from an animal who had been executed with reverence. Half of this blood he poured on an article of furniture called the *kapporeth* (site of expiation?) and then returned to the people outside. Sprinkling them with the remaining half of the blood, he assured them that their sins had been forgiven.

The external manifestations of this rite were to change through history as the Jews took on the external religious practices of the people among whom they dwelt. (Flagellation became part of the rite temporarily in medieval times.)

In modern times, the crowded synagogue is the site of this annual festival. Some of the pious faithful spend the entire twenty-four hour period of
the sacred day within the synagogue precincts. Most of the pious fast completely during this period. In a nonsacrificial liturgy, they listen to readings
from the sacred texts, sermons by the rabbi, and indulge in some periods of
silent prayer. At the conclusion of the day, the *shofar* is sounded and the
emotional release is the same for the pious modern Jew as for the Hebrew
of temple times; he is assured that his sins have been forgiven. Twentieth-
century man's need to be forgiven and the Divinity's power ever to forgive
are the constants; all that has changed is some of the externals of the ceremony.

So in many other ways has the simple religion of the desert changed,
while retaining its inner core. The development of the complexities of law
in Jewish life has had enormous cultural and religious influence. The practice of the dietary laws, for example, resulted in *de facto* segregation of Jew
from non-Jew. Since eating and drinking are the normal constituents of
most social activity, the pious Jew was compelled largely to find his social
relaxation among other pious Jews. This legislation was not "racist" in intention. It had the goal of preserving not the purity of any Jewish racial
strain, but the purity of the Jewish religious identity. In light of its enormous success, who would now suggest that a better method could have
been found?

The role of the Jew as scholar flows also from the steadily expanding
legal code. The pious Jew, as any pious religionist, wanted to make the will
of the Divinity more and more applicable to the here and now. This
required a steadily widening body of legal studies so that applications,
more and more specific, could be made. This demanded the assembling of
a large corps of scholars. One four-year-old Jewish boy understood this very
well. Barely able to read, he toddled into his father's study one afternoon to
find him poring over undeciphered texts. "I shall help you," he said, "I too
am Jewish!"

One sometimes reads that Judaism prides itself as being a religion without asceticism. This is not so. Obedience to law requires of the pious Jew an
enormous daily asceticism.

But then laws always makes demands on men. This is so whether the
law is relatively simple and stark, as the law of Sinai, or whether it is complex and detailed as the massive code which has flowed from Sinai
throughout the law history of Judeo-Christianity. But law is demanding.
Some may not realize how this enhances the dignity of man, but it does!
Even when man falls far short of the law and is laden with guilt as a result,

he has the image of law's perfection ahead of him. Even when a man's actions are terribly imperfect, law stands before him as a reminder of that perfection toward which man is called to strive. If it is ever out of reach, it is nonetheless ever in sight. As one of the sages put it, "It is not in your power to accomplish the task, still it is not your right to desist from the attempt."

SUGGESTED READINGS

A compendium of scripture citations to be used in conjunction with the reading of individual chapters of *The Threshing Floor*.

All citations are listed in order of importance so as to complement the content of individual chapters.

Judges 3,12-30 (Ehud)
Judges 9,5-21 (Jotham)

7 Reality and the Book of Ruth
   The Book of Ruth

8 Transitions: Samuel, Saul, David
   1 and 2 Samuel
   1 Chronicles 9,35-29,30

9 Solomon and the Song of Songs
   1 Kings 1,1-11,43
   2 Chronicles 1, 1-9; 31
   The Song of Songs

10 Social Justice and the Divine Tenderness
   The Book of Amos
   The Book of Hosea

11 Priesthood in the Old Testament
   The Priest as Fortuneteller
   Deuteronomy 33,8-11
   Judges 18,3-7
   Isaiah 28, 7

   Teacher
   Deuteronomy 33,10
   Malachi 2,6-8
   Hosea 4,4-6
   Jeremiah 2,8

   Mediator
   Malachi 1,6ff
   Leviticus 13-14
   Leviticus 8-10

   Priest and Levite
   Exodus 32,25-29
   1 Chronicles 23,4-5; 23,28-32; 25,1-8
   Nehemiah 10,37-39; 9,4-5; 8,7-9

   Zadok
   2 Samuel 8,17; 20,25
   1 Kings 2,26-35
   1 Chronicles 6,4-8; 24,1-3

12 Old Testament and New
        2 Timothy 3,16-17
        Acts 2,14-26

13 Notions of Covenant
        Exodus 19-24
        Genesis 12,1-9; 15,1-21
        Genesis 6,18 (Noah)
        Joshua 24,16-28
        Deuteronomy 27,11ff; 5,6-21

14 Two Views of Messianism
        Isaiah 49,1-6; 50,4-9; 52,13-53,12
        Psalm 2
        Isaiah 6, 1-9; 21
        2 Samuel 7,5-16
        1 Chronicles 17,4-14
        Psalm 89,20-37
        2 Samuel 23,1-7
        Psalm 132,11-18

15 The World of the Psalms
        Psalm 2; 20; 21; 45; 72; 89; 101; 110
        Psalm 47; 93; 96; 97; 99
        Psalm 4; 17; 23; 78; 119

16 The Literature of Isaiah
        Isaiah 6,1-9; 21; 10,5; 24,1-23
        Isaiah 40,1-2; 44,12-20; 49,1-6; 50,4-9; 52,13-53,12
        Isaiah 51,9b-11

17 The Wisdom Literature
        1 Kings 5,29-34
        Proverbs 1,1-9,18
        The Book of Ecclesiasticus
        Wisdom 6,22-10,21
        Job 38,1-42;6

18 The Old Testament and the Law
        Exodus 20,22-23,33
        Exodus 34,17-26

Deuteronomy 12,1-26,19
Leviticus 17,1-16; 26
Leviticus 1,1-7; 11,1-15,33
Numbers 28,1; 29

Note: The versification in the readings above corresponds to *The Jerusalem Bible;* there may be discrepancies with other translations.

INDEX

Note: Transliterated foreign words are not listed where the language scholar might look for them, but in English alphabetic order.